Accounting for Colleges and Universities

Accounting for Colleges and Universities

THIRD EDITION

CLARENCE SCHEPS
AND
E. E. DAVIDSON

LOUISIANA STATE UNIVERSITY PRESS
BATON ROUGE AND LONDON

1978

Type face: VIP Caledonia
Typesetter: G & S Typesetters, Inc., Austin, Texas
Printer & Binder: Kingsport Press, Kingsport, Tennessee

LIBRARY OF CONGRESS CATALOGING IN PUBLICATION DATA

Scheps, Clarence.
Accounting for colleges and universities.

Includes index.
1. Universities and colleges—Accounting.
I. Davidson, E. E., joint author. II. Title.
LB2342.S35 1978 657'.832 77-28383
ISBN 0-8071-0388-8

Contents

Charts

Forms

Annual Report

Preface

A GOOD ACCOUNTING SYSTEM is a prime requisite of sound finance, which is an inseparable part of every business enterprise. Granting that the purpose of the educational institution is instruction, research, and public service—and not profit making—finance in all of its aspects is as important in the college and university as in the commercial organization. In the educational institution, therefore, an adequate system of accounts is essential if the fullest benefits are to be realized from the educational program of the institution.

This book is concerned with the problems of accounting in the college and university and sets forth techniques for their proper handling. The scope of the book encompasses every aspect of accounting and business practice. The "accounting system" is treated in a broad sense, including not only the fundamental techniques of record keeping and entry making but also a complete discussion of budgeting, purchasing, supply and equipment inventories, cost accounting, and financial reporting.

This volume is a revised edition of *Accounting for Colleges and Universities* by Scheps and Davidson, published by the Louisiana State University Press in 1970. Its publication is timely because of the significant developments affecting institutional accounting since 1970. In 1973 the American Institute of Certified Public Accountants (AICPA), after a three-year study, published an industry guide entitled *Audits of Colleges and Universities*. Many changes in accounting principles and concepts are included in this volume, which must be complied with by colleges and universities. Following the publication of the AICPA "Audit Guide," the National Association of College and University Business Officers revised and reissued *College and University Business Adminis-*

tration, which had been published in 1968. A third important development has been the activity in the area of account classification and cost analysis of the National Center for Higher Education Management Systems (NCHEMS). Effective liaison between these three groups has produced changes that are reasonably consistent and coordinated.

The authors have made every effort to follow in minute detail the concepts of accounting and financial reporting set forth in the 1973 AICPA Audit Guide and in the 1974 edition of *College and University Business Administration*. In addition, the authors use similar account titles and generally follow the terminology, definitions, and techniques found in that volume. In a sense this book can be viewed as a companion volume to *College and University Business Administration* because it illustrates actual entries, ledger accounts, journals and registers, and forms and documents which are only described in principle in the latter volume.

The authors deeply appreciate the generous permission granted by the National Association of College and University Business Officers and the American Institute of Certified Public Accountants to use material from their publications without having to acknowledge each portion of the material so used. They are fully aware of the increased value of this publication by reason of such permission.

The authors also realize their indebtedness to the pioneering books in the field of college and university accounting and finance. They owe much to Lloyd Morey's *University and College Accounting*, E. V. Miles's *Manual of Teachers College Accounting*, G. A. Mills's *Accounting Manual for Colleges*, and Clarence Scheps's *Accounting for Colleges and Universities*. John Dale Russell's book, *The Finance of Higher Education*, was of great value as a reference source in the field of college and university finance. *College & University Business* magazine, published by McGraw-Hill, Inc., has also been a useful source of reference.

The original revision of Scheps's book was greatly facilitated by the valuable editorial assistance of George E. Van Dyke, who also edited the 1968 edition of *College and University Business Administration*.

Appreciation is expressed also to the following who read and commented on specific chapters: Felix C. Byxbe, Jesse B. Morgan, Lawrence J. Guichard, and Samuel V. Cresap, all of Tulane University; David A. Willard, Edwin E. Glover, Jack E. Coke, and R. Dean McGlamery, Oklahoma State University; and John W. Savage, Doyle L. Russell, Robert S. Shaw, and Jesse Tutor, University of Mississippi.

Much credit is due to Gilbert L. Lee, Jr., formerly of the University of Chicago, for his careful reading of the entire manuscript of the original revision and his helpful suggestions, most of which are incorporated in the text. The revised edition benefited immeasurably from the comprehensive review of Daniel Borth, former executive vice-president of Louisiana State University, and W. Harold Read, vice-president emeritus for business and finance, University of Tennessee.

The authors wish to express their special gratitude and appreciation to the Exxon Education Foundation for making available a grant which has permitted them to obtain research and editorial assistance and has made available the travel funds necessary to enable the authors to work together in revising this edition. The production of the volume would have been greatly delayed and handicapped without this generous contribution on the part of the Exxon Education Foundation.

CLARENCE SCHEPS
Tulane University
New Orleans, Louisiana

E. E. DAVIDSON
Oklahoma State University
Stillwater, Oklahoma

1

General Principles or Concepts of College and University Accounting and Finance

ACCOUNTING IS THE MEANS through which financial data necessary to the efficient administration of colleges and universities are recorded, classified, and reported to institutional officers, controlling bodies, and the general public. According to *College and University Business Administration*, "Among the objectives of accounting, whether for a commercial enterprise or a college or university, is the providing of information to assist (1) management in the effective allocation and use of resources and (2) the general public, investors, creditors, and others in evaluating the effectiveness of management in achieving organizational objectives."[1]

The accounting system of an educational institution must meet the requirements of that institution. The forms and documents employed in the recording of financial data depend upon and vary because of a number of factors. The size of the institution, the nature of its control, the amount and sources of its revenues, and the number and types of auxiliary enterprises that it operates are a few of the considerations which determine the appropriate form of its system of financial records. Regardless of the possible diversity of technical details, however, there are certain well-defined and accepted principles or concepts of college accounting and finance. The accounting and fiscal system for any institution—large or small, privately or publicly supported, independent or church related—should be based on these principles.

Principles or concepts of institutional accounting and finance reflect codification of theories and practices developed over a long period of time. Prior to 1920 very little literature on the subject of college accounting was published. In the decade 1920–1930 a

1. *College and University Business Administration* (3rd Rev. ed.; Washington, D.C.: National Association of College and University Business Officers, 1974), 177.

developing interest in governmental and institutional accounting spread to colleges and universities. The first authoritative book on the subject, *College and University Finance*, written by Trevor Arnett, was published by the General Education Board in 1922. Although the book includes a chapter on accounting, this work is concerned primarily with the financing of endowed institutions. The first modern study of accounting for educational institutions, *University and College Accounting* by Lloyd Morey, appeared in 1930, and since that date many studies on college and university financial reporting have been published. In the early 1930s Morey was the chairman of a national committee to develop standard reports for institutions of higher education. The final report of the committee appeared in 1935 under the title *Financial Reports for Colleges and Universities* and for more than a decade served as the principal source of reference for accounting and reporting principles for institutions of higher education. Following the publication of the committee report in 1935 and with the assistance of the General Education Board, the American Council of Education established the Financial Advisory Service, the purpose of which was to provide help, information, and advice for colleges and universities in financial and business administration.

The forerunner of this present volume, *Accounting for Colleges and Universities* by Clarence Scheps, appeared in 1949. In 1952 a national committee of business officers and certified public accountants brought out a volume on accounting principles, known as *College and University Business Administration*, Volume I. In 1955 a companion volume dealing primarily with college and university business administration was published by the American Council on Education. In 1968 a third national committee, under the chairmanship of Clarence Scheps, produced a revision of *College and University Business Administration*—this time a single volume dealing with accounting principles and with college and university business administration. *Accounting for Colleges and Universities* was revised in 1970, being coauthored by Clarence Scheps and E. E. Davidson. In 1974 the third revision of *College and University Business Administration* appeared as part of a series published by the National Association of College and University Business Officers known as the Administrative Service.

Before discussing the basic principles or concepts of accounting and financial reporting as enunciated in the several editions of *College and University Business Administration*, and amplified and corrected by the AICPA Audit Guide, principles related to college and university business practices are grouped and discussed. Not all of these principles are related directly to accounting functions because they cover the various functions of the office or group of offices usually referred to in college administration as the Business Office.

First, those principles concerned with the organization and responsibility of the business office and the chief business officer:

1. In most institutions, the responsibility for the business and financial functions of the college should be centralized in a single business officer responsible to the president. In unusually large or complicated institutions, there may be two or more coordinate business officers reporting to the chief executive—for example, an officer in charge of management and operations and an officer responsible for fiscal activities.

2. The chief business officer should be appointed by the governing board upon the nomination of the president. The selection of this officer is an important factor in the effective business management of the institution because of the numerous and varied responsibilities centered in the business office. He should be qualified through experience to handle the business affairs of the institution and qualified by temperament to deal with the diverse and frequently unique personalities of the campus and business world with whom he must associate. In addition to holding at least a bachelor's degree, he should have what is often termed an "educational philosophy." Finally, he must realize fully that the purpose of his office is to serve the college and to help further its educational program.

3. The more important functions that should be centralized in the business office include (a) assistance in the preparation and the control of the budget; (b) collection and custody of all institutional funds; (c) handling the funds and properties belonging to endowments; (d) establishment and operation of a proper system of accounting, financial reporting, and internal control and audit; (e) supervision of the operation and maintenance of the physical plant

and the capital construction program; (f) supervision of the purchasing of supplies and the control over inventories; (g) administration of personnel systems for nonteaching employees; (h) financial supervision of auxiliary enterprises; (i) supervision of the financial aspects of student organizations and loan funds; and (j) participation in planning programs for the entire institution.

Second, those principles concerned with the institutional budget:

1. An annual budget should be prepared covering all operations and all funds. The budget should be a carefully devised financial plan of operations for a given period of time, usually a year. The governing board should establish principles concerning the method of budget making as well as the routine of budget adjustments. Regarding the latter point, it is emphasized that every budget either should carry a contingency reserve or should leave unallocated a portion of expected revenues which can be distributed by the chief executive or the board as unanticipated needs arise.

2. The budget not only must be carefully prepared but also carefully controlled. This control can best be achieved by incorporating the budget into the accounting records. Budget control should be as rigid as practicable, seeking to prevent serious overexpenditures in individual budgets. Budget reports of both revenues and expenditures should be made available at regular intervals, usually monthly, to the governing board, institutional officers, and those responsible for individual budgets; such reports should clearly disclose actual operations as compared with budget estimates.

Third, those principles concerned with the function of purchasing and stores control:

1. Responsibility for all institutional purchasing should be centralized in the business office. If the size of the institution justifies it, a separate office of purchasing, headed by a purchasing agent, may be created. Centralized purchasing is desirable for at least four principal reasons:

(a) It effects economies through quantity buying and elimination of duplicate effort.

(b) Through the plan of requisitions, it makes possible a system of budgetary control.

(c) It facilitates in great measure the receipt, the entry, and the auditing of invoices and other documents relating to expenditures.

(d) It releases faculty members from a time-consuming responsibility.

2. A logical adjunct of the purchasing function is the control over storerooms. Even in small colleges, substantial economies can be effected through quantity purchases of standard supplies used throughout the campus. The purchasing office, or other division of the business office, should be responsible for the maintenance of an adequate inventory in the central storerooms.

3. Another subdivision of the purchasing function is the control over the physical property of the institution. In order to purchase intelligently, as well as for other reasons, a perpetual inventory of all movable equipment should be maintained by the business office and made readily available to the purchasing agent.

Fourth, those principles concerned with the operation of the physical plant:

1. Centralized management should exist in the operation and maintenance of the physical plant in all its phases. Preferably, the immediate responsibility for maintenance of plant should be vested in a superintendent or director of physical plant. This officer should be responsible directly to the chief business officer.

2. Closely allied with plant operation and maintenance is the keeping of adequate cost records for the physical plant. The accounting system should be devised so that, with the cooperation of the operation and maintenance department, a distinction can be made between the cost of operating and maintaining that part of plant devoted to educational and general purposes and that part devoted to auxiliary enterprises. In addition, a record of the cost of operation and maintenance of buildings or other units should be provided as an integral part of the accounting system.

Fifth, those principles concerned with the postaudit:

As in every other type of organization, the accounts and records of an educational institution should be audited by competent independent accountants at least once a year. There are at least four purposes of the independent post-audit—verification of the accuracy of the financial records, verification of the integrity of the employees of the institution, expert advice on accounting methods and business practices, and verification of financial statements. The institution has an obligation to the state or to its benefactors and, accordingly, should make a periodical accounting of the funds entrusted to it. The best method of making such an accounting is through the independent audit. In the case of publicly supported institutions, these audits frequently are conducted by an auditing agency of the state. In such cases the audits should conform to the generally accepted principles of institutional auditing as set forth in the AICPA Audit Guide of 1973.

Sixth, those principles concerned with the relationship of the business office to student organizations and student loan funds:

1. The finances of student organizations and activities should be subject to the supervision of the business office. The usual examples of such student organizations are student body associations, student annuals, and student newspapers. The accounts and records of such organizations should be made a part of the regular accounting system. All money collected by them should be deposited in the business office. Disbursements against these funds should be made by college checks. It is preferable for such organizations to have a faculty advisor to approve all vouchers.

2. The management of student loan funds should be predicated on principles of sound business practices and should be handled in such a manner as to insure adequate protection of the funds. Transactions involving interest and loans should be accounted for in the regular accounting system, and the business officer should be responsible for the ultimate collection of all loans. Although frequently the responsibility for making student loans vests in an officer outside the business office, the business officer should participate in policies governing the awarding of such financial assistance.

Seventh, those principles concerned with the accounting for endowment and similar funds:

A suitable organization for the administration of endowment funds should exist under the jurisdiction of the business office. The terms of each endowment gift should be adhered to and the accounts should be maintained in a way that will provide an adequate distinction between the income and principal of each fund. The business office should provide the governing board at frequent intervals with complete information regarding the status of the funds and the makeup of the investment portfolio. Responsibility with regard to the various aspects of the administration of endowments should be clearly outlined by the governing board. There should be special requirements with respect to the custody and the safeguarding of endowment securities and other investments. Responsibility for the investment program should be vested in the governing board. The audit of endowment funds should be thorough and complete.

Basic Principles or Concepts of Accounting and Financial Reporting

The 1968 edition of *College and University Business Administration* enumerated twenty-two basic principles relating to accounting and financial reporting. The 1974 edition of *College and University Business Administration* (in Chap. 5.1, entitled "Fundamental Concepts") revised and restated these basic principles, taking into consideration the changes mandated by the AICPA Audit Guide. The chapters herein, which describe in detail the forms and procedures used in college and university accounting, are based on these principles or concepts. Also, terminology used throughout this volume, as well as the general classification of accounts, is based on *College and University Business Administration*.

To meet the requirements of financial accounting and reporting for colleges and universities the following basic principles or fundamental concepts are enumerated.[2]

1. *The accounts should be classified in balanced fund groups in the books of account and in the financial reports.*

The obligations of a college or university are so varied and the use of its resources are so restricted that it is desirable to subdivide its moneys into funds. Each fund has its own resources and liabilities and is in every sense a separate accounting entity. According to *College and University Business Administration*, a fund is "an accounting entity with a self-balancing set of accounts consisting of assets, liabilities, and a fund balance."[3] The fund groups recommended are: current funds (unrestricted and restricted), loan

2. Based on *College and University Business Administration* (1968 edition) as revised and restated in *College and University Business Administration* (1974 edition).

3. *College and University Business Administration*, 178.

funds, endowment and similar funds, annuity and life income funds, plant funds (unexpended, retirement of indebtedness, renewal and replacement, and investment in plant), and agency funds.

In addition to the fund groups enumerated above, other fund groups, such as employee retirement funds, can be applicable to particular institutions. However, in the majority of institutions the six fund groups recommended should suffice.

2. *All financial transactions should be recorded and reported by fund group.*

The transactions, including receipts and disbursements, should be recorded in the appropriate fund groups and should not be intermingled. The balance sheet prepared at the end of the fiscal period provides for a disclosure of the assets, liabilities, and fund balances of each separately balanced fund group. Changes in fund balances from one fiscal period to another should be reflected in the statement of changes in fund balances.

3. *The current funds group consists of funds available for current operations, including those for restricted as well as for unrestricted purposes.*

Balances of unrestricted and restricted funds should appear separately in the current funds group, even though the assets of the fund groups may be combined. Unrestricted current funds are those funds which are available for all purposes of the institution, subject only to the discretion of the governing board. Restricted current funds are those funds which, while available for current operating purposes, are subject to limitations or restrictions placed upon them by individuals or agencies outside the institution.

4. *The loan funds group consists of funds loanable to students, faculty, and staff.*

Loan funds, classified by source and purpose, constitute a separate fund group in the accounts and reports. Examples of different kinds of loan funds include appropriations from governmental bodies; gifts; grants; bequests designated by donors to be used for student loans, some of which may be refundable under certain conditions; and funds which are otherwise unrestricted but have been designated to be used as loan funds by the governing board. Funds whose principal is to be invested with only the income available for loans are classified as endowment funds and should be included in that fund group. The income from such funds should be transferred to the loan funds group and disbursed therefrom.

5. *The endowment and similar funds group includes those funds whose principal is nonexpendable as of the date of reporting and is invested, or is available for investment, for the purpose of producing income.*

Three types of funds are included in this group:

(a) Endowment funds are those in which donors have stipulated that the principal must be maintained inviolate and in perpetuity with only the income from the investment of the funds available for expenditure.

(b) Term endowment funds are those which may be released from the status of endowment to be utilized upon the happening of a particular event or the passage of a stated period of time, as specified by the donors.

(c) Quasi-endowment funds, or funds functioning as endowment, are determined by the governing board rather than a donor, at least for the time being, to be retained and invested as though they were endowment funds.

6. *Funds held in trust by others preferably should not be included in the balance sheet with other funds administered by the institution but should be disclosed parenthetically in the endowment and similar funds group in the balance sheet or in notes to the financial statements. However, if the institution has legally enforceable rights or claims, including those as to income, such funds may be reported as assets, properly described in the financial statements.*

If the funds were established under irrevocable trusts with no discretionary powers vested in the trustees with respect to income distribution, the income should be included as endowment income with a notation of the amount, or it should be separately stated. If the funds were established under revocable trusts, or if the trustees have discretionary power in the distribution of income, the amounts received by the institution are analagous to gifts and should be so recorded.

7. *The annuity and life income funds group includes funds acquired by an institution subject to annuity contracts, living trust*

agreements, or gifts and bequests reserving life income to one or more beneficiaries.

Since annuity and life income funds have different characteristics and obligations, their transactions should be reported separately in the financial statements. Earnings from the investment of these funds should be reported in the statement of changes in fund balances—annuity and life income funds.

8. *The plant funds group consists of funds to be used for the construction, rehabilitation, and acquisition of physical properties for institutional purposes; funds already expended for plant properties; funds set aside for the renewal and replacement thereof; and funds accumulated for the retirement of indebtedness thereon.*

Properties belonging to endowment funds should be reported in the endowment funds group. Plant assets, including land, buildings, improvements other than buildings, and equipment, should be carried in the accounts at cost if purchased or constructed and at appraised values in the cases of gifts.

9. *In case of properties used for educational and auxiliary enterprise purposes, depreciation accounting as used in commercial organizations does not apply.*

Depreciation expense related to educational and auxiliary enterprise property is reported neither in the statement of current funds revenues, expenditures, and other changes nor in the statement of changes in fund balances—current funds. The reason for this departure from commercial accounting concepts is that one of the principal reporting objectives of the institutional accounting is to disclose resources received and expended rather than net income. Thus acquisitions of capital assets financed from current funds are reported as expenditures of that group in the year of acquisition. However, a depreciation allowance may be reported in the plant funds section of the balance sheet and the provision for depreciation reported in the statement of changes in fund balances—investment in plant. Moreover, the fact that depreciation is not recorded in current funds does not preclude the use of expired capital cost data in evaluating performance and in making management decisions on operating activities.

In order to protect the integrity of endowment funds principal, depreciation accounting concepts should be followed in accounting for the operations of real properties, except land, belonging to endowment and similar funds.

10. *The necessity of providing for renewals and replacements of the physical plant facilities and other real properties of an institution depends upon the class of property under consideration and the financial program of the institution.*

If an institution wishes to do so, and state regulations permit, current funds revenues may be set aside for the renewal, replacement, or expansion of educational or auxiliary plant facilities. In such cases, cash or other liquid assets should be transferred from the current funds group to the unexpended plant funds group. Current revenues so allocated should be reported in the statement of current funds revenues, expenditures, and other changes as nonmandatory transfers to plant funds.

11. *The agency funds group consists of funds in the custody of the institution but not belonging to it.*

Funds of this nature include those belonging to individual students, student organizations, faculty committees, or other groups in the institution. Receipts and disbursements of such funds do not constitute current fund revenues and expenditures and are not included in current fund operating statements.

12. *Interfund borrowings of a temporary nature should be reported as assets of the fund group making the advances and as liabilities of the fund groups receiving the advances.*

This principle insures that loans or advances made between fund groups are properly disclosed in the financial statements. In the fund group making the advance, the transaction is recorded as an asset; in the fund group receiving the advance, the transaction is recorded as a liability.

13. *All funds restricted by the donor or granting agency at the time of receipt with regard to the purpose for which they may be expended should be recorded as additions to the fund balances of the appropriate fund group.*

This principle insures that the institution uses the resources in accordance with conditions imposed by a donor or a grantor outside the institution. Funds which otherwise are unrestricted as to use but upon which a governing board has placed restrictions are not restricted funds in the sense intended by this concept.

14. *Unrestricted current funds, regardless of source, must be reported as revenues in total in the year received or accrued, in the statement of current funds revenues, expenditures, and other changes.*

The principal sources of unrestricted revenues are tuition and fees, unrestricted gifts and bequests, unrestricted endowment income, governmental appropriations for operations, indirect cost allowances, income from temporary investments of current funds, sales and services of educational departments, and the income of auxiliary enterprises.

15. *Restricted current funds must be reported as revenues only to the extent expended during the year.*

Restricted current funds represent resources received for restricted operating purposes, the related expenditures of which may be extended beyond the fiscal year in which received. Such items constitute current revenues only to the extent the money is expended in the current fiscal year in accordance with the terms of the gift or donation.

16. *Transfers and allocations of unrestricted current funds must be reported in the statement of changes in fund balances—unrestricted current funds.*

A governing board may assign unrestricted funds to fund groups other than current funds and may modify or reverse such designations at a later time. Also, unrestricted current funds, where permitted under state regulations, may be set aside by the governing board for operating purposes in future fiscal years.

17. *The accounting system should be maintained and financial reports presented on the accrual basis.*

This principle signifies that revenues should be reported when earned and expenditures when materials or services are received. Materiality of a particular item may indicate that it is unnecessary to accrue a revenue or defer an expenditure.

18. *Revenues and expenditures of auxiliary enterprises should be shown separately from other institutional operations.*

The revenues and expenditures of auxiliary enterprises should be reported separately from educational and general revenues and expenditures in the statement of current funds revenues, expenditures, and other changes.

19. *Budgets covering all operations of the institution should be prepared and adopted each fiscal year.*

The annual operating budget includes all current funds revenues, expenditures, and transfers irrespective of source of revenues and purpose of expenditure. There should be an effective budgetary control system appropriate to the needs of the institution. Budgets for organized research projects, miscellaneous sponsored programs, and physical plant projects should also be prepared and adopted.

20. *Provisions should be made for internal control and audit. In addition, there should be an annual audit by independent accountants.*

This principle emphasizes that there should be provision for adequate internal control through appropriate organization, assignment of duties, and internal auditing procedures, and that there should be an annual audit by independent accountants.

21. *A comprehensive financial report should be prepared on a timely basis for submission annually to the chief executive officer of the institution and to the governing board.*

The institution's annual report should include at least a balance sheet, a statement of changes in fund balances, and a statement of current funds revenues, expenditures, and other changes. Other schedules and exhibits may be included, depending upon the wishes of the institution and the needs of those to whom the financial reports are addressed.

2

Development, Organization, and Personnel of the Business Office

In any consideration of accounting systems, the organization and the personnel of the business office must receive attention. The administrative organization of the business office is directly related to the accounting system. Without an adequate organization and competent staff, no accounting system will perform satisfactorily.

Development of the Business Office

The business office as an independent administrative unit is a relatively recent development in the American college. Early American colleges were of small size and simple structure, and business matters were administered in part by their governing boards and in part by the academic and executive branches of the college. Each faculty member or department head did the purchasing for his own division or department, sometimes from his "share" of the institutional funds. Account keeping was performed in a similarly unbusinesslike manner. As college enrollments multiplied, as institutional revenues increased, as auxiliary enterprises grew in size and importance, and as the academic and research structure of the institution became more complicated, business administration emerged as a distinct and separate function.

Today there is universal agreement that the business office is an important major unit in the administration of a college or university. Virtually every institution, however small, has an officer with the usual responsibilities of the chief business officer. This acceptance of the business office as an essential and integral part of college organization is predicated on two facts. The first is that the complicated and increasingly diverse activities of the modern educational institution make it essential that its financial affairs be administered by specialists. When it is realized that, in addition to a complicated academic structure involving large numbers of research projects and teaching programs, most institutions operate bookstores, dining halls, residence halls, college unions, printing shops, parking garages, and photographic studios (to name some of the auxiliary enterprises generally found on campuses), the need for specialized business management is obvious.

The second factor contributing to the acceptance of the business office as an essential part of the administrative organization of educational institutions is the recognized conviction that the faculty and the president of the institution should perform only academic and administrative duties, leaving business and financial affairs to individuals specially trained in this field. This conviction is founded not only on the fact that academic officials usually lack the training and aptitude for handling complex financial matters but also on the assumption that these persons should not have to divert their energies and abilities from instruction and research.

Place of the Business Office in the Organization Chart of the College

Regarding the location of the business office in the administrative framework of the college, two general types of organization are found—the unitary type and the multiple type (illustrated in Chart

CHART 2.1

THE UNITARY AND MULTIPLE FORMS OF ADMINISTRATIVE ORGANIZATIONS

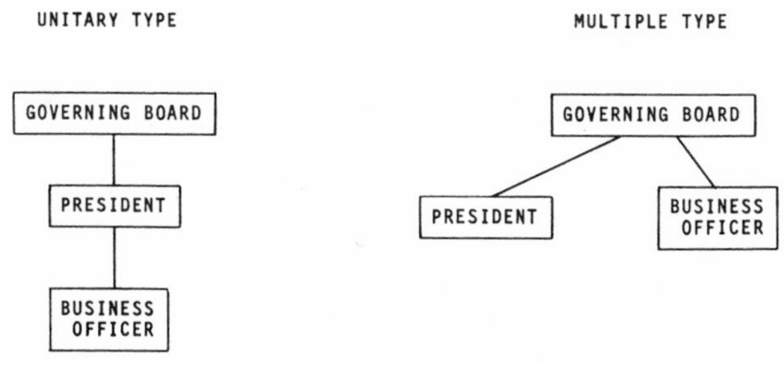

2.1). In the unitary type, the president receives his authority by delegation from the governing board and in turn delegates certain administrative functions to the other officers of the institution, including the business officer. In this form of organization the president is solely responsible to the governing board. In the multiple type of organization the president and other administrative officers each receive a delegation of authority from the governing board and operate in more or less parallel spheres of authority. For example, the president is held responsible for academic and general policies, the business officer for fiscal and accounting matters.

The unitary organization is by far the prevailing type among colleges and universities today and is the one which has proven to be administratively sound. Its chief advantage is that it allows complete centralization of authority in the president and makes the business function subordinate to the educational function. The weakness of the unitary type of organization may be that the business officer is subordinate to the president and, therefore, has no direct contact with the governing board. In actual practice, however, the business officer is directed by the president to work closely with those committees of the governing board which are involved with responsibilities in the business area—the building committee, the budget committee, and the finance committee, among others. Despite possible and theoretical weaknesses of the unitary type of organization, it is the one recommended by virtually every authority on educational administration and organization.

CHART 2.2

MODIFIED UNITARY TYPE ORGANIZATION

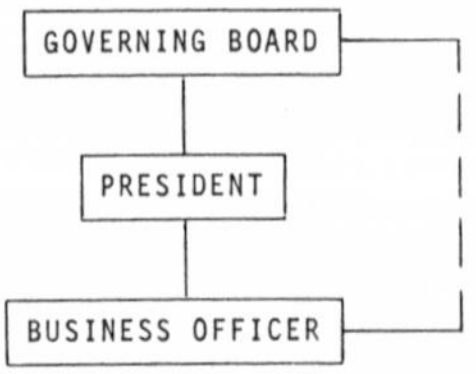

CHART 2.3

POSITION OF THE BUSINESS OFFICE IN THE ORGANIZATION CHART
OF THE EDUCATIONAL INSTITUTION

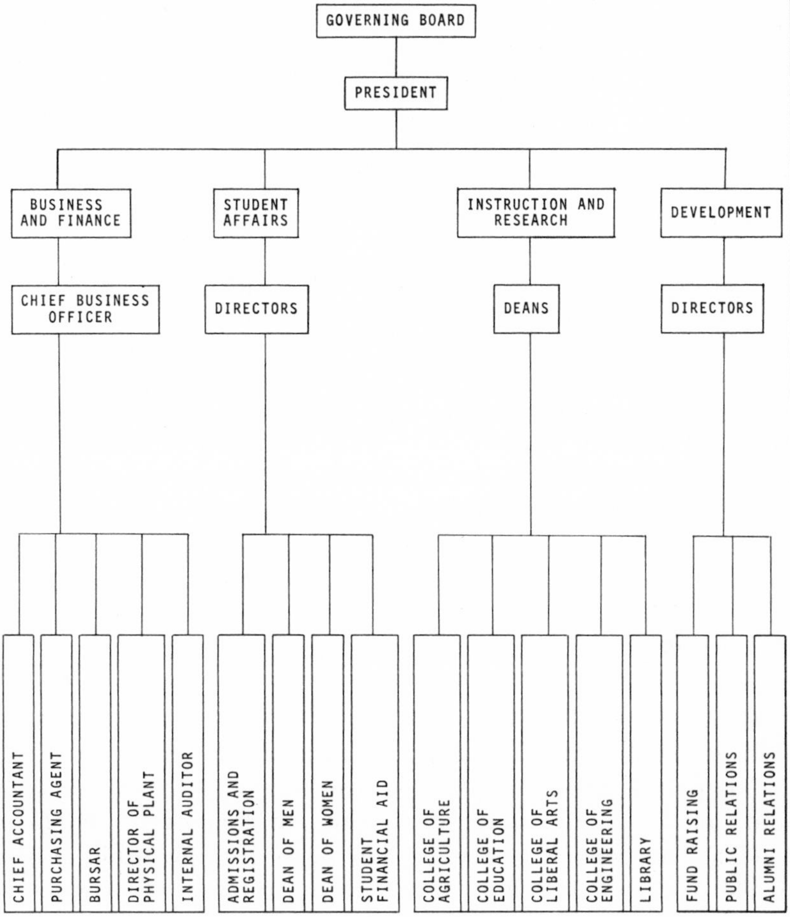

CHART 2.4

COMPOSITE ORGANIZATIONAL CHART

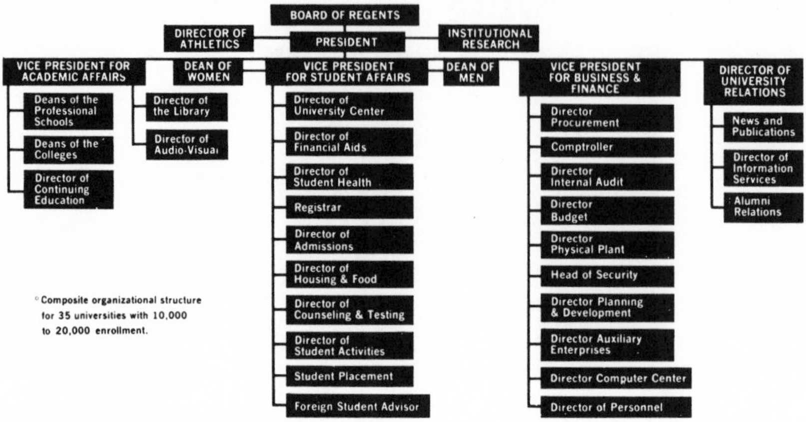

A possible modified type of unitary organization is illustrated in Chart 2.2. This arrangement makes the business officer responsible to the president in an administrative sense, but in an auditing and reporting capacity responsible directly to the governing board. It provides the business officer with that element of independence essential to any auditing agency.

Chart 2.3 illustrates the functional division of the college into four primary activities—instruction and research, business and finance, student affairs, and institutional development, the latter including public relations and fund raising. These are coordinate divisions, and, through their directors, each is responsible directly to the chief executive of the institution.

In September, 1968, *College & University Business* magazine (p. 74) published a "composite organizational chart" based on a study of 35 public universities with enrollments of 10,000 to 20,000. The general principles illustrated are applicable also to smaller colleges as well as to private institutions. The composite organizational structure is reproduced in Chart 2.4.

Functions of the Business Office

Business functions usually assigned to the business office include:

Budgets—assistance in preparation, administration, and control
Accounting

Internal auditing
Collection and custody of institutional funds
Preparation of financial reports
Purchasing and control of stores
Property control
Management of invested funds
Supervision of auxiliary enterprises
Supervision of operation and maintenance of physical plant, including planning, architectural services, and new construction
Administration of nonacademic personnel program
Fiscal supervision over student organizations and loan funds

The business office has a dual responsibility with respect to the budget. It assists in its preparation and participates in the control of the budget after it has been adopted by the governing board. Moreover, the business officer is given the further responsibility of advising the president in regard to requests for changes in the operating budget. In the preparation of the budget, the chief business officer usually acts as a financial advisor to the president. Armed with the financial history of the institution and with appropriate unit cost studies and analyses, the business officer is in an advantageous position to assist in preparing the budget. The president frequently depends on the advice and counsel of the chief academic officer, such as the dean of the college or the academic vice-president, and he works closely with the chief business officer to aid in this important task. The task of accumulating the data and of checking and typing the estimates also falls to the business officer and his staff. After the budget is submitted to and approved by the governing board, it must be controlled in order that the institution may function according to plan. A frequent method of budgetary control is to incorporate the budget into the accounting records. In the small college, however, and in a large university with sophisticated machine methods, budgetary control may be effected in other ways. Although the primary responsibility for adherence to the approved budget should rest with the budget head, the accounting office must assume the final authority in insuring that actual operations are in reasonable conformity with the financial plan as approved by the governing board.

As to the other functions of the business office, accounting and purchasing activities are important responsibilities. All records and methods of record keeping are prescribed and supervised by the business office. Although certain detailed accounting records, such as auxiliary enterprises, may be maintained in operating departments, the central business office must retain control over and responsibility for these subsidiary accounting arrangements.

Internal control is a by-product of the accounting function, growing in importance as the institution grows. The business office as custodian of institutional funds must maintain a continuous review of all activities of the institution relating to the collection and disbursement of funds. The preparation of reports to the governing board and to the president and the compilation of financial information are other functions related to accounting. In addition, the fiscal system ordinarily calls for periodic budget reports to assist those responsible for the administration of individual budgets.

Central purchasing by the business office is an important function of that office and is a necessary supplement to the accounting system. The concept of centralized procurement does not preclude the active participation of academic and other departments in the purchasing process nor the delegation of some details of purchasing to agencies outside the business office. It simply means that the ultimate responsibility for all institutional procurement rests with the business office. The control and management of storerooms are closely allied to the purchasing function, as are also the control and management of movable property.

An important function sometimes assigned to the business office is that of the management of endowment and similar funds belonging to the institution. The extent and degree of business office responsibility for the management of invested funds depends upon the procedural arrangements at a given institution. Frequently, the primary responsibility for managing the investment of endowment funds is retained by the governing board or delegated to one of its committees or to external investment managers. In other cases, this responsibility may be delegated to the chief business officer of the institution, with the board or a committee of the board acting on matters of broad investment policy. Regardless, however, of the variety of responsibilities with respect to the handling of endowment funds, the business office usually is called upon to maintain endowment funds records. It must also perform such auditing functions as will assure the safety of the assets of those funds and income in accordance with any restrictions imposed by donors.

In most institutions the fiscal supervision over auxiliary enterprises such as bookstores, residence halls, dining halls, and laundries is considered to be a function of the business office. The degree of supervision and the extent to which the business office is responsible for the management of these activities varies among institutions.

The administration of the physical plant is another important responsibility of the business office. The immediate responsibility rests in a director of physical plant or a superintendent of buildings and grounds who is under the direction of the chief business officer. This business office function includes responsibility for physical plant planning and architectural services.

In most institutions the responsibilities of the business office include the administration of the personnel program involving the nonteaching staff. The immediate responsibility is assigned to a director of personnel who is responsible to the chief business officer.

An important function of the business office which is sometimes neglected is that of exercising supervision over the financial aspects of student organizations and loan funds. Such activities include student publications and student cooperatives. Fraternities and sororities are usually, but not always, excluded from this category.

Internal Organization of the Business Office

The internal organization of the business office has a direct bearing on the adequacy of the operation of the accounting system. An accounting system, no matter how well designed, does not operate itself. Accounting personnel, however competent and well trained, cannot operate at peak efficiency without a carefully planned internal organization that clearly fixes responsibilities, eliminates duplications, and avoids vacuums in the operations of the business office. Internal audit and control is an important adjunct of the properly organized business office.

The internal organization of the business office varies among institutions, being determined by the size of the institution, available budgets, personal attributes and abilities of the officers, and many other factors. Most college business officers are charged with nearly all the functions referred to above. But whether all of these activities are performed by one official in one office or several officers in several offices, depends upon the characteristics of the institution in question. Some of the factors that influence the organization of the business office and the size of its staff include the number of students enrolled, the number of faculty members, the amount of annual revenues and expenditures, the degree of centralization of business functions, the amount of endowment, the plan for management of invested funds, the extent of research grants and contracts, the volume of auxiliary activities, general policies regarding the supervision of the financial aspects of student activities, and the relationship of the institution to the community.

It is not practicable to consider all variations in the organizational plans of college business offices. However, the following charts attempt to illustrate some of the more typical organizations found in institutions ranging from the small liberal arts college to the large university. It is emphasized that the charts are presented only for purposes of illustration and that in practice the organization of business offices will vary, even among institutions of the same size, with respect to enrollment and total budget.

Chart 2.5 illustrates the business office of a small college having a fairly simple organization. Within this organization, a functional division of responsibilities is possible, one employee acting as a check on another.

In Chart 2.6 the chief business officer, the accountant, and the bursar essentially constitute the business office. The chief business officer assumes the functions of purchasing, assistance in budget preparation, fiscal management of the auxiliary enterprises, and supervision over the physical plant. The accountant is responsible for the accounts, the reports, and internal checks and auditing, whereas the bursar assumes the cashier function. This form of organization, with or without modification, is adaptable with equal advantage to a college smaller or larger than the one illustrated. The organization illustrated in Chart 2.7 is an expansion of the organization shown in Chart 2.6. Chart 2.8 illustrates a more com-

CHART 2.5

SMALL LIBERAL ARTS COLLEGE

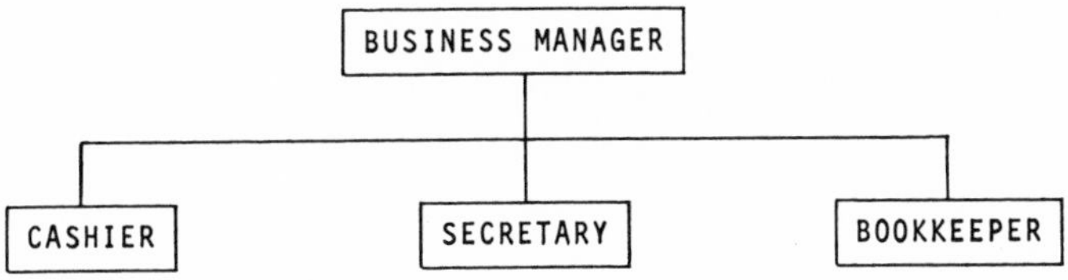

CHART 2.6

COLLEGE-- ENROLLMENT 1500, BUDGET $5,000,000

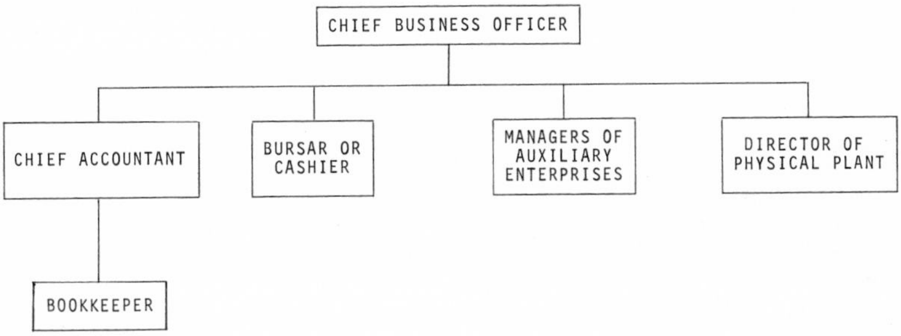

CHART 2.7

COLLEGE-- ENROLLMENT 2000, BUDGET $7,000,000

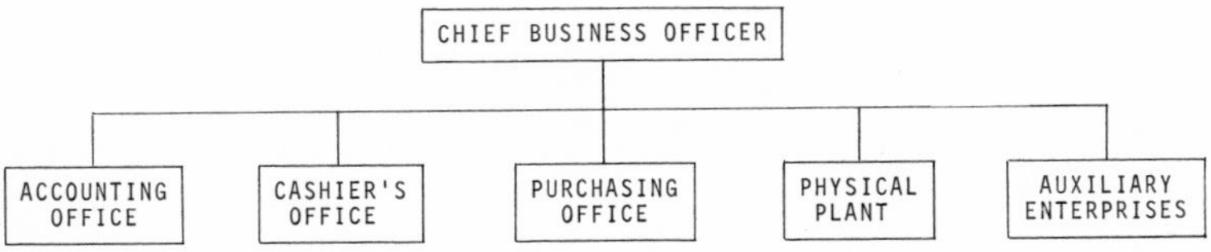

CHART 2.8

ORGANIZATION CHART*

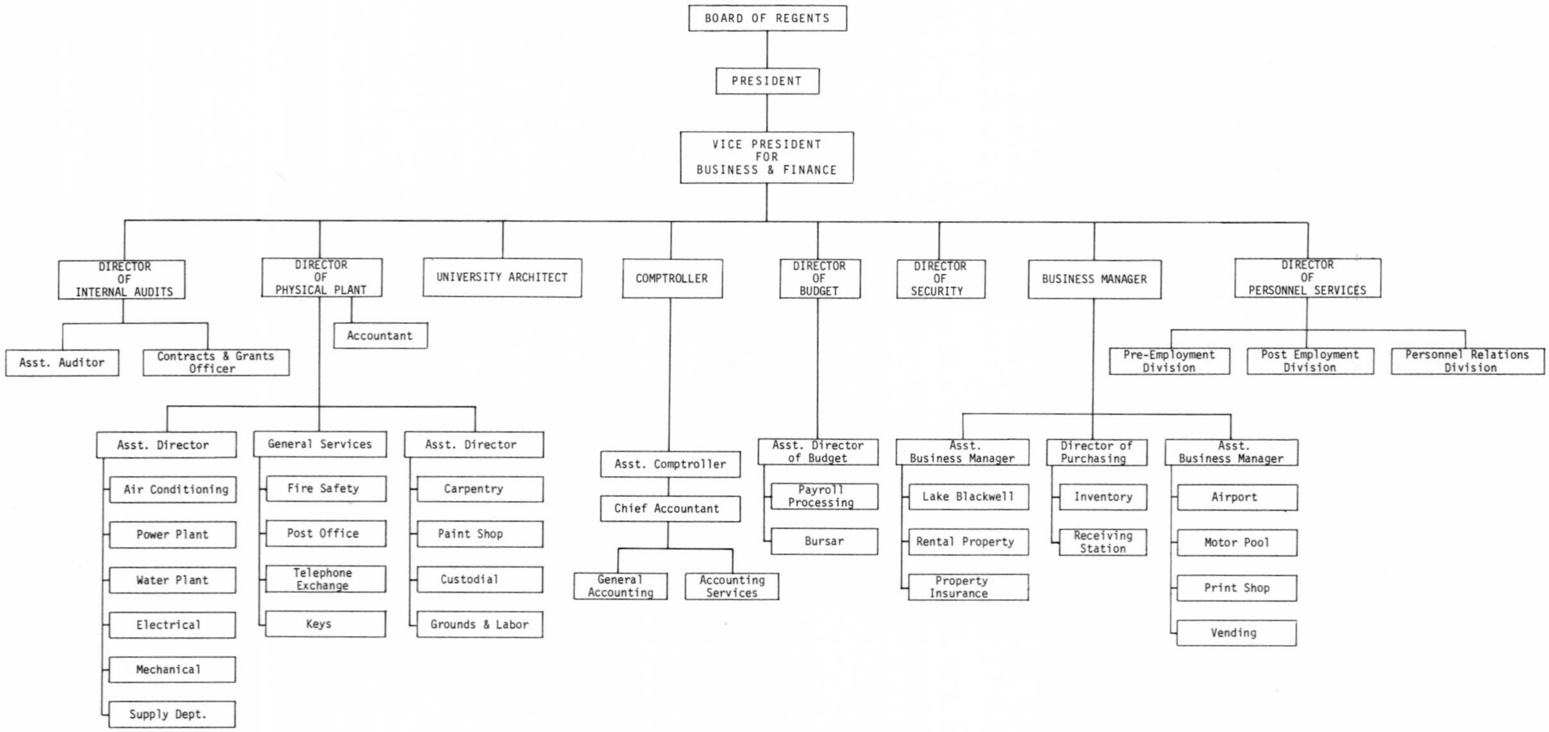

*Reproduced with the permission of Oklahoma State University, Stillwater, Oklahoma.

plicated organization of a large state institution, with certain groupings of functions which become possible as the institution grows in size and complexity.

Title of the Chief Business Officer

No particular title is suggested for the chief business officer because there is no uniformity in this respect. In previous years such titles as bursar, financial secretary, auditor, and treasurer were used to designate the chief business officer. Today, two titles are frequently used—business manager and comptroller. Many chief business officers are being given a vice-presidential title, such as vice-president for business and finance, financial vice-president, vice-president—business affairs.

Qualifications of the Chief Business Officer

It is appropriate to consider the qualifications of the chief business officer of an educational institution. He should be equipped with appropriate experience and education. Although commercial business experience is valuable, he should understand the essential differences between the problems faced in a college or university and in business. A study by the American Council on Education summarizes the principal qualifications needed by a college business officer as follows:

> In addition to special training, a position of responsibility in college and university business management calls for certain personal qualities. Among those, honesty and integrity are, of course, first. In close succession follow the qualities of tact, ability to cooperate, congeniality, and business judgment. There must then be added the essential qualities of untiring industry, initiative, and resourcefulness. An institutional business officer has contacts with a wide variety of persons. He is in contact with the members of the academic organization, with boards of trustees made up chiefly of business and professional men, with business concerns, students, and alumni. If he is in a public institution he must have contact with members of the state legislature and with state and federal officers. A wide variety of problems and personalities present themselves in rapid succession.[1]

College and University Business Administration states that "the chief business officer, as one responsible for managing the re-

1. *Training for College and University Business Administration: Series III, Financial Advisory Service*, (Washington, D.C.: American Council on Education Studies, 1937), Vol. I, No. 7, p. 10.

sources of the institution, must bring to the task high technical competence, a considerable administrative ability, and a grasp of, and a liking for, the elements of the educational environment. He must be equipped by training and experience to assume large responsibilities and must be professional in viewpoint." The volume goes on to say that the chief business officer should have academic preparation of appropriate depth and that he "must be, above all, the kind of person who, dedicated to learning, uses every opportunity for the improvement of professional knowledge and skills. The officer should be sensitive to questions of human and public relations and should be able to represent the institution before any audience interested in its mission, goals, achievements, or courses of action."[2]

2. *College and University Business Administration* (3rd Rev. ed.; Washington, D.C.: National Association of College and University Business Officers, 1974), 7–8.

3

Purchasing and Central Stores

COLLEGES AND UNIVERSITIES require a wide variety of materials, supplies, equipment, and services in their day-to-day operations, involving the expenditure of large sums of the institutions' money. Many of these items are unique and complex, and their procurement entails special problems. College and university administrators generally agree that institutional procurement can be done more efficiently and economically by those having specialized training and experience.

Centralized Purchasing. Regardless of the size of an institution, and whether the purchasing function is the full-time responsibility of a specialist or the part-time duty of some other official, the procurement operations in a college or university should be centralized within the institutional business organization.

The chief advantage in a system of centralized purchasing is economy in buying. A trained purchasing agent is able to find the most appropriate commodities at the lowest prices because he is constantly in touch with markets and sources of supply. Open competition by means of bids or other methods helps obtain goods at lower prices, and a centralized purchasing office provides the best means of performing the tasks necessary in requesting, verifying, and comparing bids. A centralized procurement organization, with its associated central storerooms, reduces costly overstocking of items, duplication of commodities, and failure to have essential items available when needed. By developing commodity specifications and enforcing these standards through centralized buying, it is possible to eliminate, or at least greatly reduce, unnecessarily wide ranges in size, color, material, and quality for the same items.

Second, centralized purchasing provides a uniform system of financial control. When purchasing is decentralized, budgetary control is difficult. Unless all purchases originate in a single office in conformity with standard procedures and unless approved requisitions precede the issuance of orders, budgetary control through the accounting system is practically impossible. In addition, the controls established through centralized purchasing make possible the systematic receipt and inspection of goods; the orderly handling, auditing, and recording of documents related to the procurement of commodities; and the orderly payment of invoices.

Third, centralized purchasing releases faculty members from tedious and time-consuming tasks which are not part of their primary functions in the institution. Academic personnel are employed to instruct and carry out research. Seeking sources of supply, negotiating with vendors, bargaining with salesmen, studying market conditions, supervising the receipt and inspection of deliveries, tracing invoices, and other similar tasks in the procurement process consume time and energy. When responsibility for all phases of procurement is placed in the purchasing department, faculty members are free to perform their functions of teaching, research, and public service.

Finally, centralized purchasing, by fixing responsibility for buying in one department, makes possible an audit control over institutional expenditures for materials, supplies, equipment, and services which is impossible when purchasing is decentralized.

Centralized Purchasing Procedures. Under centralized purchasing, a single official in the business organization of a college or university is held responsible for all institutional procurement. However, this officer, usually known as a purchasing agent or director of purchasing, is not completely independent of other officers and departments of the institution; he is not at liberty to purchase what and when he pleases. A proper procurement program requires first of all a statement, notification, or other form of request from the using department to the purchasing department listing the needed supplies, equipment, and services. This is done on a requisition form. Usually, the head of the using department has the authority to initiate requisitions for items to be charged to his departmental budget allocations, although in some instances the additional approval of a dean or director may be required.

Although the purchasing agent may have specialized training and experience in institutional procurement, he should always seek the advice and suggestions of the users when he is buying technical, specialized, and scientific laboratory equipment and supplies. Nevertheless, the performance of all the tasks related to the procurement of these items is the responsibility of the purchasing agent and the staff in his department.

The procurement of some items in an educational institution may be handled advantageously outside the routine of centralized purchasing. Examples are the day-to-day food requirements of dining halls, cafeterias, and food service departments; merchandise for resale in the student stores; and library books and periodicals.

In the area of food services, bids on a number of standard items may be obtained by the purchasing agent in cooperation with the dietician or director of the food service. A standing order may then be issued to the supplier whose bid was accepted, calling for the delivery of a commodity, at the bid price, as needed during a specified period of time. Authority is delegated to the director of the food services to purchase up to the amount of the standing order without further approval of the purchasing agent. The purchase of bread illustrates the procedure. Fresh bread is needed daily; it would be highly impractical to issue, process, and encumber individual orders for each day's purchases. Instead, bids are obtained from several bakeries, specifications calling for the delivery of bread at the price agreed upon, for a stated period of time, perhaps a month. One purchase order is issued for the estimated monthly cost of bread deliveries and goes through the regular channels of encumbrances in the accounting office. To obtain daily deliveries of bread in the quantities needed, the food service manager or his representative places an order each day without further approval of the purchasing department or the issuance of formal documents. Through this procedure the purchasing department maintains control over purchases in the food service department and the accounting office maintains control over the food service budget with a minimum of routine work, especially on the part of the food service personnel.

Another example of delegating the purchasing function is in the buying of library books and periodicals. Little "shopping around" can be done in this area; consequently, the librarian is authorized to purchase these items. Advantages of this procedure are that it eliminates writing requisitions, which serve no good purpose in this case, and typing by the purchasing office of long lists of books and magazines that are of use only in the library. Another exception to centralized purchasing may be made in the case of the student store, in which its manager is given discretionary authority to buy merchandise which is to be resold in the store.

A procedure which offers certain practical advantages in institutional procurement, although it is not entirely an exception to the centralized purchasing concept, is the issuance of monthly standing orders for certain types of recurring purchases, usually small in amount, such as automobile and truck repairs. Instead of issuing individual orders for tire repairs and minor motor adjustments, a standing order for an estimated sum is issued to a local garage at the beginning of the month. Whenever possible, specific unit prices should be quoted in such orders. For example, the standing order could provide for labor, at $8.00 per hour, and parts at list price, less 25%. Depending on the volume of business contemplated, these prices could be negotiated by the purchasing department through competitive bids or by telephone quotation. The maintenance department is then authorized to obtain the services needed by direct contact with the garage. This procedure not only reduces the total number of orders issued but also the number of confirming orders required.

To be workable, any system of centralized purchasing must provide for emergency situations. The purchasing agent should prepare, and the chief business officer should promulgate, rules and regulations concerning emergency orders, and every effort should be made to guard against their abuse. Unregulated emergency orders may nullify budgetary control as well as other advantages of centralized purchasing. In cases of an emergency, the purchase should be reported to the purchasing department as soon as possible, so that a confirming requisition can be prepared and processed through the accounting office and a confirming purchase order can be issued.

Obviously, centralized purchasing does not mean that every

item of materials, supplies, equipment, and service must be bought coldly and shrewdly on the basis of only a departmental requisition, without consulting the requisitioner. Centralized purchasing means the systematic centralization of responsibility over all institutional purchases, as well as a uniform and systematic method of channeling forms and documents involved in the procurement process. Effective purchasing, like other functions of the business office, is not an end in itself, but instead is an additional way of serving the institution in the execution of its educational program.

The purchasing agent is frequently involved in the planning for new construction and for renovation and alteration projects. His participation may be limited to the evaluation and selection of movable equipment items, but preferably he should be involved in the whole planning process. The purchasing agent may receive bids for new construction and renovation and alteration projects. These bids are handled in a fashion similar to the handling of bids on other materials and services.

In the case of state institutions, a central state agency such as a state building commission may have to approve the final contract before an award is made. In some states construction bids are received and contract awards are made by an agency of the state rather than by the institution.

Purchasing Relations to the State and Community. In some states a centralized procurement organization performs the purchasing function for all institutions and agencies in the state. This arrangement has some advantages, and many state-controlled colleges and universities may be bound by law to place all purchases through the state organization. Some disadvantages exist, however. The plan does not necessarily enable institutions to eliminate positions or reduce numbers of employees in their own business offices because of the necessity to prepare special specifications, to perform the task of encumbrance accounting, to carry out follow-up orders and receiving procedures, and to see to other functions that cannot be performed by the state office. Often, delays in deliveries to the using institutions are caused by having to place orders through a distantly removed state office. Savings in prices are not always experienced through state purchasing, and on occasion higher prices actually are paid. Frequently, there is a tendency for the purchasing function and organizations at the state level to become involved in politics.

Some of these objections can be overcome if state-controlled colleges and universities are permitted the option of placing orders either through the state purchasing system or directly with suppliers. For certain types of commodities having standard characteristics, institutions can profit by savings resulting from quantity purchasing on a statewide basis. A contract for a standard item, such as paper towels, may be awarded by the state purchasing office with all institutions participating on a voluntary basis. The question of whether an institution should participate in purchasing procedures established for all state agencies and institutions must be answered with reference to the laws of the state and practices and procedures of the state purchasing system.

Sometimes educational institutions are under pressure to purchase goods and services from local sources. The argument is advanced that because the taxes or gifts of local businesses help to support the colleges or universities, they are obligated to spend their funds in the local community. It is more important to remember that educational institutions have a stronger obligation to spend their funds as wisely as possible, whether this means purchasing locally or from other marketing areas. An institution can answer the argument, at least in part, by pointing out its total financial impact on the community through such things as the salaries and wages paid to staff and faculty, most of which is spent locally, and the purchasing power for goods and services of local merchants brought to the community by students. If all other factors in the procurement procedure are equal, such as price, quality, and service, it might well be in the best interest of an institution to buy from local sources. In any event, decisions to buy locally rather than from other areas should not be made solely by the one responsible for the purchasing function. Such decisions, especially if they involve the possibility of paying higher prices, should be made at the top level of administration and should be based on all the facts involved in the situation. In times of serious shortages of products, when bids cannot be obtained in the usual manner, it may be necessary for purchasing agents to negotiate directly with suppliers. When this situation occurs, the purchasing agent should have institutional approval to conduct such direct negotiations.

Purchasing Procedures. Procedures in a centralized purchasing system involve the following steps: (1) notification of the purchasing department by means of requisitions of the needs of using departments; (2) selection of, and negotiation with, suppliers; (3) issuance of purchase orders; (4) receipt of goods or services; (5) approval of invoices; (6) operation, supervision, and control of a system of storerooms on campus.

Issuance of Requisitions. The first step in purchasing is the issuance, by the head of the department needing the items, of a requisition addressed to the purchasing agent. Four types of requisitions may be used by an institution: the advance requisition, the purchase requisition, the stores requisition, and the work requisition.

The advance requisition is used in notifying the purchasing department of the estimated requirements for various commodities and services over a given period of time, such as a month, a quarter, or a semester. The purchasing agent is thus able to plan his buying in advance so that savings may be effected through consolidated, quantity purchases. Also, the purchasing agent is given the opportunity of taking advantage of fortuitous situations in buying certain supplies and commodities.

The purchase requisition (Form 3.1) is used for day-to-day needs. The stores requisition, illustrated and explained later in this chapter, is used when the desired items can be obtained from a storeroom on campus. The work requisition is used for requests involving maintenance and repair work to be performed by the appropriate shop or workers in the physical plant department of the institution. In most instances, the purchase requisition can be used in lieu of a work requisition.

Although variations exist among institutions in regard to the details of requisition procedures, the following points are usually applicable to all educational institutions. Requisitions should be prepared in several copies, preferably by typewriter. One copy is

FORM 3.1

BLANK COLLEGE

P U R C H A S E   R E Q U I S I T I O N

To: The Purchasing Department

Date__________ Order No.__________

Required Delivery Date__________

Department__________

Deliver To__________ (Bldg.) __________ (Room)

To Be Used For__________

Name and Address of Vendor(s) Suggested

Do Not Fill In

Promise Date__________ Ship Via__________

Cash Terms__________

F.O.B. Terms__________

Quantity	Please Give Full Description and Complete Specifications. Attach Written Quotations If Such Were Received.	Estimated Unit Price	Actual Unit Price	Total

College Policy: The Purchasing Agent Is Vested With The Sole Authority to Order Materials And Contract For Services. The College Will Honor No Obligation Except On A Previously Issued And Duly Authorized Purchase Order.

Departmental and Object Code__________

Approved If Necessary__________ President or Business Mgr.

Requested By__________

Approved__________ Purchasing Agent

Approved By__________ Dean or Administrative Head

Bid File Number__________

retained by the using department, the other copies being forwarded to the purchasing department and other offices and departments, depending on the system. Distribution of copies is simplified if they are in different colors. Usually full instructions on the purchasing procedures of an institution are included in a manual of business procedures, if such a publication is prepared. In the absence of such a manual, instructions on the preparation and use of requisitions should be printed on the reverse side of the form.

Following is an illustration of a set of instructions:

Directions for Drawing Purchase Requisitions

(Use stores requisition, Form 3.13, for materials and supplies located in institutional storerooms, office supply stores, dining hall stores, and physical plant stores.)

I. General—Prepare requisitions on typewriter in triplicate and retain one copy. Send the other copies to the office of the purchasing agent. The latter copies must be signed by the department head and approved by the dean of your college.

II. Content—Use the purchase requisition for all requests of equipment, materials, supplies (other than from stores), and service. Use this form, also, when requesting stamps from the college post office. Whenever possible include on a given requisition only items that can be ordered from one vendor.

III. Specifications—See that complete and accurate specifications are given for every item requested. Failure to do this willl cause delay in filling the request.

IV. Estimated Cost—So far as possible, estimated cost of each item should be shown. A department, however, should not go to any particular trouble or expense to obtain estimates. The purchasing agent, upon request, will be glad to assist a department in securing prices.

V. Availability of Funds—No requisition should be submitted unless the funds are available. It is the duty of the department head to keep up with his own budget, and to assist in this process the accounting office will provide each department head with a budget statement at the beginning of each month.

VI. Departmental and Object Code—All requisitions must be coded in the space headed departmental and object code. Since the accounting department determines from this code the departmental budget to be charged, it is very important that the coding be done accurately. There are two parts to the code: the departmental, which indicates the department to be charged, and the object, which indicates the particular budget to be charged. Refer to the chart of accounts to determine the proper object code.

VII. Purchase Orders—The purchasing agent will issue all purchase orders. One copy of the order will be sent to the requisitioning department. Check each order carefully and notify the purchasing agent promptly of any errors or omissions.

VIII. RECEIVING PROCEDURE

a. Supplies—All orders of supplies, materials, and equipment will be delivered to the central receiving depot, where they will be checked and compared with the original order. The receiving department will then deliver the order to the requisitioning department. The department head or his authorized representative must certify that the goods have been received in quantity and quality ordered and that an invoice based on such order is properly payable.

b. Service—All orders of service will be delivered direct to the requisitioning department. The department head will certify on a receiving report that the service has been rendered and that an invoice based on the order is properly payable. The order should be checked promptly by the requisitioning department, and the purchasing agent should be advised of any damage, improperly functioning equipment, shortages, or other service problems.

The availability of funds must be determined before a purchase order is written. Usually the requisition, or a copy of it, goes through the accounting department for this determination, which necessitates the recording of an estimated, or actual, cost of the items being requisitioned. Since the using department ordinarily has little or no knowledge of the cost, the requisition must first be sent to the purchasing department, where this information can be obtained and recorded on the form, and then sent to the accounting department for approval of funds. All this entails some time and may delay placing an order, but the step is essential if budgetary control is to function. It may be omitted when the amount in question is small. Some institutions prepare the purchase order and then check for availability of funds.

If funds are not available, the requisition should be returned to the using department with an appropriate note. A question might be raised here as to the scope of authority of the accounting office or purchasing agent in approving or disapproving requisitions. Although it is true that department heads, with perhaps the approval of deans or directors, have the right to spend their allocated funds in accordance with the approved budget, it is, nevertheless, the duty of the business office to refuse approval of requisitions calling for illegal or obviously extravagant purchases. Rather than exercise veto power over requisitions, the accountant or purchasing agent should refer questionable requisitions to the chief business officer or other appropriate administrative officer. Normally, requisitions are approved by the accounting office if funds are available in the specified accounts and budgets.

Obtaining Quotations and Selecting Vendors. The next steps in the procurement process are obtaining prices for the items requisitioned and selecting suppliers. For most large orders, written quotations should be obtained from at least three suppliers through the use of a request for quotation, illustrated in Form 3.2. This form can be printed on thin paper so that, by using carbon paper, a number of copies can be prepared at one typing, the only difference being in the name of the vendors. As a practical matter, and in the interest of conserving time, quotations often are obtained by telephone contacts. Care must be exercised on the part of buyers, however, to prevent the habitual patronizing of certain suppliers to the exclusion of others. It is a good practice to have all quotations recorded on copies of the request for quotation form so that the purchasing department files will reflect the extent to which competition has been sought and obtained. In the case of purchases involving large sums of money, sealed bids should be required of suppliers.

The statutes of many states provide that state-controlled institutions must obtain bids on all orders in which the amount involved exceeds a specified sum. These laws may specify that newspaper or other public advertisement must precede requests for bids and, also, that the lowest bidder must be awarded the order, regardless of his ability to provide service, his reliability for delivery, or even the quality of his product.

Issuance of Purchase Orders. After quotations are obtained and suppliers are selected, purchase orders are then prepared and issued. Practices among colleges and universities differ regarding the form, content, number, and use of copies of purchase orders. Variations depend on the procedures for delivery on campus and

FORM 3.2

Office of
Purchasing Agent

BLANK COLLEGE

R E Q U E S T F O R Q U O T A T I O N
(This is not an Order)

TO:

Date____________

Please submit your quotations on such items in the following list as you are able to furnish. Quotations must be in this office by ____________

BLANK COLLEGE

INQUIRY NUMBER

____
Purchasing Agent

INSTRUCTIONS

Our specifications must be strictly adhered to or full particulars given regarding proposed substitutes.
Submit quotation on this form. Address to PURCHASING AGENT, BLANK COLLEGE.
It is requested that all items be quoted F.O.B. Blank College. All quotations will be so considered unless otherwise specified.
Our terms are 2% 10 days--Net 30 days unless otherwise specified.
The right is reserved to accept or reject all or any part of quotations submitted.
The right is reserved to cancel orders unless shipping date is maintained.

Quantity	Unit	Items and Specifications	Unit Price	Total Price

BLANK COLLEGE

Date____________

We propose to furnish above items at prices listed opposite each, and guarantee that if order is placed with us, we will furnish these goods or services in accordance with your specifications shown above unless otherwise indicated.

By____________

TERMS____________

Firm____________

F.O.B.____ BLANK COLLEGE ____

Street____________

Shipment will be made within ______ days after receipt of order.

____
City State Zip

the system of accounting and financial control. The use of printing computers and other types of electronic equipment will also cause differences among institutions in the preparation and use of copies of purchase orders. It is generally agreed, however, that several copies of the purchase order should be prepared when the order is first typed in the purchasing department. Regardless of the variations, purchase orders should be prenumbered, and procedures for the issuance, use, and accounting of purchase order forms should be subject to the same audit and control as other business

FORM 3.3

BLANK COLLEGE

P U R C H A S E   O R D E R

ORDER NO.

Show this order number on invoices, packages, and shipping papers.

Date____________________

Promised Shipping Date ________________

Cash Terms________________

F.O.B. Terms________________

Ship Via________________

Requisition No.

Please Ship, Subject to the Conditions Below, the Following Materials

Item No.	Quantity	D e s c r i p t i o n	Unit Price	Total Price

Code or Fund No.

Est. Cost

Partial Liquidations

ADDRESS AND MAIL INVOICES IN DUPLICATE TO OFFICE OF THE COMPTROLLER

SHIP AS FOLLOWS:

BLANK COLLEGE
Receiving Department-ORDER NO.

BLANK COLLEGE

By____________________
Purchasing Agent

ACKNOWLEDGEMENT: Acknowledge receipt of this order and advise when and from what point shipment will be made.
SUBSTITUTIONS: Substitutions or price increases will not be accepted without prior written approval of the Purchasing Agent.
INVOICES: Address and mail invoices in duplicate to Office of the Comptroller. Show purchase order number. Do not include state or federal taxes. Purchaser will furnish tax exemption certificate upon request. Discount period to be calculated from date invoice or material is received, whichever is later.
CANCELLATIONS: Blank College reserves the right to cancel all or any part of this order not shipped in accordance with terms and conditions stated above or on vendor's quotation.
CORRESPONDENCE: Address all correspondence concerning this order to the Purchasing Dept. & refer to Order No.

FORM 3.4

PURCHASE ORDER
(Lower Portion)

PARTIAL DELIVERIES					
Voucher No.	Amount	Voucher No.	Amount	APPROVED:	Liq.
FOR ACCOUNTING OFFICE - 2				Purchasing Agent	

FORM 3.5

PURCHASE ORDER
(Lower Portion)

FUNDS AVAILABLE

Chief Accountant

FOR PURCHASING DEPARTMENT - 3

FORM 3.6

PURCHASE ORDER
(Lower Portion)

I certify that the above articles have been carefully serviced and rendered and that an invoice based on above is properly payable.	I certify that the above articles have been carefully checked for quantity and quality. Any shortages or exceptions have been noted.
Date Head of Department	Date Receiving Clerk
FOR RECEIVING DEPARTMENT - 4	

FORM 3.7

PURCHASE ORDER
(Lower Portion)

This is a copy of the order placed from your requisition. In case of error, please notify Purchasing Department at once.

FOR REQUISITIONING DEPARTMENT - 5

FORM 3.8

PURCHASE ORDER
(Lower Portion)

FOR PURCHASING DEPARTMENT - 6	

and financial documents and forms, such as prenumbered checks.

Following is a suggested list of copies of purchase order forms and the methods in which they are used:

COPY NUMBER	RECIPIENT AND USE
Original	To supplier
2	To accounting department, for encumbrance recording
3	To purchasing department, for vendor file
4	To receiving depot, to be used in reporting receipt of materials. If there is no central receiving department, this copy is sent to requesting department to be used in reporting receipt of material.
5	To requesting department, for its permanent file
6	To purchasing department, for purchase order numerical file

Receipt of Goods and Approval of Invoices. The next steps in the procurement procedure are the receipt of materials ordered and the processing of vendors' invoices. Variations in these procedures will be found among institutions because of many factors, chief of which is the method of receiving materials. In some institutions all materials are delivered to a central receiving depot; in others, materials are delivered directly tc the requisitioning department.

Central receiving has several advantages. It facilitates delivery to the institution by establishing and making known to suppliers a single point of delivery on the campus, thus obviating the problem often faced by delivery personnel of locating various departments and offices scattered over a large campus. A central delivery depot can be staffed by trained and experienced personnel, so that packages, crates, boxes, and other containers will be carefully, quickly, and efficiently examined and that the condition of materials upon arrival can be expertly noted. By comparing the goods delivered with the purchase order, verification can be made of the accuracy of shipment as far as quantity and general description are concerned. Deviations from the purchase order can then be noted in the presence of the personnel of the carrier and reported promptly to the purchasing department.

The central receiving personnel probably will not be able to determine damage to technical and scientific equipment, especially if it is internal. This means that department heads must examine deliveries promptly, even from a central receiving depot, and report any problems to the purchasing department.

The central receiving procedure is as follows. All supplies and materials, with the exception of food supplies, merchandise for resale, and heavy equipment, are delivered to the central receiving depot, where they are examined and checked by the receiving personnel. If it is possible to check an order without unloading it from the vendor's truck, this is done. After checking, the vendor then delivers the order to the proper department. In most cases, however, it will be necessary to transship the goods by the institution's trucks. The receiving department personnel fills out a receiving report (Form 3.9) for the items received. The receiving report is then signed and delivered to the requesting department. When goods are delivered to the department, a second certification is placed on the receiving report by the department head or his authorized representative. The receiving report is then sent to the accounting office with a copy to the purchasing department, where it serves as evidence of the proper receipt of the goods. In case of partial deliveries, a partial delivery receiving report follows the same channels to the accounting office with a copy to the purchasing department.

Frequently, the central receiving depot is responsible for the payment of freight and express bills and may be assigned a petty cash fund from which to pay such items. In the case of orders for services, such as repairs and printing, the delivery is made directly

FORM 3.9

BLANK COLLEGE

RECEIVING REPORT

NO.

Received From:

For Account Of:

Order Reference__________

Date Received__________

Shipped Via__________

B/L or Express Receipt No.__________

Quantity	Description	Weight

Code

I certify the above material received:

Receiving Department — Requisitioning Department — Date

to the requesting department, and the head of the department is responsible for forwarding the receiving report to the accounting office.

With regard to invoices, either of two plans may be followed. In one plan, a uniform invoice form prepared by the institution is sent with the purchase order to suppliers. One condition of the purchase agreement is that the vendor will bill the institution on this standard invoice. A system of this kind is difficult to establish among suppliers but it has many advantages. It replaces vendors' invoices, which vary widely in size, shape, content, and color. The institutional invoice results in uniformity as to signatures, approvals, account numbers, codes, and other pertinent information needed in paying and accounting for invoices.

In the second plan, vendors submit bills to institutions on their own invoice forms. Under this plan, it is necessary for the institution to prepare a remittance voucher form. Such a form sets forth the necessary information about the purchase and the payment

FORM 3.10

BLANK COLLEGE

REMITTANCE VOUCHER

Department   Date________

TO:

Cash Terms

F.O.B. Terms

Invoice Date	Vendor's Invoice Number	Receiving Report Number	Purchase Order Number	Invoice Price	Less Discount	Net Price

Charge	Amount

Invoice Checked________

Prices and Terms Correct________

Receiving Report Correct________

Code and Department Charges Correct________

Voucher Audited by:

____

Date________

Voucher No.

Check No.

For Library and Food Services Orders Only

I hereby certify that the above materials have been received or services rendered and that the voucher is properly payable:

Signed________
Director of Libraries (or)
Director of Food Services

Date________

being made in a uniform and standard manner. The remittance voucher (Form 3.10) is prepared in at least four copies.

Files and Records. The maintenance of complete and accurate files and records in the purchasing department is an integral part of the procurement system. As purchase orders are issued, they are in numerical sequence and one copy should be filed in the purchasing department by the purchase order number. A second copy is filed in a vendor file in alphabetical order; another copy is maintained in a suspense file in date-order number sequence and serves as a basis of following up on purchases for which receiving reports have not been received after a period of time, such as two weeks. The follow-up process for unfilled orders and partial shipments continues until the order is complete or outstanding items have been cancelled. Completed orders are filed by departments according to departmental account numbers. Since the purchase order number appears on all copies of the form, cross-reference between all files in the purchasing department is maintained.

The filing system for purchase requisitions, receiving reports, and remittance advices is as follows. As requisitions are received in the purchasing department they are entered in a purchase requisition register (Form 3.11), which shows the date received, name of proposed vendor, department requesting the materials, number and amount of requisition. The register may be designed to show the location of the requisition if it is necessary to send it out of the purchasing department for any reason. The requisition then serves as a basis for the preparation of the necessary bid or quotation request. Should it be necessary to receive formal bids, the bid document is filed with the requisition in an open file and held until the

FORM 3.11

BLANK COLLEGE

PURCHASE REQUISITION REGISTER

Date	Proposed Vendor	Requesting Department	Purchase Req. No.	Amount

bid opening date. When quotations or bids are received and a supplier has been selected, the purchase order is prepared and copies are distributed and filed in the manner previously described.

When the receiving report and remittance advice are received, the purchase order file can be closed on this particular transaction. The complete file consists of copies of the purchase requisition, the purchase order, the quotation document, the receiving report, and the remittance advice.

Advanced Order Processing System. Requisition and purchasing procedures can be streamlined by implementing a small order, or verbal order, procedure. The extent to which this system is utilized will vary among institutions because of the size, location relative to market, and purchasing philosophy of each institution. Under this procedure, the requisition form is modified to include additional data and is prepared in the required number of copies to meet the needs of accounting and receiving procedures. No formal written purchase order is sent to vendors; rather, the purchasing department assigns a purchase order number to each transaction and transmits the required information to the vendor by telephone. This procedure saves mailing and typing costs and reduces processing time.

Storerooms and Stores Control. The supervision of storerooms and the control of stores inventories are important functions of a college or university procurement system. In most institutions, standard commodities used by many departments can be purchased economically in large quantities and placed in storerooms for future use. A system of storerooms has definite advantages. First, it makes possible quantity buying with the resulting economies. Second, it makes available for immediate use many items which otherwise would have to be purchased through the usual procedure of requisition, bid, purchase, and delivery from a supplier who is often at some distance from the campus. Third, the system reduces the amount of clerical and paper work involved in purchasing by reducing the number of formal purchase orders written and issued.

The type and number of storerooms vary with the size of the college or university, proximity to local sources of supply, and other factors. Laboratory stores, physical plant or general stores, and office supply stores are found in nearly all institutions; medical stores, food stores, and athletic stores are other types of stores frequently found in universities.

Laboratory storerooms should serve all the teaching fields offering laboratory work—botany, biology, chemistry, geology, geography, life sciences, metallurgy, physics, and zoology. By combining the needs of many laboratories the amount of supplies needed is sufficiently large to enable an institution to realize economies through quantity buying. A storeroom in which general operating and maintenance supplies and materials are kept is necessary even in small colleges. An office supply storeroom is necessary also, since all offices on the campus use stationery and paper supplies, pens, pencils, and other office materials. The office supply storeroom may be operated in connection with the student store or the general storeroom, as is done frequently in smaller institutions, or it may be operated by the purchasing department as a separate storeroom.

Inventory Control over Storerooms. Supplies and materials in the various storerooms on a campus have a sizable monetary value and should be controlled and checked as carefully as cash. An adequate inventory accounting system requires (1) that all supplies received, on hand, and issued be accounted for both in quantity and in value; (2) that the inventory be controlled by general ledger accounts in the accounting department; and (3) that the inventory records and the general ledger accounts be verified periodically by physical count of the items in the storerooms.

Accounting control over inventories kept in storerooms is established through the use of a general ledger control account and subsidiary stores ledgers. The subsidiary stores ledgers consist of perpetual inventory cards for each type of commodity in the store and are maintained in the storerooms. A control account for each store is kept in the accounting office, and each storekeeper is held responsible for maintaining up-to-date, accurate, and complete inventory records. A type of perpetual inventory card is shown in Form 3.12. At any time after all entries are posted to these cards, the sum of the cost balances on all cards should equal the balance of the inventory account in the general ledger. Discrepancies should be investigated and explained satisfactorily, and the accounting and inventory records should be reconciled.

Central Stores Procedures. The first step in establishing proce-

FORM 3.12

BLANK COLLEGE

STORES LEDGER

Stock Number

Article__________

Description__________

Unit__________

Minimum__________

Maximum__________

Vendors			
1		4	
2		5	
3		6	

Section	Shelf	Bin

ORDERS PLACED							RECEIPTS				ISSUES					ON HAND		
Req.	Date	P.O.	Date	Quan.	Unit Price	Amount	Date	Rec. Rep.	Quan.	Amount	Date	Stores Order	Quan.	Unit Price	Amount	Quan.	Average Unit Cost	Amount

BLANK COLLEGE

No.

S T O R E S   O R D E R

Date__________

Item Number	Quantity	D e s c r i p t i o n	Price Unit	Price Total

Delivered by__________ Date__________ Posted by__________ Date__________	Maintenance Order Number Work Order Number	Charge Code__________ Department__________ Requested by__________ Received by__________

dures and records for a campus storeroom is taking a physical inventory of commodities in each store and entering quantities, unit costs, and cost balances on the perpetual inventory cards. If there are numerous items, a systematically arranged coded classification of commodities is useful. The code is arranged by commodity groups with subdivisions under each group, and inventory cards should be arranged in the same order. In many institutions, such coded classifications of items are prepared in many copies and distributed as catalogues, or commodity lists, to all departments on the campus.

The second step in the central stores procedures is ordering materials. Usually, responsibility is delegated to each storekeeper to maintain the stock of items in his store at reasonable levels. Automatic reorder procedures may go into effect when quantities reach predetermined levels. However, the purchasing agent, through consultations with department heads, should determine the items used widely by all departments and keep storekeepers informed so that as many as possible of the standard items can be well stocked in the stores on campus. When ordering materials for the inventories of stores, the regular purchase requisition should be used by storekeepers.

As goods are received at the storerooms, entries are made on the stores ledger, or inventory cards, in the columns under the heading receipts. A copy of the purchase order is used sometimes as the posting medium for these entries. However, this plan has two disadvantages: first, the unit prices on the purchase orders often differ from the actual unit prices paid for the goods; second, transportation charges, which are additional costs of the goods in stores operations, are not on the purchase orders. To meet these difficulties, a copy of the remittance voucher is sent to the storekeepers, and the actual costs of the goods are entered from this document.

New purchases should not be placed in storeroom bins and shelves or issued until the unit costs have been recorded. If it is necessary to issue new items before the inventory records are complete, the requisitions should be set aside and priced after the inventory records are posted.

The third step in the central stores procedure is issuing materials. The stores requisition, Form 3.13, is used for this purpose. It is prepared in triplicate by the using department and signed by the department head. One copy is retained in the department, the other two being presented to the store. Stores requisitions need not be approved by the accounting department for availability of funds but are certified only by department heads. This is a departure from strict budgetary control. Usually, the items requested from stores are needed immediately, and one of the advantages of the central storeroom system is to provide prompt availability of commodities. Routing requisitions for all stores items through the regular encumbrance procedures is awkward, inconvenient, and time consuming. Budgetary safeguards can be established by placing maximum limits on stores requisitions. In addition, where necessary, the accounting department should notify storekeepers of those departments whose budget allocations for supplies and materials are nearing exhaustion.

Several methods are employed in pricing commodities issued from stores inventories. The two most commonly used in colleges and universities are the first-in, first-out and the moving average methods. Under the first-in, first-out method those units which are bought first and debited to the inventory record are issued first, so that in valuing the issues on a given requisition, the unit price of the earliest purchase is used until all articles of that purchase have been issued. Then the unit price of the next purchase is used, and so on. The method is illustrated as follows:

Total stock consists of 300 units purchased as follows:

100 units @ $1.10
200 units @ $1.05

Subsequently 120 units are issued. The value of this requisition is computed as follows:

100 units @ $1.10	$110.00
20 units @ $1.05	21.00
120 units	$131.00

Under the moving average method a new unit price is calculated at the time of each purchase. All issues are valued at this unit price until another purchase is made, then a new unit price is computed. Following is an illustration of this method:

On hand, July 1	100 units @ $.50	$ 50.00
Received, July 15	100 units @ $.75	75.00
	200 units	$125.00

FORM 3.14

BLANK COLLEGE

INTERDEPARTMENTAL INVOICE

Date____________________

Credit Department of______________________________
Rendering Service or Furnishing Material

Charge Department of______________________________
Receiving Service or Material

Description	Amount

Charge: Account	Amount		Credit: Account	Amount
		POSTED CHARGE________		
Services or Materials Received:		POSTED CREDIT________	Services Rendered or Materials Delivered:	
Head of Department		APPROVED________ Chief Accountant	Head of Department	
FOR ACCOUNTING OFFICE			Voucher No.	

Average unit price	$.625	
Purchased, July 17	100 units @ $.80	80.00
	300 units	$205.00
Average unit price	$.683	
Issued, July 20	100 units @ $.683	68.30
Balance	200	$136.70

The stores requisition is the basis for posting the perpetual inventory records, and appropriate entries are shown in the column headed issues on Form 3.12. At regular intervals, the storekeeper classifies the stores requisitions by departments to be charged and summarizes these charges on the interdepartmental invoice, Form 3.14. This invoice, prepared in several copies, is used as follows:

1. One copy, to which is attached one copy of the stores requisitions which bears the signature of the department head, is sent to the accounting department and forms the basis for charging the budget of the using department and crediting the inventory control account.

2. One copy, to which is attached the other copy of the departmental requisition, is retained in the storeroom files.

3. One copy is sent to the head of the using department so that he is informed of all stores transactions affecting his budget.

4. One copy is sent to the purchasing agent so that he will be informed of items moving out of the storerooms. Variations in these forms and procedures are to be found among colleges and universities.

The final step in centralized stores procedures is taking a periodical physical inventory to check the accuracy of the accounting records and to reconcile the subsidiary stores ledgers with the controlling accounts in the general ledger. Some institutions check parts of the inventory as time permits, rather than take a complete physical inventory once or twice a year.

Accounting Entries for Storeroom Purchases and Issues. The accounting entries connected with the operation of an inventory system for storerooms are as follows:

1. Entry to set up stores inventory at the inception of a stores system, assuming goods are already on hand (journal voucher):
   Stores inventory (separate account for each storeroom)
      Reserve for stores inventory
2. Entry to record the purchase of goods for inventory (voucher register):
   Stores inventory
      Vouchers payable
3. Entry to record issues from stores (interdepartmental transfer journal):
   Expenditures control (Charge individual accounts in allocation ledger from invoices.)
      Stores inventory
4. Entries to adjust stores accounts to agree with stores inventory at end of year (journal voucher):
   Expenditures control
      Stores inventory

Reserve for stores inventory
Unrestricted current funds balances
(Reverse this entry if stores inventory has increased during the year.)

Purchasing Systems Using EDP Equipment. Many educational institutions have converted part or all of their purchasing and stores operations to data processing equipment. Some institutions have simply placed vendor payments on the EDP systems by punching data cards from the document which is normally prepared as a remittance advice. These cards serve as the basis of computer processing and are used to liquidate encumbrances, charge appropriate accounts, prepare checks in payment, and generate paper records for distribution to appropriate offices.

In order to make the most use of the computer equipment, the initial entry into the EDP system should be made when the purchase order is written. At this point, the entire purchase order (or selected details from it) can be prepared for entry into the EDP system as a by-product of typing the purchase order. Data cards punched as a by-product of typing the purchase order can be produced on a typewriter-punch unit and may contain all necessary accounting information relative to the purchase. The initial inquiry to check for available funds and to encumber the appropriate budget accounts becomes a routine computer run. As inquiry is made, the account is encumbered and, if funds are available, the purchase order is released to the vendor as explained previously. Copies of the purchase order may be used as a receiving report, or separate receiving reports may be prepared.

Invoices are received in the accounting office, where they are matched with purchase orders and receiving reports. Cards are punched from the invoice (or a prepared remittance advice), entry is made into the system to liquidate encumbrances, charge appropriate accounts, and prepare checks to vendors.

As a by-product of these runs, equipment inventories can be prepared so that all equipment can be tagged. By proper classification and coding of items purchased, it is also possible to obtain lists of supplies acquired. Further, the computer can be utilized for analyzing bids to determine lowest and best bids and for printing tabulations giving total dollars to be expended.

4

Classification of Accounts

THE PRIMARY PURPOSE of an accounting system is to furnish financial information to the management and other interested parties. In colleges and universities, adequate financial information is necessary for the efficient execution of instructional, research, and public service programs. The first step in the installation of an accounting system in educational institutions is to ascertain what information is needed.

Accounting Details Dependent on Many Factors. The information to be provided by the accounting system is conditioned by various factors. The size of the institution, the amount of its budget, and its type of organization—whether publicly or privately controlled, whether a large university or a liberal arts college—are important considerations. Another significant factor is the attitude of administrative officials toward accounting and financial information. A good accounting system should primarily furnish only the information that is needed and used. If, for example, in preparing budgets and in operating the institution generally, the management desires to use cost analyses and other detailed financial data, the accounting system should be designed to collect this information. In short, the predisposition of the administration toward accounting and business and fiscal methods is an important factor in the development of an accounting system. The desirability of having the accounting system provide financial information comparable to that of other similar institutions is an additional conditioning factor. In publicly supported institutions, state laws, as well as the requirements of the state government, may determine the kind of information required. Occasionally, the statutes and regulations prescribe a uniform system of accounts for all state agencies, including those devoted to higher education. After considering all the factors involved, both internal and external, and after ascertaining the exact nature of the information required, it is then necessary to determine what accounts will provide this information and, subsequently, to arrange these accounts into a logical and orderly system of classification.

It is not possible to prepare a chart of accounts applicable to all colleges and universities. However, *College and University Business Administration* was designed in part to provide basic principles and standards of accounting and financial reporting for institutions of higher education. Because an increasing number of institutions followed the recommendations of the predecessor volumes, it is expected that the updated principles appearing in the 1974 edition of *College and University Business Administration* will also find wide acceptance. Furthermore, because the production of comparable financial statistics is desirable and should be regarded as an important function of the accounting system, adherence to the uniform principles of classifications now recognized and followed by most educational institutions throughout the country will facilitate the production of comparable financial data.

Classification by funds in the General Ledger. The classification of accounts appearing in *College and University Business Administration* is divided into three parts: general ledger accounts, current funds revenue accounts, and current funds expenditures and transfer accounts. The general ledger, being the nucleus of the accounting system, contains or controls all the accounts comprising the system. It receives entries, in summary or in detail, of all financial transactions of the institution. The financial statements are prepared from the general ledger and supporting ledgers. Because of the nature of institutional finance, the use of resources generally is subject to limitations, restrictions, and designations. One function of the accounting system is to insure compliance with these provisions. This is accomplished by dividing the general ledger into separate funds, each being an independent financial entity composed of a group of self-balancing accounts.

College and University Business Administration recommends the following fund structure as applicable to the majority of colleges and universities:

1. Current funds
   a. Unrestricted
   b. Restricted
2. Loan funds
3. Endowment and similar funds
4. Annuity and life income funds
5. Plant funds
   a. Unexpended
   b. Funds for renewals and replacements
   c. Funds for retirement of indebtedness
   d. Investment in plant
6. Agency funds

Current funds are those funds which are expendable for ordinary operation and maintenance, as well as those restricted by donors or other outside agencies for specific operating purposes and not restricted by external sources or designated by the governing board for other than operating purposes.

In most institutions, current funds embrace the bulk of the financing of the institution. Unrestricted current funds are those which can be expended without restriction, except for the usual budgetary limitations. Restricted current funds are those which, although expendable for current purposes, are subject to provisions limiting the use of these funds. Common types of restricted funds are grants from federal or state governments and donations from private foundations, individuals, and industry for designated instructional purposes or specific research projects. Funds applicable to the operations of auxiliary enterprises, such as college bookstores and dining halls, may be reported separately as a third subdivision of current funds.

General ledger accounts for current funds are classified into asset, liability, fund balance, and operating accounts. Many of these accounts are virtually the same as those used in commercial accounting—for example, cash, petty cash, investments, accounts and notes receivable, inventory, deferred charges, accounts and notes payable, deferred revenues, and allowance for doubtful accounts. Accounts peculiar to institutional organizations are due from other funds, due to other funds, departmental allocations, estimated revenues, encumbrances, provision for encumbrances, and unallocated budget balances. Due to other funds and due from other funds relate to current funds borrowed from or loaned to other fund groups, hence they appear with contrabalances in the other fund groups affected. Departmental allocations, estimated revenues, encumbrances, unallocated budget balances, and provision for encumbrances are budgetary accounts appearing in the ledger only if transactions involving the budget are entered in the accounts. The budget allocations account represents the total of all budget allocations to departments and is equal to the estimated revenues account in those cases where total available current funds revenues are allocated to departmental budgets. If the total of such revenues is not allocated to budget units, but a portion is retained to be made available for expenditure at a later time during the fiscal year, the unallocated budget balances account is used. Obligations in the form of orders and contracts against allocations are recorded in the encumbrances and provision for encumbrances accounts. No fixed asset accounts, as used in commercial accounting, are recorded in the current funds group, even though equipment is purchased from these funds. In governmental and institutional accounting, fixed asset accounts are recorded in the plant funds group.

Loan funds include all funds the principal of which may be loaned. The excess of income over expenditures of these funds serves to increase loanable principal. Assets of loan funds include cash, investments, and notes and interest receivable on loans. These accounts are balanced on the credit side of the ledger by liability accounts such as accounts payable, due to other funds groups, National Direct Student Loan funds—repayable to government, and the loan funds balances account representing the principal of loan funds. If there are a number of loan funds, only control accounts should be maintained in the general ledger, with detailed accounts being carried in a loan subsidiary ledger.

The endowment and similar funds group includes those funds whose principal is nonexpendable as of the date of reporting and is invested, or is available for investment, for the purpose of producing income. Included in this group are three types of funds: endowment funds, term endowment funds, and quasi-endowment funds (unrestricted and restricted).

An endowment fund is one in which a donor has stipulated, as a condition of his gift, that the principal is to be maintained inviolate and in perpetuity, and that only the income from the investments of the fund may be expended or added to principal.

Term endowment funds are those which a donor, by terms of his gift, has specified for expenditure or use in other ways upon the happening of a particular event or the passage of a stated period of time. Once the use of these funds is changed, the funds should be transferred to and reported in the appropriate fund group.

Funds held in trust by outside trustees preferably should not be recorded in the records but should be reported as footnotes in the balance sheet. If the institution has legally enforceable rights to the income of such funds, they may be reported as assets in the financial statements. If the funds were established under irrevocable trusts with the trustees having no discretionary powers with respect to income distribution, income either should be included as endowment income or should be separately stated. If the funds were established as revocable trusts with the trustees having discretionary powers as to income distribution, income should be reported as gifts.

Quasi-endowment funds are those funds which the governing board of an institution, rather than the donor or an outside agency, has determined are to be retained and invested. The term *funds functioning as endowment* may also be used to identify such funds. A governing board may determine at any time in the future that such funds may be used in some other manner. They may be expended for any operating purpose, either designated or undesignated; they may be expended for plant purposes; or they may be used as loan funds. When this occurs, quasi-endowment funds should be transferred from the endowment and similar funds group to the appropriate fund group as indicated by the new use to which the funds are to be put.

The usual asset accounts of the endowment and similar funds group are cash, accounts receivable, notes receivable, and investments, unless the funds are pooled for investment purposes, in which case the asset account would be pooled investments. The usual accounts on the credit side of the general ledger include accounts and notes payable and, if improved real properties is one type of investment, mortgages payable and reserve for depreciation.[1] Accounts for the balances of the three types of funds—endowment funds balances, term endowment funds balances, and quasi-endowment funds balances—are also included here.

The annuity and life income funds group includes funds acquired by an institution that are subject to annuity contracts, living trust agreements, or gifts and bequests reserving a portion of principal and/or life income to one or more beneficiaries. The asset accounts of these funds include cash, accounts receivable, notes receivable, investments, and due from other funds. The equity accounts include those for payables or other forms of indebtedness of the funds, including annuities payable, due to other funds account, undistributed income account, and fund balance accounts for annuity funds balances and life income funds balances.

Plant funds are divided into at least two balanced sections—unexpended plant funds and investment in plant. The first section includes funds designated for or restricted to the construction, rehabilitation, and acquisition of physical plant. The second section includes funds already expended on fixed property and equipment.

The asset accounts of the unexpended plant section include cash, investments, receivables, due from other funds groups, and construction in progress. The equity accounts include accounts payable, notes payable, bonds payable, mortgages payable, and unexpended plant fund balances.

The asset accounts of the investment in plant section include land, buildings, improvements other than buildings, equipment, library books, and art museums and collections. Construction in progress may be included as an asset account if capitalization of such accounts during construction is desired. Allowances for depreciation may be included as offsets to the appropriate asset accounts. The liability accounts for this section include accounts payable, notes payable, bonds payable, mortgages payable, due to other funds groups, and net investment in plant.

If needed, two additional balanced sections of plant funds may be used—funds for renewals and replacements and funds for retirement of indebtedness. The former represents cash or other as-

1. Provision or allowance for depreciation is frequently used as an alternative account title.

sets designated for or restricted to the renewal and replacement of plant assets. Asset accounts include cash, accounts receivable, investments, deposits with trustees, and due from other funds groups. Liability and fund balance accounts include accounts payable, due to other funds groups, and fund balances. The latter represents funds available for the retirement of indebtedness. Asset accounts include cash, accounts and notes receivable, investments, deposits with trustees, and due from other funds groups, whereas the liability and fund balance accounts are accounts payable, due to other funds groups, and fund balances.

Agency funds are those funds over which the institution exercises custodianship, though they are not controlled or owned by it. Examples are student deposits and deposits of fraternities and other student or faculty organizations. Cash, accounts receivable, notes receivable, due from other funds groups, and investments are asset accounts typical of this group, while accounts payable, due to other funds groups, and deposit liabilities are the liability accounts.

Relative to the classification of accounts in the general ledger, several points should be emphasized. Each fund group exists in complete independence of the other fund groups, being contained in a separate section of the general ledger. Each of these fund sections is balanced in itself. To illustrate this fund relationship, consider the entries required to record a loan from one fund group to another group, for example, from unrestricted current funds to endowment funds. In the lending fund group (unrestricted current funds), the entry is a debit to due from endowment and similar funds and a credit to cash; in the borrowing fund group (endowment and similar funds), the entry is a debit to cash and a credit to due to unrestricted current funds. Also, consider the entries required to record the purchase of equipment out of current funds. In unrestricted current funds, the entry is a debit to expenditures (supported by debits to individual departmental or office budgets) and a credit to cash. In the plant funds group (investment in plant section), the entry is a debit to equipment and a credit to the account for net investment in plant.

In order to illustrate the classification of accounts by funds, a *pro forma* balance sheet is presented on pages 64–65, herein.

Classification of Revenues and Expenditures. Regarding classification of revenues and expenditure accounts, it is to be noted that these accounts reflect the current operations of an institution and relate only to current funds. The transactions of the other fund groups are additions to and deductions from the balances or principal of the funds and are reflected in the statements of changes in balances of the appropriate fund groups.

Classification of Revenues. In regard to the classification of current funds revenues, *College and University Business Administration* recommends a breakdown by sources of revenue. The volume states that current funds revenues include: "(1) all unrestricted gifts, grants, and other resources earned during the reporting period and (2) restricted resources to the extent that such funds were expended. Current funds revenues do not include restricted current funds received but not expended or resources that are restricted by external persons or agencies to other than current funds."[2] Following is an outline of the recommended classification of revenues by source of funds.

A. Tuition and fees
B. Federal appropriations
C. State appropriations
D. Local appropriations
E. Federal grants and contracts
F. State grants and contracts
G. Local grants and contracts
H. Private gifts, grants, and contracts
I. Endowment income
J. Sales and services of educational activities
K. Sales and services of auxiliary enterprises
L. Sales and services of hospitals
M. Other sources (includes expired term endowments and expired life income agreements)

The extent to which each of the categories of revenues is detailed in the accounting records depends upon conditions at, and the desire of, individual institutions. Some itemizing of the main divisions is usually desirable. Obviously, the revenue from each auxiliary enterprise should be reported separately. The accounting system can be made to provide the amount of detailed information

2. *College and University Business Administration* (3rd Rev. ed.; Washington, D.C.: National Association of College and University Business Officers, 1974), 182.

desired by increasing or decreasing the number of accounts in the revenue chart.

Classification of Expenditures and Transfers. Expenditures and transfers may be classified in terms of function, organizational unit, and object. Expenditures for auxiliary enterprises, hospitals, and independent operations should be distinctly separated from those for educational and general functions.

Classification by function is the grouping of expenditures according to the general end or purpose for which the funds were expended. The following list of functional classifications meets the requirements of most colleges and universities:

- I. Educational and general
  - A. Expenditures
    1. Instruction
    2. Research
    3. Public service
    4. Academic support
    5. Student services
    6. Institutional support
    7. Operation and maintenance of plant
    8. Scholarships and fellowships
  - B. Mandatory transfers
  - C. Nonmandatory transfers
- II. Auxiliary enterprises
  - A. Expenditures
  - B. Mandatory transfers
  - C. Nonmandatory transfers
- III. Hospitals
  - A. Expenditures
  - B. Mandatory transfers
  - C. Nonmandatory transfers
- IV. Independent operations[3]
  - A. Expenditures
  - B. Mandatory transfers
  - C. Nonmandatory transfers

The grouping by function is simply a logical arrangement of the accounts for purposes of financial statements and the facilitation

3. This category applies to those activities that are independently organized but enhance the primary missions of the institution. It is generally limited to expenditures of major, federally funded research laboratories.

FORM 4.1

BLANK COLLEGE

BALANCE SHEET

At End of Fiscal Year

ASSETS	
I. CURRENT FUNDS	
A. Unrestricted:	
Cash	
Investments	
Accounts receivable	
Less: Allowance for doubtful accounts	
Inventories	
Prepaid expenses	
Total unrestricted current funds	$
B. Restricted:	
Cash	
Investments	
Accounts receivable	
Due from agency funds	
Total restricted current funds	$
TOTAL CURRENT FUNDS	
II. LOAN FUNDS	
Cash	
Investments	
Notes receivable	
Interest receivable	
Due from unrestricted current funds	
TOTAL LOAN FUNDS	$
III. ENDOWMENT AND SIMILAR FUNDS	
Cash	
Investments	
Notes receivable	
TOTAL ENDOWMENT AND SIMILAR FUNDS	$

LIABILITIES AND FUND BALANCES	
I. CURRENT FUNDS	
A. Unrestricted:	
Accounts payable	
Due to other funds:	
Agency funds	
Loan funds	
Deferred revenues	
Unrestricted current funds balances	
Provision for encumbrances	
Total unrestricted funds balances	$
B. Restricted:	
Accounts payable	
Restricted current funds balances	
Total restricted current funds	$
TOTAL CURRENT FUNDS	
II. LOAN FUNDS	
U.S. government grants refundable	
Loan funds balances	
TOTAL LOAN FUNDS	$
III. ENDOWMENT AND SIMILAR FUNDS	
Endowment funds balances:	
Endowment funds	
Term endowment funds	
Quasi-endowment funds:	
Unrestricted	
Restricted	
TOTAL ENDOWMENT AND SIMILAR FUNDS	$

FORM 4.1 (continued)

IV. ANNUITY AND LIFE INCOME FUNDS	
Cash	
Investments	
TOTAL ANNUITY AND LIFE INCOME FUNDS	$
V. PLANT FUNDS	
A. Unexpended:	
Cash	
Investments	
Accounts receivable	
Total unexpended plant funds	$
B. Renewals and replacements:	
Cash	
Investments	
Accounts receivable	
Deposits with trustees	
Total renewals and replacements funds	$
C. Retirement of indebtedness:	
Cash	
Investments	
Deposits with trustees	
Total retirement of indebtedness funds	$
D. Investments in plant:	
Land	
Buildings	
Improvements other than buildings	
Equipment	
Library books	
Total invested in plant funds	$
TOTAL PLANT FUNDS	$
VI. AGENCY FUNDS	
Cash	
Investments	
Due from unrestricted current funds	
TOTAL AGENCY FUNDS	$

IV. ANNUITY AND LIFE INCOME FUNDS	
Annuities payable	
Annuity funds balances	
Life income balances	
TOTAL ANNUITY AND LIFE INCOME FUNDS	$
V. PLANT FUNDS	
A. Unexpended:	
Accounts payable	
Notes payable	
Bonds payable	
Unexpended plant funds balances	
Total unexpended plant funds	$
B. Renewals and replacements:	
Renewals and replacements funds	
Balances:	
Unrestricted	
Restricted	
Total renewals and replacements funds	$
C. Retirement of indebtedness:	
Retirement of indebtedness funds	
Balances:	
Unrestricted	
Restricted	
Total retirement of indebtedness funds	$
D. Investments in plant:	
Bonds payable	
Mortgages payable	
Net investment in plant:	
From governmental appropriations	
From gifts	
From current funds	
Total invested in plant funds	$
TOTAL PLANT FUNDS	$
VI. AGENCY FUNDS	
Due to restricted current funds	
Deposits held in custody for others	
TOTAL AGENCY FUNDS	$

of uniformity among institutions. Obviously, more detailed information is required. Actually, individual accounts bearing the captions shown above would not be set up in the books of account; but accounts should be set up to the extent needed and grouped according to the functions shown, to provide the desired amount of detailed information regarding the expenditures of an institution.

Classification of expenditures by organizational unit is the primary classification for recording detailed expenditures. An organizational unit is a department, office, or a subdivision of either, which comprises a distinct administrative unit such as the president's office, business office, or each of the various departments of instruction. The budget, like the accounts, should be set up by organizational units, and funds should be allocated to these various units.

The object classification is a method of classifying expenditures according to that which is received in return for the expenditures —for example, personnel compensation, supplies and expense, and capital expenditures. Although the budget is established by organizational units, frequently it is broken down further into objects and allocated on this basis to organizational units. Thus, the budget for the vice-president's office may be subdivided into personnel compensation, supplies and expense, and capital expenditures; the funds so allocated must be expended in this manner. The object breakdown may be carried further by subdividing supplies and expense into office supplies, instructional supplies, travel, and so forth. This classification process may be carried still further by breaking down office supplies and instructional supplies into more detailed categories. However, the advantages derived from the use of detailed classifications must be balanced against the increased cost of obtaining the information.

The following chart summarizes the classification of expenditures and indicates the subdivision of expenditure accounts:

I. Educational and general (general function)
    A. Academic support (specific function)
        1. Office of the vice-president for academic affairs (organizational unit)

a. Personnel compensation (general object)
b. Supplies and expense (general object)
   (1) Office supplies (specific object)
   (2) Telephone (specific object)
   (3) Travel (specific object)
c. Capital expenditures (general object)
   (1) Desks (specific object)
   (2) Filing Cabinets (specific object)

Thus, an expenditure by the vice-president's office for office supplies may be classified first by organizational unit, then by general object, and finally by specific object. For statement purposes, the vice-president's office is classified as to specific function under academic support and as to general function under educational and general. From the point of view of the actual accounts, the general objects—personnel compensation, supplies and expense, and capital expenditures—would be account titles. In small institutions, one account for the vice-president's office might be sufficient, with a further analysis of expenditures made possible through the use of codes. To facilitate the planning process and to assist in decision making, expenditures and transfers may be further classified in terms of programs, which frequently cut across functional, organizational, and even fund groups.

Transfers from Current Funds. Transfers from current funds are reported in the transfer sections of the statement of current funds revenues, expenditures, and other changes. *College and University Business Administration* distinguishes between mandatory and nonmandatory transfers, stating that mandatory transfers "should include transfers from the Current Funds group to other fund groups arising out of (1) binding legal agreements related to the financing of educational plant, such as amounts for debt retirement, interest, and required provisions for renewals and replacements of plant, not financed from other sources, and (2) grant agreements with agencies of the federal government, donors, and other organizations to match gifts and grants to loan and other funds. Mandatory transfers may be required to be made from either unrestricted or restricted current funds."[4]

4. *College and University Business Administration*, 189.

The nonmandatory category "should include those transfers from the Current Funds group to other fund groups made at the discretion of the governing board to serve a variety of objectives, such as additions to loan funds, additions to quasi-endowment funds, general or specific plant additions, voluntary renewals and replacements of plant, and pre-payments on debt principal. It also may include the retransfer of resources back to current funds."[5] These criteria for current funds are applicable to mandatory and nonmandatory transfers from auxiliary enterprises, hospitals, and independent operations.

Chart of Accounts. A chart of accounts, based on the principles enumerated above and suitable for a college or university, is presented below and serves as a basis for the accounting system explained in the following chapters. Because the use of codes or symbols is useful in college accounting, a suggested code of accounts is presented with the chart. This chart probably contains more detailed accounts than would be needed by some institutions, particularly smaller colleges, and is intended to be illustrative of the possibilities for proper classification of data. Institutions must adapt the chart and coding system to their own needs and requirements.

The chart of accounts comprises four sections. The first section presents a chart of general ledger accounts. The second section presents a chart of expenditure accounts classified by function and organizational unit. This classification applies to the allocations ledger. The third section presents a chart of revenue accounts and hence applies to the revenues ledger. The fourth section presents a chart of expenditure accounts classified by general object and also by detailed object.

The same chart of accounts is readily adaptable to electronic data processing systems; however, a different coding system may be required. This coding system is discussed in detail in Chapter 8 herein, "Data Processing Systems."

5. *Ibid.*

CHART OF ACCOUNTS

General Ledger—Current Funds—Unrestricted

Asset Accounts

Number	*Title*
1001	Cash—general account
1002	Cash—monthly salary payroll account
1003	Cash—weekly wage payroll account
1004	Petty cash
1005	Bank transfers
1006	Cash over and short
1011	Due from other funds
1012	Investments
1015	Accounts receivable—student (control)
1016	Accounts receivable—others (control)
1020	Notes receivable (control)
1023	State appropriations receivable
1030	Inventories (detail as needed)
1035	Physical plant stores
1041	Work in process
1051	Prepaid expenses and deferred charges
1061	Expenditures and other changes (control)
1062	Restricted expenditures (control)
1063	Transfers to other funds (control)
1071	Encumbrances
1091	Estimated revenues

CHART OF ACCOUNTS

General Ledger—Current Funds—Unrestricted

Liability and Fund Balance Accounts

Number	*Title*
1201	Vouchers payable
1211	Due to other funds
1221	Notes payable
1231	Employee life insurance deductions
1232	Retirement system deductions
1233	Withholding tax deductions
1234	Social security deductions
1236	Deposits
1241	Deferred revenues
1251	Revenues (control)
1252	Restricted revenues (control)
1261	Budget allocations for expenditures and other changes

1271	Provision for encumbrances
1275	Allowance for doubtful accounts
1310	Unallocated budget balance
1351	Unrestricted current funds balances—allocated (detail as needed)
1356	Unrestricted current funds balances—unallocated

CHART OF ACCOUNTS

General Ledger—Current Funds—Restricted

Asset Accounts

Number	*Title*
1501	Cash—First National Bank
1511	Due from other funds
1512	Investments
1521	Accounts receivable (detail as needed)

Liability and Fund Balance Accounts

1701	Vouchers payable
1711	Due to other funds
1851	Restricted current funds balances—allocated (control) (detail as needed)
1856	Restricted current funds balances—unallocated (control)

CHART OF ACCOUNTS

General Ledger—Loan Funds

Asset Accounts

Number	*Title*
2001	Cash—First National Bank
2011	Due from other funds
2012	Investments
2020	Notes receivable (control)
2031	Interest receivable

Liability and Fund Balance Accounts

2201	Vouchers payable
2211	Due to other funds
2215	Allowance for doubtful loans
2241	National Direct Student Loan funds—repayable to government
2242	National Direct Student Loan funds—institutional share
2251	Loan funds balances (control)

CHART OF ACCOUNTS

General Ledger—Endowment and Similar Funds

Asset Accounts

Number	*Title*
3001	Cash—First State Bank
3011	Due from other funds
3012	Investments—securities (control)
3013	Investments—real estate (control)
3061	Accounts receivable
3111	Unamortized premiums on bonds

Liability and Fund Balance Accounts

3201	Vouchers payable
3211	Due to other funds
3221	Reserve for depreciation on real estate
3224	Mortgages payable
3231	Reserve for accumulation of bond discounts
3241	Undistributed pool income
3242	Income (control)
3301	Net adjusted gains and losses
3351	Endowment funds balances (control, if number of such funds is large)
3352	Term endowment funds balances (control, if number of such funds is large)
3353	Quasi-endowment funds balances—unrestricted (control, if number of such funds is large)
3356	Quasi-endowment funds balances—restricted

CHART OF ACCOUNTS

General Ledger—Annuity and Life Income Funds

Asset Accounts

Number	*Title*
4001	Cash—Second State Bank
4002	Accounts receivable
4004	Notes receivable
4011	Due from other funds
4012	Investments—securities (control)
4013	Investments—real estate (control)

Liability and Fund Balance Accounts

4201	Vouchers payable
4211	Due to other funds
4215	Annuities payable

4301	Undistributed income—annuity funds (control)
4302	Undistributed income—life income funds (control)
4401	Net adjusted gains and losses
4551	Annuity funds balances (control)
4651	Life income funds balances (control)

CHART OF ACCOUNTS

General Ledger—Unexpended Plant Funds

Asset Accounts

Number	*Title*
5001	Cash—Third State Bank
5002	Accounts receivable
5005	State appropriations receivable
5011	Due from other funds
5012	Investments
5091	Construction in progress

Liability and Fund Balance Accounts

5101	Vouchers payable
5104	Notes payable
5111	Due to other funds
5123	Bonds payable
5151	Unexpended plant funds balances (control, if more than one such fund; funds should be divided between restricted and unrestricted.)

CHART OF ACCOUNTS

General Ledger—Funds for Renewals and Replacements

Asset Accounts

Number	*Title*
5201	Cash—First National Bank
5202	Accounts receivable
5211	Due from other funds
5212	Investments
5271	Assets of funds on deposit with trustees

Liability and Fund Balance Accounts

5301	Vouchers payable
5311	Due to other funds
5351	Renewal and replacement funds balances (control; funds should be divided between restricted and unrestricted.)

CHART OF ACCOUNTS

General Ledger—Funds for Retirement of Indebtedness

Asset Accounts

Number	*Title*
5401	Cash—Second National Bank
5402	Accounts and notes receivable
5411	Due from other funds
5412	Investments
5471	Funds on deposit with trustees

Liability and Fund Balance Accounts

5501	Vouchers payable
5511	Due to other funds
5551	Retirement of indebtedness funds balances (control; funds should be divided between restricted and unrestricted.)

CHART OF ACCOUNTS

General Ledger—Investment in Plant

Asset Accounts

Number	*Title*
5605	Land (control)
5606	Buildings (control)
5607	Improvements other than buildings (control)
5608	Equipment (control)
5609	Library books
5610	Art museums and collections
5611	Due from other funds
5691	Construction in progress

Liability and Fund Balance Accounts

5701	Vouchers payable
5711	Due to other funds
5722	Notes payable
5723	Bonds payable
5724	Mortgages payable
5751	Net investment in plant (control)

CHART OF ACCOUNTS

General Ledger—Agency Funds

Asset Accounts

Number	*Title*
6001	Cash—Third National Bank

6002	Accounts Receivable
6004	Notes receivable
6011	Due from other funds
6012	Investments
	Liability and Fund Balance Accounts
6201	Vouchers payable
6211	Due to other funds
6251	Deposit liabilities (control)

EXPENDITURE ACCOUNTS
(classified by function and organizational unit)

I. Educational and General
- A. Instruction
  - College of Liberal Arts
    - 2 Aerospace studies
    - 3 Art
    - 5 Biology
    - 6 Chemistry
    - 7 Classics
    - 10 English
    - 11 History
    - 12 Home economics
    - 14 Mathematics
    - 15 Military science
    - 16 Modern languages
    - 17 Music
    - 20 Naval science
    - 21 Philosophy
    - 22 Physics
    - 23 Psychology
    - 25 Sociology and anthropology
    - 26 Speech and theater
  - College of Business and Government
    - 32 Accounting
    - 33 Economics and business administration
    - 34 Journalism
    - 35 Business education and office administration
    - 36 Political science
  - College of Education
    - 42 Health, physical education, and recreation
    - 43 Library science
    - 44 Reading clinic
  - College of Engineering

52 Chemical engineering
53 Civil engineering
54 Geology and geological engineering
55 Mechanical engineering
56 Electrical engineering
57 Seismological observatory

School of Law
61 School of Law
62 Law extension
63 Legal Institute for Agriculture and Resource Development

School of Pharmacy
71 School of Pharmacy

Graduate School
82 City planning

Summer session
92 University
93 School of Law

Other instructional expenditures
95
96

B. Research
101 Institutes and research centers
102 Project research

C. Public services
111 Community service
112 Cooperative extension
113 Conferences, institutes, and short courses
114 Radio
115 Television

D. Academic support
151 Academic administration
152 Computing services
153 Audiovisual services
154 Curriculum development
155 Libraries
156 Museums and galleries

E. Student services
160 Registrar
161 Admissions
162 Student counseling and guidance
163 Dean of students
164 Financial aids
165 Cultural activities

166 Health services
167 Intramural athletics
168 Intercollegiate athletics (if operated as part of Department of Physical Education)
169 Student organizations
170 Remedial instruction

F. Institutional support
181 Governing board
182 President or chancellor
183 Chief academic office
184 Business office
185 Comptroller's office
186 Budget office
187 Bursar
188 Legal services
189 Administrative data processing
190 Internal audits
191 Security
192 Safety
193 Alumni activities
194 Development office
195 Commencement
196 Convocations
197 Catalogues, bulletins, etc.
198 Personnel services
199 Memberships
200 Public relations
201 Publications
202 Printing
203 Purchasing
204 Telephone services
205 Transportation services
206 Service departments (interim accounts only)

G. Operation and maintenance of physical plant
321 Administration
322 Custodial services
323 Maintenance of grounds
327 Trucking service
329 Fire protection
331 Utilities
333 Property insurance
334 Other maintenance, renovations, and alterations of physical plant

H. Scholarships and fellowships
351 Scholarships

355 Fellowships
358 Fee waivers

I. Mandatory transfers
371 Loan fund matching grants
372 Provision for debt on educational plant

J. Nonmandatory transfers
381 Transfers to loan funds
382 Transfers to quasi-endowment account
386 Transfers to plant accounts

K. Auxiliary enterprises, hospitals, and independent operations:
Auxiliary enterprises
411 Student union
412 Cafeteria
416 Residence halls—single
418 Residence halls—married
420 Bookstore
Hospitals
Accounts as needed
Independent operations
Accounts as needed

REVENUE ACCOUNTS
(classified by source of revenues)

A. Student tuition and fees
501 Resident tuition and fees
502 Nonresident tuition and fees
503 Late registration fee
504 Course change fee
505 Deferred test and examination fee
506 Advanced standing examination fee
507 Music fee
508 Diploma fee
509 Thesis fee
510 Summer session
511 University extension

B. Governmental appropriations
601 State appropriations—general support
602 Federal appropriations
603 Local appropriations

C. Federal grants and contracts
621 Accounts as needed

D. State grants and contracts
631 Accounts as needed

E. Local grants and contracts
641 Accounts as needed

F. Private gifts, grants, and contracts
 651 Business grants
 652 Business and industry contracts
 653 Business and industry training grants
G. Endowment income
 661 Unrestricted
 662 Restricted
H. Sales and services of educational departments
 701 Dairy operation
 702 Testing services
 703 Film library rentals
I. Sales and services of auxiliary enterprises
 721 Student union
 722 Residence halls—single
 723 Residence halls—married
 724 Cafeteria
 725 Bookstore
J. Sales and services of hospitals
 731 Patient services
 732 Nursing services
 733 Professional services
 734 Clinics
K. Sales and services of independent operations
 741 Accounts as needed

OBJECT CLASSIFICATION OF EXPENDITURES

A. Personnel compensation
 011 Salaries—teaching
 012 Salaries—other professional
 013 Salaries—nonprofessional
 014 Staff benefits
 021 Wages—graduate teaching
 022 Wages—other graduate
 023 Wages—other professional
 024 Wages—nonprofessional
 025 Wages—undergraduate students
 026 Staff benefits
B. Supplies and expense
 031 Instructional supplies
 032 Office supplies
 033 Janitorial, cleaning, and laundry supplies
 034 Printing, binding, and reproducing
 035 Repairing and servicing to equipment
 036 Postage and freight

037 Telephone and telegraph (unless charged to institutional support)
038 Travel (unless charged to institutional support)

C. Capital expenditures
041 Scientific equipment
042 Office machines and equipment
043 Furniture and furnishings
044 Physical plant machines and tools
045 Motor vehicles
046 Books
047 Livestock

Name of subsidiary ledger—by funds	Name of control account in general ledger	Description
I. *Current funds*		
A. Unrestricted		
1. Accounts receivable	Accounts receivable	Includes an account for each debtor. Total of detail accounts equals control account.
2. Allocations	Expenditures	Includes accounts with organization units listed in chart of accounts, Section II. Totals of different columns in subsidiary agree with respective control accounts in general ledger.
3. Revenues	Revenues Estimated revenues	Includes accounts with each type of revenue. Totals of different columns agree with respective control accounts in general ledger.
B. Restricted		
1. Restricted funds	Restricted funds balances	Includes an account with each restricted fund. Total of balances of restricted funds equals control account.
II. *Loan funds*		
1. Notes and interest	Note receivable Interest receivable	Includes an account with each person to whom a loan has been made. Account is subdivided to show amount due on principal and interest. Totals of columns agree with respective control accounts.

Name of subsidiary ledger—by funds	Name of control account in general ledger	Description
2. Loan funds	Loan funds balances	Includes an account with each separate loan fund. Total of all funds agrees with control account.
III. *Endowment and similar funds*		
1. Investments	Investments	Includes an account with each security or parcel of real estate. Total of all accounts in subsidiary ledger agrees with control accounts.
2. Endowment funds Term endowment funds Quasi-endowment funds	Endowment funds balances Term endowment funds balances Quasi-endowment funds balances	Includes an account with each separate endowment fund. Total of individual funds agrees with control account.
IV. *Annuity and life income funds*		
1. Annuity and life income funds	Annuity and life income funds balances	Includes an account with each separate annuity and life income fund. Total of individual funds agrees with control account.
V. *Plant funds*		
A. Unexpended plant funds		
1. Unexpended plant funds	Unexpended plant funds balances	Includes an account with each fund in the unexpended plant funds group. Total of all funds equals control account.
B. Renewals and replacement funds		
1. Renewals and replacement funds	Renewals and replacement funds balances	Includes an account with each fund in the renewals and replacement fund group. Total of all funds equals control account.
C. Retirement of indebtedness		
1. Retirement of indebtedness funds	Retirement of indebtedness funds balances	Includes an account with each fund in the retirement of indebtedness funds group. Total of all funds equals control account.

Name of subsidiary ledger—by funds	Name of control account in general ledger	Description
D. Investment in plant		
1. Plant	Land Buildings Improvements other than buildings Equipment Library books	Includes accounts with each type of plant asset. The ledger is subdivided to provide the details under each of the four control accounts.
VI. *Agency funds*		
1. Deposit	Deposit liabilities	Includes an account with each student or organization having funds on deposit with the college. Total of funds on deposit equals control account.

5

Preparation and Control of the Current Funds Budget

THE EVER-EXPANDING PROGRAMS and needs of educational institutions create financial problems and pressures of a magnitude experienced in few other organizations. The dollars for financing these programs and needs are usually limited. Because demands on institutional resources normally exceed such resources, some workable plan of coordinating demands and revenues is essential. The document designed to accomplish this objective in colleges and universities is the institutional budget. A budget should be formulated covering all current funds activities of the institution, including auxiliary enterprises, sponsored research, and other institutional programs. The current funds budget is discussed in this chapter.

Definition and Functions of the Budget.[1] The budget is defined as "an itemized, authorized, and systematic plan of operation, expressed in dollars, for a given period."[2] It is an authorization, after approval by the governing board, to incur the expenditures and to collect the revenues. In the business world, the budget formulates a program of sales, production, and finance which assures management that a plan to insure an approximately known profit is being followed. In the field of education, the budget serves other purposes. It is both an instrument of control and limitation and a comprehensive financial plan for efficient and serviceable operation.

From a negative point of view, the budget places limitations on the administration of the institution and its subdivisions. This purpose of the budget is illustrated in the state institution, which is

1. The term *budget* in institutional finance generally refers to the budget of current funds. Although the operations of other funds may be covered by some type of working plan or budget, it is in the current funds group that the budget assumes the most importance.

2. *College and University Business Administration* (3rd Rev. ed.; Washington, D.C.: National Association of College and University Business Officers, 1974), 157.

financed largely through the contributions of the taxpayers. The taxpayers vest the authority of control in a board of laymen, variously known as supervisors, trustees, or governors. This board meets infrequently and its members give but little of their time to the actual administration of the institution. In order that the governing board may exercise its prerogatives—to guide the institution and to determine its policies—a financial plan must be formulated in advance outlining the operations of the institution for a given period of time. The governing board thus extends its control over the institution by means of this plan or budget, which places limitations on the president's powers of control and supervision over the detailed expenditures of funds for the various divisions of the college. In like manner, the budget enables the president of the institution to extend his control over the detailed operation of the institution.

One purpose of the budget is to insure that the institution does not obligate itself in a given period of time in excess of resources available during such period. This applies to private as well as to state-controlled colleges and universities. In privately controlled schools, overspending results in the impairment of the endowment funds of the institution, or even in bankruptcy. In publicly controlled institutions, overspending results in legal complications. The budgets of most state institutions are approved by the legislature and a state budget agency and, hence, cannot be legally exceeded.

Too often these negative purposes are regarded as the sole function of the budget. The budget has greater significance as a positive, constructive device. The purposes of the educational institution are instruction, research, and public service. The activities of the institution, which in the aggregate promote these purposes, must be financed. The budget embodies the educational program in terms of dollars. It coordinates not only needs and finances but also the various interests which coexist in the college. It is the financial plan through which the various activities of the institution are carried on most efficiently. Moreover, the budget typifies the working of the democratic process. The budget as adopted is not the product of the president's desires, the desires of the business office, or the desires of a segment of the faculty. Instead, it meets the requirements of the faculty, president, deans, business officers, and students. The budget is a plan without which a college cannot function satisfactorily.

Relationship of the Budget to the Institutional Organization and Accounting System. The budget is related both to the functional organization of the institution and its accounting system and must be devised in conformity with the organization chart of the college or university. In most institutions, the nucleus of the budget is the department—the instructional department, the administrative unit, or the organized division, such as the bookstore, dining hall, or athletic department. The head of each organizational unit prepares a budget and is guided by it. Logically, the head of a department must also be the head of a budget unit. Although one person may be required to administer two or more budgets, two department heads should not administer a single budget. The subbudgets of academic support, covering such activities as commencement and audiovisual services, may be placed under the jurisdiction of a faculty member whose field of interest is akin to the purpose of that budget in question. Frequently committees are appointed to prepare and execute budgets of a general nature. Budgets for expenditures incurred in connection with finances, such as pension contributions, group insurance, and sinking fund contributions, are usually prepared and supervised by the chief business officer.

Because the accounts conform to the lines of the college organization, the budget should conform to the chart of accounts. Referring to the suggested chart of expenditure accounts presented in Chapter 4, one finds one or more accounts each for expenditures of the president's office, the business office, the department of art, the operation and maintenance department, the bookstore, and so on. The budget not only follows the accounting system, it is reflected also in the periodic financial statements.

It is sometimes said that two budgets are involved in the operation of state colleges and universities—the legislative budget and the internal or operating budget. The legislative budget, as its name implies, is a request for funds submitted to the legislature, whereas the operating budget is the financial plan based on the legislative appropriation. The budget for the legislature is a summary of the detailed budget which is designed for and later serves as a basis for the preparation of the operating budget. Of course, if the legislature fails to appropriate as much as is requested, the detailed budget must be adjusted accordingly before being implemented.

The appropriation made by the legislature may be either in a lump sum or in detail. A lump sum appropriation means that a certain amount of money is made available to be spent at the discretion of the institution. A detailed appropriation binds the institution to conform to each item of its budget. Between these extremes are many possibilities. For example, many legislatures appropriate one sum for ordinary operating expenses and a separate sum for capital outlay, allowing the institution to exercise discretion in the expenditure of funds from each appropriation. There exists a tendency on the part of state legislatures to appropriate a lump sum for ordinary operating expenditures, but to make "line item" appropriations for equipment, special repairs, and building projects.

However the legislative appropriation is made, the internal allocations in the operating budget of the institution are detailed under major classes of expenditures. Institutions subdivide departmental budgets into such categories as personnel compensation, supplies and expenses, and capital expenditures. Note that any important item of expense can be elevated into the position of a coordinate budget, for example, traveling expenses—the type of expenses over which the institution desires to exercise a specific control. In many colleges, particularly the small ones, only one allocation is made to each department. The account for this department, through the use of object codes, is maintained in such a manner that it may be analyzed periodically in order to obtain details of expenditures.

Preparation of the Budget. There are two broad phases in the preparation of the budget: the estimation of expenditures and the estimation of revenues. Theoretically, in institutional finance, the estimate of expenditures, representing needs, precedes the estimate of revenues. In practice, however, this procedure seldom is followed, since resources usually are limited. Instead, an attempt is made to relate, or balance, necessary expenditures and expected revenues simultaneously. Although the determination of needs is the paramount consideration in the preparation of the budget, it is necessary at the same time to estimate the expected revenues. In the state institution, the predominant sources of revenues are appropriations by the state and federal governments, grants and contracts, tuition and fees, sales and services of educational activities, and sales and services of auxiliary enterprises. Revenues from the last three sources may be estimated in advance with a reasonable degree of accuracy, but estimating the amount the state or federal government will appropriate presents difficulties. Usually the institution estimates as carefully as possible the revenues that are more or less under its control and then forecasts the appropriations obtainable from government sources. In some states, funds are dedicated to the college by constitutional provision, so that the total revenue can be estimated with greater accuracy. In preparing estimates of revenue from tuition and fees and from sales made by auxiliary enterprises and educational activities, statistics of past enrollment and the number of scholarships to be offered, as well as business and financial conditions, are considered. Regarding state appropriations, the political situation may be a factor. Many states maintain budgetary departments that correlate needs of the various state agencies with anticipated revenues before budgets are presented to the legislature. Under such conditions, the state institution secures aid from the budget department in estimating legislative appropriations. The major sources of revenue accruing to the privately controlled institution include tuition and fees; earnings from endowment investments; private gifts; grants and contracts; federal, state, and local contracts and grants; and sales of auxiliary enterprises. In recent years, the private institution increasingly has received from the state legislature financial assistance which has to be anticipated in the budgeting process.

In preparing estimates of revenue, the business office, assisted by the institutional research office, plays the major role, particularly in estimating tuition and fees, income from endowments, state appropriations, and federal grants and contracts. To assist in estimating revenue from auxiliary enterprises and miscellaneous sources, the manager or director of each enterprise submits a formal estimate.

Some institutions, after estimating revenues as accurately as possible, issue a tentative allotment to each department head. This allotment is not final but is used to initiate the budget process and to prevent departmental requests from greatly exceeding available resources. After issuing tentative allotments, department heads are given an opportunity to justify requested changes in them. Throughout all steps of budget preparation, a definite calendar should be followed. This calendar should call for the completion of the budget well before the end of the fiscal year but should afford sufficient time at each stage of the process to allow for needed deliberation.

After the issuance and revision of tentative allotments, the budgetary process is as follows:

Step One: Budget request forms, described later in this chapter, are sent out by the president to deans and department heads (with a letter setting forth guidelines, including such items as percentage increase for salaries, new positions, supplies and expense levels, etc.).

Step Two: Formal requests are obtained from heads of departments or other organizational units after they have been developed with the advice and cooperation of their respective faculties.

Step Three: The deans of colleges and directors of other organizational units are called upon to approve requests from the departments of their respective colleges or divisions. In small colleges, the deans and department heads may work together in preparing the budget requests so that steps one and two tend to merge.

Step Four: The business office consolidates all budget requests and prepares a tentative or preliminary budget for guidance of the president in making revisions.

Step Five: The president and his representatives study the departmental requests and begin their revision in view of needs and available resources. The chief business officer, with the assistance of the institutional research office, provides statistics and unit cost studies to assist at this stage of the budgetary process. A committee consisting of the president, chief business officer, chief academic officer, and representatives of the faculty may be established to review the budget. In such review, each department head should be given opportunity to present reasons for the adoption of his own budget. If departmental requests exceed available or anticipated resources of the college, the paring process begins. This process may consist of elimination of new projects or services; reduction of increases in existing services; reduction of expenses in connection with a planned expansion of enrollment; elimination of increases over last year's budget.

In paring the budget, there is a tendency to conform too closely to past expenditures. If a given department has been uneconomical in the past, basing the budget entirely on past performance encourages future excesses. Throughout the budgetary process intelligent consideration should be given to new trends and new developments—in short, to future needs as well as to past performance. Program budgeting, discussed later in this chapter, assists in an intelligent review of needs. Zero-base budgeting, also discussed later in this chapter, is another form of budgeting.

Step Six: The final step in the budgetary process is approval of the budget by the president and, in turn, his submission of it to the governing board for final approval.

Unallocated Budget Balance. As fully explained later in this chapter, the budget as adopted must be controlled rigidly. The easiest way to disparage the budget and to limit its usefulness in institutional administration is to permit departmental budgets to be overspent. This practice thwarts the financial plan, however laboriously worked out. On the other hand, any budget, however carefully prepared, will have to be revised in some respects to meet contingencies arising during the year. Thus, in a well-prepared budget, provision is made for reasonable changes. The required elasticity is accomplished by including a contingency reserve in the budget. This reserve may be created by leaving unallocated some institutional revenue. The reserve is ordinarily placed under the control of the president of the institution and becomes effective only after the department head requesting the change obtains written approval (see Form 5.8).

Budget Forms. Uniformity of procedure is of prime importance in preparing the budget. For this reason, definite rules and instructions, together with necessary forms, should be provided for those who engage in the budgetary process. These forms include:

1. Letter of Explanation (Form 5.1). This form, the letter of transmittal from the department head to the president, is primarily

FORM 5.1

BLANK COLLEGE BUDGET REQUEST 19__-19__	Chemical Engineering Department	Code

LETTER OF EXPLANATION

Use this form for any necessary explanation of Budget Requests, including reasons for any increase or unusual items. (If necessary, use more than one sheet--------please do not use plain paper.)

Budget Item	Explanation	*Do not use this space*
PERSONNEL COMPENSATION	Department Position No. 7 - New position, Assistant Professor. The justification for a new position in Chemical Engineering was set forth in a memorandum to the Dean of the College of Engineering of October 7. Points developed included the need to keep teaching loads at a reasonable level, the need to provide increased manpower to handle the growing graduate program, the need to devote more effort to research, the need to provide increased staff flexibility, the need to engage in more public relations activity and professional activity. Because of steadily rising demands for qualified engineering personnel, it is expected that a salary of $12,000 will be required to attract the type of teacher-researcher desired.	
SUPPLIES & EXPENSE	The increase requested in the amount of $1,920 is a simple reflection of the increased cost of supplies and services and the demand for more instructional supplies as the number of graduate students increases.	
CAPITAL EXPENDITURES	The amount requested, $7,500, will provide for one item of equipment which has been scheduled for addition to the laboratory (Unit Operations) for the past three years. Additional equipment is actually needed, but it is anticipated that some of this equipment can be procured in connection with the equipping of the addition to Carrier Hall to be built as Phase IV of the Science Center.	
	Department Chairman	

used to justify any unusual budgetary requests and to state reasons for any increases. It also may be used to suggest improvements in the department or to explain its future plans and objectives.

2. Personnel Compensation (Form 5.2). All positions with required explanatory details are listed on this form. In addition to

FORM 5.2

BLANK COLLEGE BUDGET REQUEST 19__-19__	Chemical Engineering Department	Code

Salaries

Dept. Pos. No. (1)	NAME Title of Position (2)	No. of Mos. (3)	Present Salary Rate (4)	Increase Decrease* Requested (5)	Recommended By Dept Chairman (6)	Approved By Dean (7)	Approved By President (8)
1.	FRANK A. SMITH Associate Dean of the School of Engineering and Professor of Chemical Engineering	12	$25,000	$3,000	$28,000	$28,000	$28,000
2.	RUSSELL E. BAKER Professor and Radiation Safety Officer	9	18,000	2,500	20,500	20,500	20,500
3.	BILL E. CARTER Professor	9	16,000	2,500	18,500	18,500	18,500
4.	J. ROGER JOHNSON	9	-0-	-0-	-0-	-0-	-0-
5.	JAMES JONES Associate Professor	9	14,000	1,250	15,250	15,250	15,250
6.	TED MILES, JR. Assistant Professor and Research Engineer (Paid by Engineering Experiment Station)	9	10,500 (2,500) (13,000)	750 (250) (1,000)	11,250 (2,750) (14,000)	11,250 (2,750) (14,000)	11,250 (2,750) (14,000)
7.	__________ Assistant Professor		New	12,000	12,000	12,000	Not Approved
8.	DORA McHENRY	12	7,000	800	7,800	7,800	7,800
	TOTAL SALARIES → (List Totals on Last Page Only)				$113,300	$113,300	$101,300

Prepared and Approved By

Dept. Chairman		Division Head		Checked By	
Dean		President		Entered On Budget	Business Manager

the entries shown in the illustration, Form 5.2 might include persons on part-time, persons transferred from one position to another, promotions, and persons on leave. To achieve the greatest possible uniformity in personnel service requests, a model form, meeting all possible requirements, should be sent to each department head.

3. Supplies and Expense (Form 5.3). Each department head is required to list on this form the items needed for his department. Only the important requirements with respect to supplies and expense need be itemized.

FORM 5.3

BLANK COLLEGE

BUDGET REQUEST

19__-19__

Chemical Engineering
Department

Code

Supplies and Expense

Object Code (1)	Items (2)	Budget For 1967-1968 (3)	Increase Or Decrease* (4)	Requested By Dept. Chairman (5)	Approved By Dean (6)	Approved By President (7)
201	Building and Electrical Supplies					
202	Food Supplies					
204	Fuel, other than motor vehicle					
205	Instructional Supplies	$1,700	$1,050	$2,750	$1,700	
206	Janitorial, Laundry and Cleaning Supplies					
207	Motor Vehicle Supplies					
209	Office Supplies	300	100	400	300	
217	Power Plant Supplies					
218	Dues and Subscriptions	50	-0-	50	50	
219	Heat, Light, Power, and Water					
220	Insurance and Bond Premiums					
221	Postage and Freight on Commodities	100	-0-	100	100	
222	Printing, Binding and Reproducing	100	100	200	100	
223	Repairing and Servicing Property	450	350	800	450	
225	Telephone and Telegraph	380	320	700	700	
226	Travel	1,100	-0-	1,100	700	
227	Contractual Services					
230	Fees for Professional Services					
231	Advertising					
232	Health Service Supplies					
	TOTALS	$4,180	$1,920	$6,100	$4,100	$4,100

Prepared and Approved By

Dept. Chairman		Division Head		Checked By	
Dean		President		Entered On Budget	Business Manager

FORM 5.4

BLANK COLLEGE

BUDGET REQUEST

19__-19__

Chemical Engineering
Department

Code

Equipment

Items (1)	Requested By Dept. Chairman (2)	Approved By Dean (3)	Approved By President (4)
Five-Stage, Liquid-liquid Denver Extraction Unit (new apparatus to fill major gap in stage-wise laboratory apparatus)	$7,500	$7,500	$7,500
TOTALS	$7,500	$7,500	$7,500

Please list all equipment in detail using estimated cost where actual cost is not known.
If additional sheets are required use Detail Sheet (Form 2) and summarize above.

Prepared and Approved By

Dept. Chairman		Division Head		Checked By	
Dean		President		Entered On Budget	Business Manager

4. Capital Expenditures (Form 5.4). As regards equipment, the department head lists separately each item requested. The equipment budget frequently is controlled in detail; that is, the expenditure of funds for equipment must follow the detailed items of the budget. Deviations are allowed only upon properly approved requests.

5. Departmental Summary (Form 5.5). This form summarizes requests for personnel compensation, supplies and expense, and capital expenditures.

6. Estimated Revenues (Form 5.6). The head of each department or division which produces any revenue submits revenue estimates on Form 5.6. Revenues that do not pertain to a particular division, such as those from state appropriations or endowments, are estimated on this form by the chief business officer.

7. Budget Summary (Form 5.7). After all requests from departments have been collected and estimates of revenue prepared, they are accumulated and summarized on Form 5.7. This summary is supported by detailed revenue estimates and expenditure budgets.

At least four copies of the completed budget documents are necessary for internal operating purposes. These copies go to the president, the chief business officer, the auditor, and the chief academic officer, respectively. A special summary is usually prepared for presentation to the governing board. Regarding the budget submitted to the state legislature, the budgetary forms in some states are prescribed. These forms usually require summarized information for the institution as a whole and can be prepared easily from the detailed operating budget.

Budgets of Self-Supporting Activities and Enterprises. Generally, all current revenues and expenditures should be included in

FORM 5.5

BLANK COLLEGE BUDGET REQUEST 19__-19__	Chemical Engineering Department	Code

Summary of Departmental Requests and Approved Budget

Budget	Budget For Prior Year	Increase or Decrease* Requested	Requested By Dept. Chairman	Approved By Dean	Approved By President
Personnel compensation	$90,500	$22,800	$113,300	$113,300	$101,300
Supplies and expense	4,180	1,920	6,100	4,100	4,100
Capital expenditures	5,000	2,500	7,500	7,500	7,500
TOTALS	$99,680	$27,220	$126,900	$124,900	$112,900
Comments:					

Prepared and Approved By

Dept. Chairman		Division Head		Checked By	
Dean		President		Entered On Budget	Business Manager

FORM 5.6

BLANK COLLEGE BUDGET REQUEST 19__-19__	Auxiliary Enterprises College or Division Bookstore Department 65 Code No. 5 Sheet No.		
ESTIMATED REVENUES			
Items	Budget Estimated Revenue Prior Year	Estimated Revenue Current Year	Increase or Decrease* Over Prior Year
Sale of textbooks	$200,000	$240,000	$40,000
Sale of supplies	20,000	30,000	10,000
Sale of wearing apparel	19,000	20,000	1,000
TOTAL REVENUE	$239,000	$290,000	$51,000

the current funds budget. Operations of all departments, including those producing revenues sufficient to finance themselves, should be controlled by the institutional budget. In cases where the department is wholly self-supporting, such as a cafeteria, dining hall, or bookstore, estimates of revenue and proposed expenditures may be incorporated in the budget with the understanding that the entire revenue from such enterprise is available for expenditure by that enterprise. If operations result in increased revenues, the expenditure budget should be increased by an amount sufficient to finance the enhanced operations. In other words, the budget for self-supporting departments should be flexible and should be expanded or contracted in proportion to actual operations. Some institutions handle self-supporting activities in a revolving or working-capital fund, which is not a part of or controlled by the

FORM 5.7

BLANK COLLEGE

BUDGET SUMMARY

19__-19__

	Estimated Prior Year	Approved Current Year	Increase or Decrease* Over Prior Year
REVENUES			
Tuition and Fees			
Federal Appropriations			
State Appropriations			
Local Appropriations			
Federal Grants & Contracts			
State Grants & Contracts			
Local Grants & Contracts			
Private Gifts, Grants, & Contracts			
Endowment Income			
Sales & Services of Educational Activities			
Sales & Services of Auxiliary Enterprises			
Sales & Services of Hospitals			
Other Sources (including expired term endowments & expired life income agreements if not material; otherwise, separate category)			
Independent Operations			
TOTAL REVENUES			
Educational and General EXPENDITURES			
Instruction			
Research			
Public Service			
Academic Support			
Student Services			
Institutional Support			
Operation & Maintenance of Physical Plant			
Scholarships & Fellowships			
Educational and General Expenditures			
Mandatory Transfers			
Nonmandatory Transfers			
Total Educational and General			
Auxiliary Enterprises			
Expenditures			
Mandatory Transfers			
Nonmandatory Transfers			
Total Auxiliary Enterprises Expenditures & Transfers			
Independent Operations			
Expenditures			
Mandatory Transfers			
Nonmandatory Transfers			
Total Independent Operations Expenditures and Transfers			
TOTAL EXPENDITURES AND TRANSFERS			

current funds budget. This procedure is satisfactory, provided the self-supporting enterprise is considered part of the regular operations of the institution. If the financing of auxiliary or self-supporting activities in a revolving fund fosters or encourages the notion of separate ownership, then such a plan is not satisfactory. In the event certain activities are financed through a revolving fund, for statement purposes the expenditures and revenues of such activities should be combined with the expenditures and revenues of other current funds.

Control of the Budget. The budget, having been prepared, reviewed, and approved by the president, the governing board, and the legislature or state budgeting agency, is placed in operation. There are two phases of control exercised over budgets of educational institutions. The first, pertaining only to the state institution, is external control exercised by some agency of the state. Ordinarily this agency is interested in ascertaining that the total budgetary appropriation is not exceeded. In some states such control is exercised through the medium of the postaudit, normally conducted by the state auditing agency. The control may be of a continuous nature, being exercised by a state budgetary department through the use of work programs and a system of periodic allotments. Under this plan, the institution submits a work program broken down into periods—frequently quarters—and requests that funds be allotted to it on this basis. In approving these requests, the state budgeting department issues allotments authorizing the institution to expend a stipulated amount for the period in question. The purpose of this system is to enable the state to correlate cash receipts with disbursements continuously throughout the fiscal year. The privately controlled institution is not concerned with this type of budgetary control. In a few states, control is by line item.

Second, and more important from the accounting point of view, is the internal control over the detailed operating budget exercised by the institution itself. If the budget is to have meaning and if the wishes of the governing board relative to the budget are to be carried out, the accounting system must provide for budgetary control. Institutions usually exercise this control by recording the budget in the accounting records, so that the progress of each budget is reviewed constantly. Through a system of requisitions and the encumbrance of purchase orders that are entered as a charge against the appropriate budget, strict budgetary control is effected. In small institutions, budgetary control may be predicated on files of outstanding purchase orders and a system of periodic reports on the progress of the departmental budgets. Regardless of the size of the institution, however, two factors are of fundamental importance to budgetary control: centralized purchasing and a requisitioning system under which the accounting office approves most requisitions (or purchase orders) prior to the issuance of purchase orders. Requisitions for small amounts need not have prior approval.

An outline of the steps necessary to obtain complete budgetary control over expenditures follows:

1. The budget is recorded in appropriate detail in the accounting records.
2. Personnel services are controlled through personnel action forms set up by the accounting office only if funds are available. No payroll voucher is processed if funds are not available.
3. All purchasing is done by the business office upon the requisition of the department head.
4. Prior to the issuance of the purchase order, the accounting office approves the requisition or the purchase order relative to the availability of funds.
5. When issued, the purchase order is entered as a charge or encumbrance against the appropriate departmental budget, thus effecting a reduction of the available balance.
6. The accounting office prepares monthly statements for each budgetary unit, showing the exact status of its budget.
7. Adjustments of budgets for unanticipated needs are formally approved and entered in the accounts.

Budgetary control should also be related to revenues. Obviously, the expenditure budget can be executed fully only if all estimated resources are realized. If, for example, the enrollment unexpectedly declines, resulting in decreased revenues, it will be necessary to adjust budget allotments accordingly, unless new sources of revenue are found. If it is possible to relate decreased revenue to a particular department—for example, if bookstore sales are less than estimated—it may be possible to reduce the bookstore budget of expenditures correspondingly, without affecting other budgetary units. Budget adjustments may be made on a request for budget revision, Form 5.8.

Recording the Budget in the Records. As soon as the accounting department receives an approved copy of the budget, entry is

FORM 5.8

BLANK COLLEGE

R E Q U E S T   F O R   B U D G E T   R E V I S I O N

No.______________ ______________ Date

	Chemical Engineering			
	Name of Unit / Code No.			
Account	Present Budget	Revisions Requested: Increases	Revisions Requested: Decreases	Revised Budget
Personnel Compensation				
Supplies and Expense	$4,100.00	$600.00	-0-	$4,700.00
Capital Expenditures				
TOTAL	$4,100.00	$600.00	-0-	$4,700.00

(The above section may be detached and used for continuation sheets where necessary.)
Explain fully the reasons for this request for revisions in the above budget. Attach extra sheets if necessary.

The budget was reduced to $4,100 from our actual budget of $4,180 for the prior year. We cannot operate the full year without additional funds. This request will provide new funds for instructional supplies only.

Personnel Compensation Rates Approved (where required) ______________ Director of Personnel

Requested by

____
(Department Chairman or Administrative Head)

Approval Recommended

____
Dean

Approval Recommended

____
Division Head

Recommended Means of Financing Request:

Charge Increase to: Unallocated Budget Balance $ 600.00

Credit Decrease to: ______________ $______

____
Business Manager

Approved Date______ ______________ President

FORM 5.9

BLANK COLLEGE

JOURNAL VOUCHER

No.____________

Year 19__-19__

Date____________

	Account Number	Subsidiary		General Ledger	
		Debit	Credit	Debit	Credit

Explanation:________________________

Prepared By:____________ Approved:____________

made on a journal voucher (Form 5.9) to record the estimated revenues and the budget allocations to departments:

Estimated revenues	$10,000,000	
Departmental budget allocations		$9,900,000
Unallocated budget balance		100,000
To record the budget as approved by the governing board June 1, 19_		

Entries in subsidiary accounts:

IN REVENUES LEDGER (see Forms 5.10 and 5.6)

Debit individual revenue accounts, for example:

Resident tuition	$2,000,000
Nonresident tuition	50,000
Bookstore (from Budget Form 5.6)	
Textbooks	240,000
Supplies	30,000
Wearing apparel	20,000
Dining halls (from Budget Form 5.6, not shown)	
Sales	600,000

IN ALLOCATIONS LEDGER (see Forms 5.11, 5.12, and 5.13)

Credit individual departmental budget accounts, for example:

Chemical Engineering (from Budget Form 5.5)

Personnel compensation	101,300
Supplies and expense	4,100
Capital expenditures	7,500
Electrical Engineering (from Budget Form 5.5, not shown)	
Personnel compensation	80,000
Supplies and expense	4,000
Capital expenditures	3,000

The above entry indicates that the total estimate of revenues is $10,000,000 and that $9,900,000 is allocated to the various organizational units. The balance of $100,000 remaining in the unallocated budget balance account constitutes a budgetary contingency reserve. The general ledger account estimated revenues controls the detailed estimates in the revenues ledger. Similarly, the departmental budget allocations account in the general ledger controls the individual allocations accounts in the allocations ledger. As revenue is actually realized, credits are made to the current funds revenues control account in the general ledger. Charges against departmental allocations are recorded as debits to the expenditures control account.

Form 5.10 illustrates one of the subsidiary revenue accounts appearing in the revenues ledger. The budget is recorded as a debit in the estimated revenues column of this account. Subsequently, as revenues are realized, the amount collected or accrued is entered in the revenues realized column. The balance, at any time, represents the amount of revenue yet to be realized from that particular source. In some institutions there may be a requirement to identify separately interdepartmental transactions. In such cases, separate columns can be used in the revenues ledger to record cash transactions and interdepartmental transactions.

Forms 5.11, 5.12, and 5.13 illustrate how the detailed allocation accounts are recorded in the allocations ledger. Following the outline of the budget, separate ledger sheets are set up for personnel compensation, supplies and expense, and capital expenditures for each department or other organizational unit. The amount budgeted for each respective allocation is entered as a credit in the allocations column. As requisitions are approved for the department (Chemical Engineering in the illustration) and orders are issued, the amounts of such orders are entered in the orders placed

FORM 5.10

BLANK COLLEGE

R E V E N U E S L E D G E R

Account Bookstore

Account No. ______

Sheet No. 1

Date	Description	Voucher Number	Unrealized Revenues Amount	Unrealized Revenues Total To Date	Revenues Realized Amount	Revenues Realized Total To Date	Unrealized Balance
7-1-8	Set Up Budget	JV 1	$290,000	$290,000			$290,000
7-5-8	Cash Receipts	CV 1		290,000	$4,000	$4,000	286,000
7-6-8	Interdepartmental Sales	JV 2			1,000	5,000	285,000

FORM 5.11

BLANK COLLEGE

A L L O C A T I O N S L E D G E R

Division College of Engineering

Department Chemical Engineering

Sheet No. ______

Budget Personnel Compensation

Orders Placed, Paid, or Cancelled	Order Number	Date	Name or Description	Voucher Number	Object Code	Amount Paid		Allocation		Balance	
		7- 1-	Set up budget	JV 1	100			101,300	00cr	101,300	00cr

FORM 5.12

BLANK COLLEGE

A L L O C A T I O N S   L E D G E R

Division College of Engineering — Department Chemical Engineering

Sheet No. ______ — Budget Supplies and Expense

Orders Placed, Paid, or Cancelled	Order Number	Date	Name or Description	Voucher Number	Object Code	Amount Paid	Allocation	Balance
		7- 1-	Set up budget	JV 1	300		4,100 00cr	4,100 00cr
100 00	79240	7-20-	Brown Electronics		300			4,000 00cr
100 00cr	79240	8- 1-	Brown Electronics	784	300	100 00		4,000 00cr

FORM 5.13

BLANK COLLEGE

A L L O C A T I O N S   L E D G E R

Division College of Engineering — Department Chemical Engineering

Sheet No. ______ — Budget Capital Expenditures

Orders Placed, Paid, or Cancelled	Order Number	Date	Name or Description	Voucher Number	Object Code	Amount Paid	Allocation	Balance
		7- 1-	Set up budget	JV 1	400		7,500 00cr	7,500 00cr

column. This results in a decrease in the unencumbered or free balance of that particular budget. Subsequently, when the materials are received and the actual amount of the expenditure is determined, the encumbered order is liquidated by entering a credit in the orders paid column and a debit in the expenditures column. The free balance is adjusted automatically for any difference between the amount of the order and the actual cost of materials. At any time, after all vouchers have been posted, the available balance in any budget can be ascertained readily. This procedure assists in the approving of requisitions—a step in budgetary control. The illustration of this process refers to the supplies and expense budget, but it applies to all other budgets except that for personnel compensation. As the number of employees and the amounts of their pay are known in advance, it is not absolutely necessary to encumber personnel compensation. However, some colleges follow the practice of encumbering the personnel compensation budgets at the beginning of the year and liquidating for each payroll. Methods of payroll control are discussed in Chapter 6.

The importance of rendering budget reports to the department heads has been explained. One way to obtain this report is to design the allocations ledger so that a duplicate sheet is provided by inserting a carbon between two identical ledger sheets. Thus, the budget statement becomes a by-product of posting and is obtained without additional work. Moreover, providing the department head with an exact duplicate of the formal ledger sheet assists the business office in the discovery of errors and differences. Computerized and tabulating systems produce duplicate copies for budget heads. In a hand-posted system, a summarized monthly report showing the condition of each budget takes the place of the duplicate ledger sheet.

Revising the Budget. There are at least four methods of effecting budget revisions: (1) increasing both revenue estimates and departmental allocations; (2) decreasing revenue estimates and departmental allocations; (3) increasing one allocation and decreasing another; (4) transferring credits from the unallocated budget balance account to a departmental budget. The entries to record each of these types of changes are as follows:

1. Increased revenues from bookstore sales to increase the bookstore allocation for supplies and expense:

Estimated revenues
  Departmental budget allocations

In the revenues ledger, debit bookstore revenues (estimated) account. In the allocations ledger, credit the bookstore supplies and expense account in the allocations column.

2. Decreased revenues from registration fees absorbed by decreasing the supplies and expense budget of the accounting office.

Departmental budget allocations
  Estimated revenues

In the revenues ledger, decrease the budget estimate originally set up for registration fees. In the allocations ledger, reduce the supplies and expense budget of the accounting office by a debit in the allocations column.

3. The supplies and expense budget of the department of chemistry is increased. This increase is offset by a decrease in the capital expenditures budget of the department of history.

Departmental budget allocations
  Departmental budget allocations

In the allocations ledger, the appropriate budgets of the two departments are increased and decreased, respectively.

4. An increase in the salaries budget of the registrar's office is financed by a transfer from unallocated budget balance.

Unallocated budget balance
  Departmental budget allocations

In the allocations ledger, the salaries budget of the registrar's office is increased.

Closing Budgetary Accounts. The final phase of the budgetary process relates to the closing entries required at the end of the year and the disposition of unused allocations in particular departments. For convenience and clarity in describing closing entries, the following example is presented:

Original revenues estimate	$10,000,000
Actual revenue realized	9,900,000

Original budget allocations	8,000,000
Subsequent budget allocations	1,900,000
Actual expenditures	8,900,000
Encumbrances at end of year	800,000

Using the above figures, an incomplete trial balance of the general ledger is prepared as follows:

	Debit	*Credit*
Departmental budget allocations		$9,900,000
Estimated revenues	$10,000,000	
Unallocated budget balance		100,000
Revenues		9,900,000
Expenditures	8,900,000	
Encumbrances	800,000	
Provision for encumbrances		800,000

The following closing entries are made on journal vouchers:

1. Departmental budget allocations	$ 9,900,000	
Unallocated budget balance	100,000	
Estimated revenues		$ 10,000,000

To close budgetary accounts for revenues and expenditures into unallocated budget balance.

2. Revenues	9,900,000	
Expenditures		8,900,000
Unrestricted current funds balances		1,000,000

To close nominal accounts for revenues and expenditures into unrestricted current funds balances.

3. Provision for encumbrances:		
Current year	800,000	
Encumbrances		800,000

To close current year encumbrances.

4. Unrestricted current funds balances	800,000	
Provision for balances carried forward to cover encumbrances		800,000

To provide for balances carried forward to cover prior-year encumbrances.

In the above illustrations, transactions for the year produced an increase in the unallocated balances of unrestricted current funds of $200,000. This balance may be used to finance expenditures in the succeeding year or, in the publicly supported institution, it may have to be turned back to the state treasurer as an unexpended appropriation. Since encumbrances are not to be considered either expenditures or liabilities, the provision for balances carried forward to cover encumbrances should be shown as a segregation of unrestricted current fund balances.

Referring to the illustration, observe that although $9,900,000 was allocated to various departmental budgets, only $9,700,000 (expenditures plus encumbrances) was actually expended and/or committed. This means that there are free balances in the allocations ledger totaling $200,000.

There are several methods of handling unused departmental balances. In some public institutions, as has been stated, the unallocated balance reverts to the state. In such cases, unrestricted current funds balances is debited and cash is credited to record the refund. If the balance can be retained, there are three possible methods available to the institution. First, all free departmental balances can be lapsed at the end of the year and closed into unrestricted current funds balances. This is the procedure assumed in the above illustration. Entry 2 is supported by debits to detail accounts of those departments having free balances. Second, the departments may be allowed to retain their unspent balances. If such is the case, it can best be handled by closing all accounts, as outlined, but allocating in the new budget the current balance of $200,000 to those departments which had unexpended balances. Third, unexpended departmental balances can be closed into unrestricted current funds balances but earmarked for general institutional purposes or for the particular departments from which they were recovered.

Although a difference of opinion seems to exist as to the preferred method of disposing of unused departmental allocations, most accountants feel inclined toward the first plan discussed above—that is, the lapsing of all balances into a general unallocated balances account. Any reservations of balances in the name of departments endow those departments with a strong sense of ownership; hence, accumulated unallocated balances may be difficult to obtain for institutional purposes if emergencies should arise.

Regarding the revenues ledger, it is necessary to close the detail accounts that have balances, since detail estimates were $100,000 greater than actual revenues realized. In actual practice, it is seldom possible to estimate exactly the amount of revenue from each source; thus, at the end of the year some revenue accounts are overrealized and other accounts are underrealized. In the illustration, the net underrealization of revenue is $100,000.

Program Budgeting. Currently in limited use by a number of colleges and universities is a system of financial planning called program budgeting. Program budgeting—or planning-programming-budgeting systems—began to be used by the United States Department of Defense in 1961, and since 1965, efforts have been under way to extend the system to other federal departments and federal agencies. This system, generally referred to as P.P.B.S. or program budgeting, focuses on the most effective use of available resources to meet predetermined goals.

Program budgeting is designed for long-range planning and budgeting and, as such, is generally developed to cover five- or ten-year periods. Institutional programs are the central factor in program budgeting, rather than the organizational unit, as in the traditional budget system. The program budget attempts to establish and clarify the relationships among the goals, the resultant programs and activities derived from the goals, the economic impact of the proposed programs, and expression of costs in financial terms in a long-range budget. It also contributes to the decision-making process by providing analyses of alternative program decisions in terms of anticipated costs and expected benefits.

It might be well to mention at this point that the program budgeting concept may in certain instances make extensive use of computers and computer technology. However, it does not necessarily attempt to computerize the decision-making process, even though it makes use of quantitative analytical methods.

In relating program budgeting to colleges and universities, it is essential to develop the basic concept of the system. The institution's goals are usually set out in institutional documents and in many instances will be clearly defined. For example, the goals may be expressed in terms of programs such as instruction, research, and extension and public service. Such statements of goals do not provide the specifics that would permit programs to be formulated and evaluated. Goals of the institution, therefore, must be defined in terms of "program categories" that have identifiable end products. For example, if one of the major goals of the institution is instruction in business-related techniques, then the end product, "program categories," becomes the degree programs in the respective fields, *i.e.*, B.B.A. degree in accounting. A specific degree, such as the one just named, must be defined in terms of identifiable units generally referred to as "program elements." For a degree, the program elements usually consist of a specified set of courses; however, a degree program may consist of program elements from other than instructional functions, for example, student activities and student health services. A program classification structure (PCS) enables the institution to cut across program lines to obtain costs of a given degree.

The program classification structure is a mechanism that can be employed to do budgeting by the program budgeting method. This type of structure may be illustrated as follows for the bachelor's degree as a product of an institution:

- I. Instruction (program)
  - A. Instruction leading to a bachelor's degree (subprogram)
    - 1. Instruction in department A (program subcategory)
      - a. Level of instruction by department (program sector)
        - (1) Courses (program elements)
          - (a) Personnel costs } measures of program elements
          - (b) Supplies } measures of program elements
    - 2. Instruction in department B
      - a. Level of instruction by department
        - (1) Courses
          - (a) Personnel costs
          - (b) Supplies
  - Etc.
- II. Academic support (program)
  - Etc.
- III. Student services (program)
  - Etc.
- IV. Institutional support (program)
  - Etc.

Institutional programs, such as the ones listed above, will have inputs to the cost of a degree. This format will reflect the necessary input by each program area of an institution, thus defining the composition of a degree. It should be noted that end products other than degrees exist for an institution. For example, the composition of actions that lead to development of a new cure for a disease may be an end product for an institution.

Historically, budget making typically was concerned with decremental and incremental costs of continuing the same programs, operations, or functions, or with adding new ones. It generally is assumed that the expenditure base on which the budget-making process begins is correct. Program budgeting, on the other hand, makes no such assumption but attempts to set out programs and apply analytical tools to measure the cost-benefit/cost-effectiveness before alternative decisions are made.

Program budgeting cuts across conventional department lines and measures the performance of a program in terms of its output. In this manner, program elements that are possible substitutes for others may be given full consideration. Thus, program budgeting introduces a degree of competition designed to achieve greater effectiveness. Effectiveness may be considered as a measure of the extent to which a general program accomplishes its objectives and is related to benefits, which may be considered as the utility to be derived from a given program. This is the cost-benefit/cost-effectiveness as employed in program budgeting.

Another objective of program budgeting is control. Historically, budget control was identified solely with expenditure control. Program budgeting implies monitoring of program achievement as well as control of expenditures.

The final objective of program budgeting involves data and information. The system, if properly designed, will produce certain data that was not previously in evidence. This will enable the institution to make its decisions in terms of total program rather than on a departmental basis, which is possible because the programs relate to end products rather than to the administrative organization or function of the institution. The incremental emphasis of program budgeting becomes more appropriate as a system in view of the increased orientation toward interdisciplinary programs. As further study is given to program budgeting, it is likely that wide use will be made of this type of system as an approach to various institutional programs.

In summary, the important features of program budgeting are as follows:

1. The time frame for budgeting is extended from the usual one-year period to a minimum of five years and may be extended to a longer period.
2. The purpose of program budgeting is planning. Thus, it becomes essential to examine the cost and benefit implications of alternative courses of action for the future. The program budget shows existing programs extended over time and the effects of decisions already made.
3. The full cost of programs and program alternatives must be calculated if correct decisions are to be made. Certain support programs must be allocated to academic programs to determine full cost. It may be necessary to construct a cost model in order to be able to review the interrelationship of resources and costs.
4. Program budgeting is dynamic, aiming at a continuous management process.

Although program budgeting as considered above would require a reconstructing of the present function-departmental-object systems in use in colleges and universities, it is possible to construct computer systems that would permit the conversion of the present systems to the equivalent program budgeting. Such a system might be referred to as a "crosswalk" or "bridge." It remains to the future to see a fair evaluation of the program budgeting system. In the meantime, the program budgeting philosophy can be used as a tool to improve the efficiency and management of institutional programs while the present accounting system is continued to be used in collecting expenditure data.

Zero-Base Budgeting. The zero-base budgeting technique assumes nothing about prior budgets; it starts from zero each year to build a new budget. This kind of budgeting establishes standard workloads for the respective departments or colleges. If credit-hour production in a given department or college decreases and is expected to continue to decline, fewer instructional personnel, travel allowances, and supplies might be required; thus, less money should be budgeted than in the previous period. This is a partial adaptation of program budgeting and forces better management of the institution's resources. Whereas the detail supporting an allocation in this type of budgeting is different, the final budget is prepared in the traditional manner. An alternate approach to zero-base budgeting would be to have each department list the lowest 5 or 10 percent of its priorities.

Obviously, the reductions or additions called for in the zero-base budgeting approach cannot be achieved easily and sometimes not at all. This is so because the institution cannot quickly or easily adjust its costs in the organization. It may be extremely difficult to relocate or terminate personnel in a short period of time. Fixed costs that have been financed over a period of several years make budget changes difficult in the short run. Although zero-base budgeting has much to offer from a management point of view, the inflexibility that college management faces makes its adoption and strict implementation difficult.

6

Accounting for Current Funds: Expenditures, Disbursements, and Interfund Transfers

IN THIS CHAPTER, the routine accounting procedures employed in the recording and posting of expenditures of current funds are explained, and the records and documents used are illustrated. Although the discussion pertains to current funds, it is emphasized that the accounting routines for all funds are merged into one integrated system; hence, some of the forms and records may be used in funds other than current. The system is described from the point of view of both unrestricted and restricted current funds.

The ledgers used in recording expenditures of current funds are the general ledger (Form 6.1) and the allocations ledger (Forms 5.11, 5.12, and 5.13). The general ledger contains control accounts and receives, in summary or in detail, entries representing all financial transactions. It is posted monthly from the journals. In larger institutions, because of the volume of transactions, postings may go directly to general ledger accounts, obviating the need for some or all original entry journals. Subsidiary to, and controlled by, the general ledger is the allocations ledger, which contains

FORM 6.1

BLANK COLLEGE

GENERAL LEDGER

Account Title ______________ Account Number__________

Sheet Number__________

Date	Description	Reference	Debits		Credits		Balance
			Amount	Total To Date	Amount	Total To Date	

ledger accounts for each department listed in the budget. (See Chart of Accounts, pp. 74–77, herein, for complete list of allocations ledger accounts.) The allocation or allotment to each department may be divided into three parts—personnel compensation, supplies and expense, and capital expenditures—with a ledger account for each part of the allocation. To facilitate proving the accuracy of postings to the various suballocations and to localize errors, there are three subcontrol accounts over the allocations ledger, one each for personnel compensation, supplies and expense, and capital expenditures.[1] The sum of the various columns of these three subcontrol accounts, after all entries are posted, equals the control accounts in the general ledger (expenditures, encumbrances, and departmental allocations).[2] At least monthly, each group of suballocation accounts in the allocations ledger is balanced against its respective subcontrol account and, in turn, the total of the subcontrol is checked against the general ledger controls.

Use of Mechanical Accounting Equipment. Colleges and universities, like other organizations handling a large volume of financial transactions, are realizing more and more the advantages of mechanical accounting devices. Most modern installations of college and university accounting systems make use of one or more accounting machines or computers. It should not be understood, however, that every institutional business office, irrespective of its volume of business, needs mechanical equipment. Moreover, it is not to be inferred that in cases where mechanical equipment should be used, such equipment can be used to advantage in all operations of the accounting system. Individual colleges have their particular needs. Different types of accounting machinery are constructed to meet varying situations. Before mechanical equipment is installed, an intelligent survey should be made to ascertain, first, whether machines should be installed, and, second, what types of

1. This procedure is a routine that may not be applicable or desirable in some systems. It is merely suggested as an assisting device in setting up the allocations ledger. Obviously, a single general ledger control account would be sufficient, and a number of institutions use only one.

2. Expenditures controls the amount paid column of the allocations ledger, encumbrances controls the orders placed, paid or cancelled (the balance at the end of the posting period is the amount of orders outstanding), and departmental allocations controls the allocation column.

machines would be most efficient and appropriate for the various kinds of accounting work to be performed.

There are many advantages to be derived from using mechanical accounting devices such as computers. Of great value is the accuracy which results from the use of machines. Not only is the legibility of the records enhanced, but the machine itself is equipped with various devices to prevent the occurrence of errors or to provide automatic methods of discovery should errors be made. Also, mechanical equipment lends itself well to the assembly-line process of accounting. By reducing most accounting procedures to a routine, fewer highly trained accountants are needed in the business office. The work can be performed satisfactorily at a lower cost with the assistance of accounting machines. Finally, the ability of accounting machines to make multiple copies brings about a tremendous saving of time and effort. Such statements as budgetary reports to department heads can be produced as a part of the ledger posting process. Journals can be produced as a by-product of writing checks or posting ledgers. All payroll documents, including checks, check registers, and earnings records, can be produced simultaneously in one operation.

Some of the more important accounting functions that can be performed with accounting machines include: (1) maintenance of budgetary control records; (2) preparation of vouchers and voucher register; (3) writing of checks and check register for payment to vendors; (4) writing of payroll checks, payroll register, and earnings records; (5) keeping of investment records; (6) posting of accounts receivables; (7) keeping of revenue and general ledger records; and (8) preparation of reports to departments. Many of the functions listed above will be described fully in this chapter.

There are several types of accounting machines on the market. A number of companies manufacture several types of machines which are particularly adaptable to certain kinds of operations. Each institution will want to investigate the market before making a decision as to what type best fits its needs.

Use of Electronic Data Processing Equipment. Institutions of higher education, like business and commercial organizations, are realizing more and more the advantages of electronic data processing systems. Not only are many large institutions converting their accounting systems to computers, but plans are being made to institute total information systems in the future. The number of accounting and administrative procedures that can be programmed into an EDP system is almost limitless. The result is greater accuracy and speed, and, for large institutions, substantial savings in labor costs. Oftentimes, an institution may not have the volume of paperwork to justify the use of EDP equipment. In such instances, a careful survey should be made to ascertain whether some other type of mechanical equipment should be used. See Chapter 8 for a detailed discussion of the data processing systems.

Procedure in Machine Posting. Because many college and university business offices use mechanical accounting equipment, the authors will outline at this point the procedure in machine posting.[3] The first step in posting documents, such as purchase orders, invoices, payrolls, and interdepartmental invoices, to the allocations ledger is to accumulate a number of like documents into a batch or group. This group, known as a "run," is sent to the machine operator with a prelist or proof total, so that the correctness of the posting may be determined immediately after the batch is posted. A convenient procedure is to face the whole batch with a posting proof sheet (Form 6.2). Since three subcontrols are maintained in the allocations ledger, it is desirable to segregate the documents according to these subdivisions, with a predetermined total for each division, as illustrated in Form 6.2. Within each subdivision, the documents are arranged in the order of the accounts in the allocations ledger. The operator posts the documents by divisions and obtains an automatic machine total for each division. This result is checked by an employee other than the machine operator against the predetermined total on the posting proof sheet, and, if the two totals agree, the accuracy of the operation is proved. The posting proof sheet serves also as the medium of posting to the three subcontrol accounts.

Original Journals. In describing the original journals used in accounting for expenditures, it is assumed that a separate set of journals is employed for each group of funds. Thus, current funds expenditures are recorded in voucher and check registers devised

3. The routines described here can be applied, with some adaptation, to a handwritten accounting system.

FORM 6.2

BLANK COLLEGE

POSTING PROOF SHEET

No. 1

Date 7/1/75

	Item	Total
DEBIT		
Expenditures--Total		17,000
Personnel Compensation	9,300	
Supplies and Expense	7,300	
Capital Expenditures	400	
CREDIT		
Orders Liquidated		8,000
Supplies and Expense	7,550	
Capital Expenditures	450	

DOCUMENTS AND NUMBERS

Debits

Invoice vouchers 1 through 25

Credits

Purchase orders 1 through 20

Prepared by: ____________

Posted O.K. ____________ Operator

especially for that group. Disbursements of other funds—plant, endowment, loan, and agency—are recorded in separate sets of the same type journals. This method is not the only one employed in college accounting systems. Frequently, one series of journals is used to account for the expenditures or disbursements of all funds. In other words, all disbursements, irrespective of the fund to which they are charged, are recorded in the same voucher and check register. In such systems, the charges are distributed to proper fund accounts either by means of special columns or by codes.

In the system herein described, the following journals are used in connection with the accounting for expenditures and disbursements:

1. The voucher register (Form 6.3) is used to record all current funds vouchers other than payroll vouchers and interdepartmental transfer vouchers.

2. The check register (Form 6.4) is used to record the issuance of all checks in payment of vouchers other than payroll vouchers.

3. The payroll check register (Form 6.16) is used to record payroll checks for personnel compensation.

FORM 6.3

BLANK COLLEGE

VOUCHER REGISTER

Date	Payee	Reference		Vouchers Payable	Expenditures	Miscellaneous		
		Voucher No.	Check No.			L.F.	Account	Amount

FORM 6.4

BLANK COLLEGE

CHECK REGISTER

Posted By________ Checked By________ Sheet No.______

Check Number	Date	Voucher Number	Payee	Amount of Check	Reconciliation

FORM 6.5

BLANK COLLEGE

ORDERS PLACED AND LIQUIDATED JOURNAL

Date	Reference	Orders Placed	Orders Liquidated

FORM 6.6

BLANK COLLEGE

INTERDEPARTMENTAL TRANSFER JOURNAL

Date	Invoice No.	Debits			Credits		
		Expenditures	Stores	Revenues	Expenditures	Stores	Revenues

4. The orders placed and liquidated journal (Form 6.5) is used to record the amount of orders placed and liquidated.

5. The interdepartmental transfer journal (Form 6.6) is used to record interdepartmental invoices.

6. The general journal (Form 5.9) is used to record transactions which cannot be entered in any other journal. Such transactions include opening and closing entries, correction of errors, and budgetary adjustments. This journal usually consists of a series of individual journal vouchers.

The above journals, with the exception of the check registers, are standard columnar journal sheets, having appropriately printed column headings. The check registers result automatically from writing checks on the accounting machine.

In the following several sections, the accounting for expenditures of current funds is considered.

Accounting for Orders and Invoices. Purchasing routine has been explained in Chapter 3. An initial phase of purchasing is the routing of the requisition to the purchasing office in order to secure quotations and bids and the preparation of the purchase order. The purchase order, before it is released to the vendor, is audited both as to the availability of funds and as to extensions and codings. The audit is performed by the accounting office. The auditing of codes on the purchase order is important, inasmuch as this code indicates the account to be charged in the allocations ledger. The purchase order is checked as to availability of funds by reference to the free balance column in the proper account in the allocations ledger. If funds are available, one copy of the approved purchase order is sent back to the purchasing department authorizing release of the order to the vendor. The copy retained in the accounting office is placed in a departmental order file until the order is received. If funds are not available in the departmental allocations account, both copies of the purchase order are returned to the purchasing office with such notification.

Approved purchase orders are sorted as to code sequence and tabulated on a posting proof sheet. The orders in the batch are then posted as encumbrances against the proper allocations accounts. The amount of each order is entered in the orders placed, paid, or cancelled column of the allocations ledger, resulting in a decrease in the free or unencumbered balance of the account.

After details have been posted to the subsidiary ledger, the total amount of the orders placed, as shown by the posting proof sheet, is entered in the orders placed column of the orders placed and liquidated journal. At the end of the month, when this journal is summarized, the following entry is posted to the general ledger:

Encumbrances
  Provision for encumbrances—current year

The individual orders are then filed by departments, awaiting delivery of the goods.

As explained in Chapter 3, the receiving report, certifying that the goods have been properly received, is sent by the receiving clerk to the accounting department. When both the receiving report and the invoice have been received in the accounting office, these documents are matched with the purchase order. A copy of the requisition may also be provided by purchasing if necessary.

The proper audit of the voucher includes a checking of extensions, additions, and codes; a comparison of the vendor's invoice with both the receiving report and the order; and a verification of all signatures and approvals. Under this procedure, duplicate payments are virtually impossible, since the voucher document consists of the purchase order and receiving report, in addition to the vendor's invoice. For a double payment to occur, it would be necessary to duplicate not only the vendor's invoice but also the purchase order and the receiving report—an extremely unlikely series of duplications.

After the voucher is properly audited, it is sent to the voucher clerk to be numbered and entered in the voucher register. Invoices eligible for cash discount are paid early enough to take advantage of such discounts. At the end of the month, the summarized voucher register is posted to the general ledger as follows:

Expenditures
Miscellaneous accounts (itemized)
  Vouchers payable

Having been audited and entered in the voucher register, the voucher is prepared for machine posting in the same manner as the purchase order—that is, it is grouped with other invoices, separated into classes of expenditures, and arranged by departments within each class. A posting proof sheet is prepared, showing the total charges to the subcontrol accounts and the credits to those accounts for the amount of orders liquidated. The entry in the allocations ledger is made by recording the amount of the purchase order in the orders placed, paid, or cancelled column and the amount of the invoice in the amount paid column. The machine adds back to the free balance the amount of the purchase order credit, deducts from that balance the amount of the invoice, and automatically calculates and prints the new balance of the allocation. By means of object codes a detailed analysis of expenditures is possible.

In the case of partial deliveries, it is necessary to liquidate only the completed portion of the order. This end is accomplished by subtracting, on the posting margin of the purchase order, the amount to be liquidated from the total amount of the order.

The machine posting of invoices may be facilitated by designing the purchase order and invoice voucher so that the machine operator is able, without having to turn several documents to get the information, to liquidate the amount of the purchase order and to charge the amount of the invoice. Referring to the illustration of the purchase order on page 39, herein, observe that the right-hand margin of that document contains the amount of the encumbrance to be released and that the departmental code is indicated on the same line in the center of the order. All necessary posting information is furnished at a glance.

After the invoice has been posted to the detail account in the allocations ledger, the amount of orders liquidated is entered in the orders liquidated column of the orders placed and liquidated journal. At the end of the month, this column is posted in total to the general ledger as follows:

Provision for encumbrances—current year
  Encumbrances

The balance of the encumbrances account, after all entries have been posted at the end of the month, reflects the total orders outstanding and serves as a control over the sum of all open orders in the orders placed, paid, or cancelled columns in the allocations ledger.

The final step in accounting for the invoice is the preparation of a check in payment thereof. Some institutions follow the practice of paying each invoice with a separate check as soon as it is audited. This plan is profitable, however, only in large organizations, being advantageous because it results in an even flow of routine clerical work. It has the disadvantage of reducing cash balances, thus providing less funds to invest in short-term securities. More practicable for the smaller college is the procedure of filing the audited invoices by vendors and drawing one check weekly or bimonthly covering all the invoices of a particular vendor. Of course, if an invoice affords a discount for prompt payment, a check should be drawn in time to obtain the discount. Form 6.7 illustrates the type of check used to pay invoices in a machine accounting system. Entry in the check register (Form 6.4) is written simultaneously with the check. Many colleges use a voucher-check in which the vouch-

FORM 6.7

GENERAL FUND CHECK

BLANK COLLEGE
GENERAL FUND

No. 1

Check Number	Date	Voucher Number	Pay to the Order Of	Amount

BLANK COLLEGE

To
FIRST NATIONAL BANK
BLANK, STATE

50-309

Chief Accountant

Business Manager

er and the check are inseparable documents. At the end of the month, the check register is summarized and posted to the general ledger as follows:

Vouchers payable
  Cash

The balance of the vouchers payable account represents the outstanding current obligations at the end of the month and controls the file of unpaid invoices.

In the state-supported institution, the above procedure for invoices and checks may have to be modified to conform with the state's fiscal procedure. The following are typical fiscal relationships existing between the state college and the state government:

1. The funds of all agencies, including those concerned with higher education, are deposited and kept in a state depository. The institution certifies vouchers to the state treasurer, and state warrants are issued in payment.

2. The funds available to the institution are divided into two classes: (a) the state appropriation, which is kept and disbursed by the central government; and (b) fees and sales revenues, which are kept and disbursed locally by the institution.

3. The state maintains a central fiscal organization which not only purchases and writes checks for state institutions but also keeps many of the accounting records which otherwise would be kept by the institution. Invoices and payrolls are approved by the

college and sent to a central state office, where checks are prepared and issued.

4. The college withdraws its appropriation in lump sum or in installments and does its own purchasing, disbursing, and accounting.

In concluding this discussion of accounting for orders and invoices, attention is directed to handling orders outstanding at the end of the fiscal year. According to the AICPA Audit Guide, "Encumbrances representing outstanding purchase orders and other commitments for materials or services not received as of the reporting date should not be reported as expenditures nor be included in liabilities in the balance sheet."[4] Thus, encumbrances and provision for encumbrances at the end of the year are carried forward into the new year to cover these items in the new period. The provision for balances carried forward to cover encumbrances should be shown in the balance sheet as a segregation or earmarking of fund balances. Notice from the entries below that the departmental budget allocations will have to be increased in the new accounting period by the amount of the encumbrances carried forward.

The old allocations accounts are closed out completely; thus, financial statements are based upon expenditures without inclusion of outstanding encumbrances. As invoices on the encumbered orders are received in the current year, they are charged against current budgets in the same manner as current expenditures. The entries, illustrated in journal form, are as follows:

1. Entry to close departmental allocations at end of fiscal year:
   Unrestricted current funds balances
   Expenditures

   In the allocations ledger, close out all accounts completely.

2. Entry to set up provision for balances carried forward to cover encumbrances:
   Unrestricted current funds balances
   Provision for balances carried forward to cover encumbrances.

   Encumbrances and provision for encumbrances are carried forward into the new year and are used to account for current orders.

4. *Audits of Colleges and Universities* (New York: American Institute of Certified Public Accountants, 1973), 7.

At the beginning of the new fiscal year, the current departmental budgets are increased by the amount of the balances carried forward to cover encumbrances, as illustrated below:

Provision for balances carried forward to cover encumbrances
  Departmental allocations
    In the allocations ledger, individual accounts are credited.

Invoices on unencumbered orders are charged to current budgets in the usual manner by debiting expenditures and crediting vouchers payable.

Accounting for Payrolls. Three general types of payrolls are used in colleges and universities: (1) salary payrolls for instructional, administrative, and clerical personnel; (2) wage payrolls for laborers who work by the hour; and (3) payrolls for student labor. Many institutions have incorporated student and wage payrolls into one, as both are paid on an hourly basis.

The first step in accounting for the above types of payrolls is determining the personnel to be paid. There are several sources from which the authorized record of personnel may be compiled. Salaried employees are usually listed by name in the annual budget approved by the governing board. In addition, some form of annual employment contract is usually issued by the institution, a copy of which is received in the payroll office. Labor personnel ordinarily do not appear by name in the annual budget, and contracts are not issued to this class of employees. For such personnel, the establishment of the payroll is predicated upon written advices of employment from the various employing departments or from a central employment or personnel office. Generally, student employment is handled through a student employment office or is maintained as a separate and distinct function of the central personnel office. From these various sources, the institutional payroll, or roster, is compiled, taking the form of a roster card (Form 6.8) for each employee. These roster cards serve as a perpetual record, because once they are set up, they require adjustment only when there is a change in the status of an individual employee. The student labor section of the file may consist of work cards, supplied at the beginning of each semester by the student employment office.

FORM 6.8

BLANK COLLEGE

ROSTER CARD

Name__________________________________

Address________________________________

________________________________ Phone____________________

Date	Title	Department	Salary

From the roster cards, an earnings record (Form 6.9 or Form 6.16) is prepared for each employee. This record serves several important purposes. It is used as the voucher or payroll in case of salaried employees, no other document being required to initiate the salary payroll check. For all salaried employees, it provides an accumulated record of earnings used in reporting to the federal and state governments for purposes of income taxes and social security. It is also a valuable source of information in preparing the budget. The earnings record serves as a check on duplicate salary payments because an individual record is set up for properly authorized employees only. Further, it calls attention to changes in earnings from the prior period, thus assisting the auditor in ascertaining whether salary increases are authorized. Finally, because it records all deductions made from the employee's salary, it serves as a valuable aid in checking and verifying deduction accounts. Under a machine accounting system, the earnings record is written at the same time as the salary check and, hence, is produced with little additional effort. Under an electronic data processing system, earnings record information would be generated as a by-product of running the payroll, and a hard copy printout would be available for review.

One problem that arises in connection with the establishment of the salary payroll is that of split salaries, whereby an employee

FORM 6.9

BLANK COLLEGE

EARNINGS RECORD

Name

Social Security No. | Withholding Exemptions

Title

	Department	Code	Monthly Amount
Split			
Salary			
Detail			
		Gross Pay $	

Remarks

Dept. Code | Position Number

Department

Salary Rate | Per

Effective Date

Annuity Amount

Adjusted Contract Amt.

Monthly Group Life

Monthly Blue Cross

Monthly Income Protection

F.I.T. Specified Amt.

Retirement Member | FICA Member

Period Ending	Gross Pay	Add Emol.	Adj. Gross	FIT	FICA	State Retire.	Group Life	Blue Cross	Income Protect. Insur.	Emol.	Misc. Ded. Amount	Misc. Ded. Code	Net Pay
Jul													
Aug													
Sep													
Oct													
Nov													
Dec													
Jan													
Feb													
Mar													
Apr													
May													
Jun													
Jul													
Aug													

Budget Amount		Encumbrance		Liquidation	
Increase		Date	Amount	Date	Amount
Decrease					

teaches or works in more than one department. In such cases, the salary of the employee must be allocated or split between the two or more organization units involved. If the employee is a faculty member, his salary may be divided in proportion to the number of credit hours or other measurement of effort he devotes to teaching and/or research in each department. In the case of nonteaching personnel, the allocation is based on the relative amount of time devoted to each department. If costs are to be collected accurately, the allocation must be changed when the duties of the employee change. Ordinarily, the accounting office can determine the allocation at the start of each year by reference to the approved budget.

Although the establishment of the official payroll is an important beginning in payroll procedure, equally important is a well-defined channel through which the accounting department receives prompt notice of the addition of new employees, changes of status, and terminations. This end may be accomplished through the use of the request for personnel action form (Form 6.10). In many state institutions, the employment of certain clerical and wage personnel is regulated through a state civil service system. In such cases, it may be necessary to establish a procedure for obtaining from the state civil service department a written certification for all additions or changes in the payroll.

The use of time records and reports as required by wage and hour laws is widespread in colleges and universities. The application of minimum wage legislation to colleges and universities has forced uniformity in hours of employment, wage rates at the lower levels, and overtime pay. Many institutions have well-developed sick leave, vacation, retirement, and sabbatical leave plans. Good business practice requires that the institution establish rules and regulations to be applied uniformly throughout the college and administered through the business office. In all colleges and universities, time reports are now required for all employees who are covered by the Fair Labor Standards Act as amended in 1966.

A well-organized accounting system should include a procedure under which time reports, kept in each department and covering nonexempt employees (under the Fair Labor Standards Act as amended in 1966), are submitted to the accounting office in sup-

BLANK COLLEGE · FORM 6.10 · REQUEST FOR PERSONNEL ACTION

SOCIAL SECURITY NO	CLASSIFICATION GROUP		NEW APPOINTMENT	REAPPOINTMENT
MR.	LAST NAME	FIRST NAME	MI. PERMANENT	TEMPORARY
MRS.			FULL TIME	PART TIME
MISS			TRANSFER	FUND CHANGE
HOME ADDRESS	STREET	CITY	STATE ZIP CODE	TELEPHONE · HA · TITLE CHANGE / BUDGET CORRECTION
CAMPUS ADDRESS	BUILDING NAME	BLDG. CODE ROOM NO.	EXTENSION · CA · SALARY ADJUSTMENT / RETURN FROM LEAVE	

PRESENT STATUS		OCCUPATION CODE	PROPOSED STATUS		OCCUPATION CODE
TITLE OR POSITION			TITLE OR POSITION		

DEPARTMENT NAME	DEPARTMENT NUMBER	BUDGET POSITION NO.	MONTHLY SALARY DISTRIBUTION	DEPARTMENT NAME	DEPARTMENT NUMBER	MONTHLY SALARY DISTRIBUTION

SALARY RATE	$	TOTAL MONTHLY	$	$	HOME AG	HOME DEPT.	TOTAL MONTHLY	$

PERQUISITES

ACADEMIC APPOINTMENT PERIOD	2 MO.	9 MO.	10 MO.	12 MO.	OTHER	ACADEMIC APPOINTMENT PERIOD	2 MO.	9 MO.	10 MO.	12 MO.	OTHER
	40 HOUR	42 HOUR	44 HOUR				40 HOUR	42 HOUR	44 HOUR		
1 YR	FROM	TO				1 YR	FROM	TO			
3 YR						3 YR					
4 YR						4 YR					
PERM						PERM					

IT IS HEREBY CERTIFIED THAT THE STATUS OF THE AFORESAID INDIVIDUAL IS AS FOLLOWS:

STUDENT? YES___ NO: HOURS___ CLASS: FR___ SO___ JR___ SR___ GRAD___ STUDENT? YES___ NO: HOURS___ CLASS: FR___ SO___ JR___ SR___ GRAD___

EXEMPT WAGE & HOUR? YES___ NO: PERCENT OF FULL TIME___% EXEMPT WAGE & HOUR? YES___ NO: PERCENT OF FULL TIME___%

REPLACEMENT AND/OR AUTHORIZED POSITION ☐ FOR WHOM?_____ BUDGET POSITION NO.___

PRIOR SERVICE: DEPARTMENT _____ TITLE _____ APPROX. DATE ___

IF THE APPOINTEE HAS RELATIVES EMPLOYED BY THE UNIVERSITY, INDICATE:

EMPLOYEE NAME _____ DEPARTMENT NAME _____

REFERENCES _____

QUALIFICATIONS OF CANDIDATE (DEGREES HELD, INSTITUTIONS, ETC.) _____

REMARKS:

RECOMMENDED	DATE	RECOMMENDED	DATE
HEAD OF DEPARTMENT		DEAN OR ADMINISTRATIVE OFFICER	

APPROVED FOR THE ADMINISTRATION

COMPTROLLER'S OFFICE	PRESIDENT
	BOARD APPROVAL DATE · PAYROLL AUTHORIZATION NUMBER

port of the payroll voucher and salary check. A type of report commonly used is the attendance report (Form 6.11). If this kind of time report is used, it may be made to serve as support for a payroll voucher and as an independent time report. A leave and vacation card (Form 6.12) is a necessary part of the payroll records.

FORM 6.11

BLANK COLLEGE

A T T E N D A N C E   R E P O R T

Date (Month and Year) ____________ Department ____________

Name	1	2	3	4	5	6	7	8	9	10	11	12	13	14	15	16	17	18	19	20	21	22	23	24	25	26	27	28	29	30	31	Deductions

Code: X = Worked
A = Sick Leave, No Deduction
B = Vacation
C = Absent Without Leave, Deduction
D = Holiday

Signed:
____________ Department Head
____________ Employee

FORM 6.12

BLANK COLLEGE

LEAVE AND VACATION RECORD

Name____________________ Department____________________

Address____

Year:				Year:				Year:			
Code	From	To	Total Time	Code	From	To	Total Time	Code	From	To	Total Time

Code: A = Sick Leave With Pay
B = Vacation
C = Leave Without Pay
D = Other

In colleges and universities, the usual procedure is to prepare payroll vouchers for nonsalaried or labor personnel only, the earnings record serving as an individual voucher in the case of salaried employees. Form 6.13 is suitable for use as a wage payroll voucher for all employees and student labor. Labor payrolls are prepared in duplicate by the head of the organization unit and submitted to the accounting office. An important part of the payroll procedure for labor is the establishment of definite dates for submission of payrolls and the drawing of payroll checks. A good plan is to close the payroll period several days before checks are to be issued. This procedure affords the accounting office time to make the necessary audit of the payroll vouchers and to prepare checks. An example of payroll dates for a semimonthly labor payroll follows:[5]

First period—from the first through the fifteenth—
Payroll vouchers due in the accounting office on the sixteenth and payroll checks ready for distribution on the twenty-first.

5. Because the Fair Labor Standards Act requires that covered employees be paid overtime for time worked in excess of forty hours per week after February, 1969, a number of institutions find it convenient to pay these employees every two weeks. Some institutions have placed all covered employees on an hourly basis and all exempt employees on a salary basis.

Second period—from the sixteenth through the last day of the month—Payroll vouchers due in the accounting office on the first and payroll checks ready for distribution on the sixth.

If the number of employees on all payrolls is considerable, it may be advisable to stagger the payroll dates—that is, arrange for each of the different types of payrolls to fall due on a different date, so that the work of auditing payrolls and writing checks is fairly evenly distributed throughout the month. Staggering of payrolls is particularly important under a machine accounting system in which one machine is required to write all records in addition to writing payroll and other checks.

The recommended procedure in distributing payroll checks is to issue them to department heads for distribution to the individual employees of their particular departments. All undistributed checks should be returned promptly to the accounting office. This method is preferable to that under which each individual employee

FORM 6.13

BLANK COLLEGE

WAGE PAYROLL VOUCHER

Department______________________________

For Period Beginning________________, 19___ Through ________________, 19___

Payroll No.	Check No.	Name	Pay Basis	Time	Rate	Gross Amount	With-holding Tax	Social Security Tax	State Retire-ment	Blue Cross	Net Amount

Charge		Pay Basis	Certification and Approval
Account	Amount	1 Hour 2 Day 3 Week 4 Month 5 Special	I certify that the services for which payment is requested have been rendered. } ________ Department Head Approved for payment ________ For the Chief Accountant

Auditor________	Rates Verified	Computed by	Checked by	Wage Voucher No.

calls in person at the business office for his check. However, it is a good practice for a representative of the accounting office to be present occasionally when checks are distributed to workers, as a partial safeguard against padded payrolls. If a student employment office is maintained, students are usually required to call at that office for their checks. Some institutions may find it convenient to send payroll checks to the respective banks for deposit to the employees' accounts.

After an audit of the payroll vouchers, in the case of laborers, and of the earnings records, in the case of salaried personnel, the payroll checks are written by machine. Because more information is needed on the payroll check than on the general check and because bank reconciling and postauditing are facilitated, it is customary to use separate payroll bank accounts and a separate series of payroll checks. Different colors of paper may be used for the wage and salary checks, respectively. A payroll check is illustrated in Form 6.17. The entries in journal form required to effect a transfer of funds from the general bank account to the payroll bank account are as follows:

1. On bank transfer voucher (Form 6.14) and entered in voucher register:
   Bank transfers
      Vouchers payable

2. In the check register (general bank account):
   Vouchers payable
      General bank account

3. In cash receipts journal (check is routed through the cashier as with all other receipts):
   Payroll bank account
      Bank transfers

One advantage of the mechanical method of payroll check writing is that the payroll check register, the earnings record, and the payroll check are written simultaneously in a single operation. This operation is accomplished through the use of carbon paper inserted between the documents. The relationship between these records is illustrated on page 134, herein.

The final steps in the payroll process are the distribution and posting of the payroll to the proper allocations ledger accounts and

FORM 6.14

BLANK COLLEGE

Voucher No.__________

B A N K   T R A N S F E R   A N D   R E I M B U R S E M E N T
V O U C H E R

Date____________________

Issue check in the amount of $_______________ payable to ____________________

on ______________________________ Bank, ____________________________ Fund,

for purpose of ____

	General Ledger		Subsidiary
	Account	Amount	Account
DEBIT			
CREDIT			

Prepared By____________________	Entered Voucher Register______________
	Posted Allocations Ledger______________
Approved____________________ Chief Accountant	Paid by Check Number______________

the entries made at the end of the month in the general ledger. The method of posting payroll vouchers to the detail departmental accounts has been explained. Since salary payrolls are based solely on the earnings records, there are no individual vouchers from

FORM 6.15

BLANK COLLEGE — P A Y R O L L   C H E C K   R E G I S T E R

Posted By — Checked By — Sheet No.

Pay Period	Gross Earnings	Date	Deductions: Group Ins.	Deductions: Tchr. Ret.	Deductions: Accts Rec.	Deductions: With-holding Tax	Deductions: Misc.	Code	Check No.	Net Earnings	Date	Pay Period Ending	Pay to the Order of	Amount of Check	Recon-ciliation
Jan.	500.00	1/31/76	20.00	20.00					1	460.00	1/31/76	Jan.	John Doe	460.00	

FORM 6.16

E A R N I N G S   R E C O R D

Year______ Salary - Reg.______ Basis______ Salary - S.S.______ P.I.K.______ Charge:

Name______ Dept.______

Year______ Salary - Reg.______ Basis______ Salary - S.S.______ P.I.K.______ Charge:

Deductions: Teachers Ret.	Deductions: Group Ins.	Deductions: Other

Deductions: Teachers Ret.	Deductions: Group Ins.	Deductions: Other

Pay Period	Gross Earnings	Date	Deductions: Group Ins.	Deductions: Tchr. Ret.	Deductions: Accts Rec.	Deductions: With-holding Tax	Deductions: Misc.	Code	Check No.	Net Earnings
Jan.	500.00	1/31/76	20.00	20.00					1	460.00

FORM 6.17

EMPLOYEE'S STATEMENT OF EARNINGS

Pay Period	Gross Earnings	Date	Deductions: Group Ins.	Deductions: Tchr. Ret.	Deductions: Accts Rec.	Deductions: With-holding Tax	Deductions: Misc.	Code	Check No.	Net Earnings
Jan.	500.00	1/31/76	20.00	20.00					1	460.00

Please Detach This Statement Before Depositing This Check

SALARY PAYROLL ACCOUNT
BLANK COLLEGE

Date	Pay Period Ending	Pay to the Order of	Amount
1/31/76	Jan.	John Doe	460.00

BLANK COLLEGE

To: Second National Bank
Blank, State
56-501

______ President

______ Business Manager

FORM 6.18

BLANK COLLEGE

MONTHLY SALARIES DISTRIBUTION

No.____________

Date____________

Code	Budget Unit	Object	Amount
351	President	012	
		013	
354	Business Manager	012	
		013	
355	Accounting Office	012	
		013	
358	Purchasing	012	
		013	
411	Student Union	013	
412	Cafeteria	013	
416	Residence Halls - Single	012	
		013	
418	Residence Halls - Married	012	
		013	
420	Bookstore	012	
		013	
	TOTAL		

which to post. Therefore, a salary distribution sheet (Form 6.18) is prepared from the payroll check register and used as the basis for posting the departmental salaries accounts in the allocations ledger. The general ledger entries for all cash payrolls come from a monthly summary of the payroll check register. This summary is illustrated in the following journal entry:

Expenditures (for total amount of payroll):
  Due to Acme Life Insurance Company (for deductions from salaries for group life insurance)

Due to retirement system (for deductions from salaries for the retirement system)
Withholding tax deductions—federal (for income tax deductions)
Withholding tax deductions—state (for income tax deductions)
F.I.C.A. deductions (for Social Security deductions)
Second National Bank—salary payroll account (for net amount of salary payroll)
Third National Bank—wage payroll account (for net amount of wage payroll)

Accounting for Traveling Expenses. The regulations of many institutions relative to travel by employees on institutional business include the provision that a travel request or authorization must be submitted and approved before each trip. In the case of employees who travel constantly or seasonally, then monthly or even annual travel requests are used. The use of a travel authorization (Form 6.19) has three advantages. First, it serves the same function as the purchase requisition in a system of budgetary control. Second, it gives the business office an opportunity to learn about anticipated trips before such trips are made. Third, it assists the accounting office in the auditing of expense vouchers, in that it prevents disagreements (after the trip has been made) as to what items are to be reimbursed. Fourth, it safeguards against duplicate payments of expense vouchers.

Upon completion of a trip, the individual making the trip submits a travel expense voucher (Form 6.20 and reverse). One of the regulations covering travel vouchers is that the voucher must be typewritten on a special form so that the preparation of a new voucher document is unnecessary. Some colleges encumber the travel requests. In such cases, it is necessary to liquidate the amount of the request at the time the expense voucher is entered.

The travel expense voucher follows the same channels as do the other vouchers. It is audited, entered in the voucher register, posted to the allocations ledger, and paid.

Accounting for Petty Cash. One requirement of a voucher system, such as the type described here, is that all disbursements be made by check. Under such a system, it is necessary to have on hand cash from which to pay small bills. The generally accepted method of doing this is through the use of the imprest petty cash fund. Under the imprest system, a fixed sum is established as a

FORM 6.19

BLANK COLLEGE

TRAVEL AUTHORIZATION

Submit One Set
Per Individual

Date________________

To: Business Manager, Blank College

From:________________ Title________________

In compliance with college regulations and state laws permission is respectfully requested for authorization to attend the following convention, association, or meeting.

Name of Convention, Association, or Meeting ________ Place of Meeting ________

Date of Meeting ________ Mode of Transportation ________

PURPOSE OF CONVENTION, ASSOCIATION, OR MEETING:

Departmental Code ________ Signature ________

ESTIMATED COST:

Transportation________

Meals and Lodging________

Other________

Total________

APPROVED:

1. ________ Department Chairman ________ Date

2. ________ Dean or Administrative Head ________ Date

3. ________ President (if necessary) ________ Date
Subject to
Availability of funds

________ Funds Available - Accounting ________ Date

White Copy for Accounting
Blue Copy for Auditor
Yellow Copy for President
Green Copy for Department Chairman
Pink copy for Individual

See back of pink copy for University Travel Policy

This space for use by Accounting Office

________ Travel Request Number

________ Code

________ Est. Cost

petty cash fund. The exact amount of the fund depends on the specific requirements of the department in question. A voucher is prepared and a check is drawn payable to the individual designated as custodian of the fund. The entry in the voucher register to record the establishment of the fund is a debit to petty cash (with

FORM 6.20
(front)

Standard Form No. 223E
Form Prescribed By
State Auditor
April 1964

VOUCHER FOR REIMBURSEMENT OF EXPENSES
INCIDENT TO OFFICIAL TRAVEL

BLANK COLLEGE ________ Dr.
(Department)

To____________________

Address____________________

____

____
(Official Duty)

For mileage for privately owned motor vehicle used by me for transportation, and/or lieu allowance, and for reimbursement for subsistence (meals and lodging) and other expenses paid by me in the discharge of official duty

from ____________ 19___ to ____________ 19___, as per itemized statement within.

Amount Claimed			Amount Due (as per office verification)		
For	Dollars	Cents	For	Dollars	Cents
Subsistence					
Travel					
Other					
Total			Amount Verified: Correct For		

Subject to any differences determined by verification, I certify that the above amount claimed by me for travel expenses for the period indicated is true and just in all respects, and that payment for any part thereof has not been received.

Approved for Payment:____________________ Payee____________________
(Department Chairman)

____________________ Title Business Manager Verified By____________________

ACCOUNTING CLASSIFICATION

The Above Claim Is Requested To Be Charged To:				The Above Claim Is Verified For Charge To:			
Department	Code	Amount		Department	Code	Amount	
Travel Authorization				Travel Authorization			
No.__________				No.__________			

a corresponding entry to a subsidiary account) and a credit to vouchers payable.

The check is cashed by the payee (custodian of the fund) and disbursed in accordance with specific regulations. When cash is disbursed, a receipt or voucher (Form 6.21) is obtained from the

FORM 6.20
(back)

STATEMENT OF TRAVELING EXPENSES INCURRED BY ____________________

From __________ 19__ to __________ 19__

Date	Points of Travel: From	Points of Travel: To	Motor Vehicle: Miles	Motor Vehicle: Mileage Amount	Air or Rail Fare	Date	Items	Amount
Total Amounts (carry to page 1)						Total (carry to page 1)		

Statement of Cost of Meals and Lodging

Date	Break-fast	Lunch	Dinner	Hotel Room	Daily Total	Place Where Expense Incurred
Total						
Total Subsistence (carry to page 1)						

State Place and Purpose of Visit

Complete the following if travel was out of state and by auto-mobile:

Meeting commenced at ______ __M

on ____________ (date) and terminated

at ______ __M on ____________ (date)

Accompanied by:

____

____

Note: Receipts for amounts paid for lodging and other expenses, other than for meals, must accompany this voucher.

payee. At definite intervals, or whenever necessary, a check is drawn payable to the custodian to reimburse the petty cash fund to its original amount. A petty cash reimbursement voucher (Form 6.22) is used to support the reimbursing check. The entry in the voucher register to record the reimbursement voucher is a debit to

FORM 6.21

BLANK COLLEGE
BUSINESS OFFICE

PETTY CASH VOUCHER

Paid To ____________________ $ ________

For ____________________

Approved __________ Received Payment __________

Accounts to be Charged __________

FORM 6.22

BLANK COLLEGE Voucher No. ________

PETTY CASH REIMBURSEMENT VOUCHER

Date ________

Date	Paid To	Explanation	Amount

Pay To: ____________________ $ ________
Signed (Custodian of Fund)

Charge Accounts:
________ $ ____ ________ $ ____
________ $ ____ ________ $ ____
________ $ ____ ________ $ ____
________ $ ____ ________ $ ____

Entered:
Allocations Ledger
Revenue Ledger
General Ledger

Approved for Reimbursement ____________________
Auditor

expenditures or revenues (for refunds of revenues) and a credit to vouchers payable. The allocations ledger accounts are charged from the individual petty cash vouchers, which are permanently attached to the reimbursement voucher. If expenditures made from petty cash are chargeable to funds other than current funds, petty cash is reimbursed by separate checks on the proper funds.

Where numerous petty cash funds are needed, a single large working cash fund might be established from which small petty cash funds and expense advances could be set up.

Care must be taken to safeguard the petty cash fund. It is sometimes necessary to advance sums of cash to various auxiliary enterprises for making change and to the receiving clerk for paying small freight and express bills. In such cases, audits should be made of these funds from time to time. Since petty cash is misused easily, the amount of the fund should be small and its use should be restricted to specific types and amounts of expenses.

Accounting for Interdepartmental Transactions. Interdepartmental transactions are of a noncash nature, yet they have an important effect on the accurate determination of costs and operating results. At least three types of transactions fall within this category: (1) sales by auxiliary enterprises and organized activities to other institutional departments, (2) sales and services of the maintenance department, and (3) miscellaneous sales or transfers between departments. These types of interdepartmental transactions differ, and each is treated differently in the accounting records.

The first type, sales to a department by an auxiliary enterprise (such as a bookstore) or by an organized activity (such as a dairy), must be recorded for two reasons. First, the selling agency is judged by its profit and loss statement; hence, it must receive credit for all its sales. Second, the buying department has expended some of the funds allotted to it in the budget, and so it must be charged with the cost of the purchase. Many interdepartmental transactions of this type occur. For example, the bookstore sells office supplies to nearly every department; the farm sells produce to the dining hall; and the dairy sells raw milk to the creamery, which, in turn, sells milk to the dining halls. In journal form, the entry to record interdepartmental transactions of this type is as follows:

Expenditures (in the allocations ledger, debit the account of the purchasing department)
    Revenues (in the revenues ledger, credit the account of the selling department)

If there is a requirement that interdepartmental expenditures and revenues be kept separate from so-called cash expenditures and revenues, appropriate adjustments would have to be made in the accounts to reflect the distinction between the two types of transactions.

The second type of interdepartmental transaction arises from the sales and services of the maintenance department, which renders service to the academic and administrative departments and to the auxiliary enterprises. The former departments are not charged with ordinary upkeep and maintenance but are billed only when the maintenance department serves them in a special manner, for example, by the construction of a cabinet or bookcase. Auxiliary enterprises, however, must be assessed for all overhead costs occasioned by the existence of the enterprise on the campus, such as repairs to equipment, trucking services, utilities, and janitorial services. The following entry, in journal form, illustrates a transaction in which service rendered by the maintenance department is charged to some other department:

Expenditures (in the allocations ledger, charge budget of the department receiving the service)
    Expenditures (in the allocations ledger, credit appropriate maintenance account)

The third type of interdepartmental transaction arises from incidental transfers between instructional departments; for example, the department of art "buys" some supplies from the department of history. The entry to record this transfer is as follows:

Expenditures (charge supplies and expense budget of the art department)
    Expenditures (credit supplies and expense budget of the history department)

All interdepartmental transactions originate on interdepartmental invoices (Form 3.14), which are made out in triplicate by the selling department and approved by the department receiving the service or supply. The accounting department, the selling department, and the receiving department receive a copy of the invoice. The accounting department's copy of the interdepartmental invoice is numbered and entered in the interdepartmental transfer journal. The detail charges and credits are posted directly from the invoices; the general ledger is posted from a monthly summary of the interdepartmental transfer journal.

Interfund Transfers

Mandatory and Nonmandatory Transfers. Mandatory transfers include transfers from current funds to other funds. Such transfers may be required for the following reasons: first, because of grant and contractual agreements with federal government agencies, donors, and other organizations to provide matching funds for gifts and grants; second, because of legal requirements relating to the financing of the institutional plant, such as funds to pay for bond obligations or other debt obligations, and required funding for renewals and replacement of plant which is not financed from other resources and similar transactions.

Nonmandatory transfers include those made at the discretion of the institution's governing board, not those made because of legal or contractual requirements. These transfers from current funds to other fund groups may be made for a number of purposes, such as additions to physical plant, increases in loan and/or endowment funds, prepayment of debt, voluntary allocations for renewal and replacement of plant, and similar purposes.

The following entries, in journal form, illustrate a transaction in which funds are transferred to meet legal debt service requirements (a mandatory transfer) on educational plant:

IN UNRESTRICTED CURRENT FUNDS:
  Transfers to funds for retirement of indebtedness
    Cash

IN FUNDS FOR RETIREMENT OF INDEBTEDNESS:
  Cash
    Retirement of indebtedness fund balances
    (separate subsidiary accounts established as required)

The following entries, in journal form, illustrate a transaction in which funds are transferred at the board's discretion (a nonmandatory transfer) to increase loan funds.

IN UNRESTRICTED CURRENT FUNDS:
  Transfers to loan funds
    Cash

IN LOAN FUNDS:
  Cash
    Loan fund balances
    (credit appropriate subsidiary account)

Analysis of Expenditures. The primary accounts for expenditures are set up for purposes of budgetary control and therefore are broken down no further than the budget classes of expenditures—that is, personnel compensation, supplies and expense, and capital expenditures. It is essential, however, that the accounting system furnish more detailed information within each general object class. Thus, for each entry in the amount paid column of the allocations ledger a code number is placed in the object code column, designating the specific object of the expenditure. At the end of the month, these codes are analyzed and the detailed information desired is accumulated. One method of accumulating this information is by means of a columnar analysis sheet. Another method makes use of unit tickets or cards. The advantages of the second plan lie in the ease of handling and filing the unit tickets, as compared with manipulating the bulky columnar analysis sheets, and also in the fact that it makes possible a greater division of labor. These tickets (Form 6.23) may be spread in a binder so that a comparative analysis is readily made available for all previous months. If an EDP or a tabulating machine system is being used, the analysis of expenditures is produced electronically.

Accounting for Expenditures of Restricted Current Funds. Restricted current funds are those funds that are expendable for operating purposes but restricted by an outside agency or person as to use, as distinguished from unrestricted current funds, which are available for any current purpose. A fund is not to be classified as restricted if its use is subject to the control of the governing board of the institution. Since restricted current funds are expendable for current purposes, the expenditures and revenues of these funds may be combined with those of unrestricted current funds in financial statements. Common types of restricted current funds are gifts for scholarships and fellowships or for the purchase of books or equipment; grants from foundations, industries, individuals, and governmental bodies for research projects and other sponsored programs; and income from investments of endowment funds restricted by donors as to use.

There are several methods of accounting for the expenditures of restricted current funds. Three of these methods will be explained and illustrated. In the first method, restricted funds are made a part of the regular unrestricted current funds budget, and separate

FORM 6.23

BLANK COLLEGE

ANALYSIS OF EXPENDITURES

Department ____________________

Expenditures for Month	Object Classification			Expenditures to Date
	010	Personnel Compensation (Salaries)		
	011	Teaching Salaries		
	012	Other Professional Salaries		
	013	Nonprofessional Salaries		
	016	Staff Benefits		
	010		Subtotal	
	020	Personnel Compensation (Wages)		
	021	Graduate Teaching Wages		
	022	Other Graduate Wages		
	023	Other Professional Wages		
	024	Nonprofessional Wages		
	025	Undergraduate Student Wages		
	026	Staff Benefits		
	020		Subtotal	
	030	Supplies and Expense		
	031	Instructional Supplies		
	033	Janitorial Supplies		
	030		Subtotal	
	040	Capital Expenditures		
	041	Scientific Equipment		
	042	Office Machines and Equipment		
	043	Furniture and Furnishings		
	044	Machines and Tools		
	045	Motor Vehicles		
	046	Books		
	047	Livestock		
	040		Subtotal	
			Grand Total	

accounts are included for them in the allocations ledger. The routine of requisitioning, purchasing, and invoicing is identical with the routine for regular unrestricted current funds transactions. As restricted current funds are received, however, they are taken into the restricted current funds group as credits to the proper balance accounts. Periodically, usually each month, the unrestricted current funds group is reimbursed by the restricted current funds group for expenditures made on its behalf during that period, this reimbursement being credited to revenues. The amount of the reimbursement is determined by reference to those allocation ledger accounts designated as restricted. Revenue taken in from restricted current funds, according to *College and University Business Administration*, is limited to the amount actually expended from restricted funds during the year. Receipts of the restricted current funds group not expended are reflected in the accounts and on the balance sheet as part of restricted current funds balances. Journal entries, illustrating this method of accounting for the transactions of restricted current funds, are given below:

1. To record receipt of funds, expendable for current purposes, but subject to designated restrictions:

   a. In Restricted Current Funds:
      Cash
         Restricted current funds balances
      In subsidiary restricted current funds ledger, credit individual accounts.

   b. In Unrestricted Current Funds:
      No entry required.

2. To record expenditures chargeable to restricted current funds:

   a. In Restricted Current Funds:
      No entry required.

   b. In Unrestricted Current Funds:
      Restricted expenditures (control)
         Vouchers payable
      In subsidiary allocations ledger, charge proper account (designated as restricted current funds).

3. To record monthly reimbursement from restricted to unrestricted current funds:

   a. In Restricted Current Funds:
      Restricted current funds balances
         Cash
      In subsidiary restricted current funds ledger, charge proper accounts.

   b. In Unrestricted Current Funds:
      Cash
         Restricted revenues (control)
      In revenues ledger, credit appropriate revenues accounts.

There are several advantages in this method of handling restricted funds. First, the handling of restricted funds expenditures along with those of the unrestricted current funds results in a smoother accounting routine. Second, this method fits in with a system of budgets and budgetary control and, in addition, obviates the necessity of preparing two budgets—one for unrestricted current and another for restricted current expenditures. Third, it makes unnecessary any merging of expenditures for purposes of financial statements, as all current funds expenditures can be determined from the allocation ledger without consolidating the unrestricted accounts with the restricted accounts.

A second method, closely related to the one just described, is used in many institutions. The unrestricted current funds budget includes restricted revenues and expenditures, and the budget allocations and unrealized revenues accounts include estimates of these funds. All transactions involving restricted funds are recorded entirely within the restricted current funds group. At the end of each month, expenditures and revenues of restricted current funds are brought into the unrestricted current funds section of the general ledger. Revenues, as in the first method, are limited to the amount of restricted current funds expended. The following entries, in journal form, illustrate the second method of handling restricted current funds transactions:

1. To record receipt of funds, expendable for current purposes but subject to designated restrictions:

   IN RESTRICTED CURRENT FUNDS:
   Cash
   Restricted current funds balances
   In subsidiary restricted current funds ledger, credit individual accounts.

2. To record expenditures of restricted current funds:

   IN RESTRICTED CURRENT FUNDS:
   Restricted current funds balances
   Cash
   In subsidiary restricted current funds ledger, charge proper accounts.

3. To transfer to unrestricted current funds the revenues and expenditures of restricted current funds:

a. In Unrestricted Current Funds:
Expenditures
Revenues
In allocations ledger, debit individual accounts. In revenues ledger, credit individual accounts.

b. In Restricted Current Funds:
No entry required.

A third method of handling restricted current funds is to record all transactions involving such funds entirely within the restricted current funds group. This method necessitates the use of practically all of the original journals explained above, as well as the subsidiary expenditure ledger for individual restricted accounts. Each entry in the detail ledger is coded with the standard object code number, and at the end of the year the expenditures of the restricted current funds group are merged with those of the unrestricted current funds group. In like manner, revenues of restricted current funds are consolidated with unrestricted current funds revenues.

Accrual Accounting. In connection with the accounting systems of colleges and universities, it is required that current funds revenues be reported as these revenues become due; and expenditures should include charges for materials received and services rendered. Expenditures incurred at the balance sheet date should be accrued and expenditures applicable to future periods should be deferred. The only acceptable basis of deviating from the accrual method is that the omission has no material effect on the financial statements.

Good judgment must be exercised in determining whether minor items of revenues and expenditures are to be accrued. If the items are not material in nature, it is expected that such items would not be accrued. Those items which should be accrued are material in amount, so that the financial statements will properly reflect the actual revenues and expenditures of the institution. Accrual accounting methods should be applied to all funds of the institution.

7

Accounting for Current Funds: Revenues and Receipts

THE LEDGERS USED in accounting for revenues are the general ledger and the subsidiary revenues ledger. The revenues account in the general ledger represents the total revenues realized to date and controls the detailed revenue accounts in the revenues ledger. The estimated revenues account is a budgetary account,[1] indicating the total estimated revenue for the period. It remains unchanged during the year, unless the revenue budget is revised. Postings to the general ledger for revenues and other cash receipts are made from the cash receipts journal, and postings to the revenues ledger are made directly from the daily cash receipts records. At least once a month, the detailed accounts in the revenues ledger are reconciled with the control accounts in the general ledger.

Relationship Between Fiscal Systems of State and Institution. Before discussing the accounting procedure for revenues, consideration must be given to the fiscal relationship existing between institution and state because the form of this relationship is an important factor in determining how the publicly supported institution must account for its revenues. From the point of view of the handling of revenues, state fiscal systems fall into four major groups. First, in some states, publicly supported institutions are permitted to retain all receipts from student fees and sales of auxiliary enterprises and to receive an additional appropriation from the state for the balance of their needs. Second, in some states, institutions remit all receipts to the state treasury and receive credits for their receipts, against which warrants may be drawn. Third, in some states, institutions turn over all receipts to the state and receive an appropriation from the legislature to cover their entire

1. Some accountants consider the estimated revenues account as both a budgetary and a proprietary account. Budget estimates of revenues are debited to this account and realized revenues are credited.

budgets. Fourth, in some states, institutions retain certain specified funds, such as revenues from student activities, but remit all other receipts to the state treasury.

The first plan, which is the one employed in many of the states and applies to all privately controlled institutions, serves as the basis for the present discussion. The second plan differs but slightly from the first in that receipts are deposited in the state treasury instead of a college depository. Under this plan, accounting procedure for revenue requires that a receivable account (such as funds in state treasury), instead of a bank account, be charged with receipts. Under the third plan, whereby institutions remit all receipts to the treasury and receive all monies through state appropriations, colleges have only that revenue received from the state through legislative appropriation. Therefore, as receipts from student fees and other institutional revenues are accrued or collected, they are credited, not to a revenue, but to a liability account, since they represent debts to the state treasurer. When this plan is followed, however, a detailed revenue ledger should be kept to accumulate statistical information relative to sources of receipts and to control these receipts from a budgetary point of view. Although these receipts are not retained, they must be budgeted and collected on behalf of the state treasury. Under this plan, as receipts are collected from various sources, they are credited to revenues due to state and are posted in the usual manner to detailed revenue accounts. As payments of these collections are made to the treasurer, a remittances of revenue to state account is charged. The revenues due to state account remains open until the end of the year and thus serves as a control over the detailed ledger, which is regarded as a memorandum or statistical ledger. Under the fourth plan, whereby institutions retain only specified funds, such funds should be retained as restricted funds and accounted for as such. Some accounting problems arising in connection with revenues and cash receipts are segregated and considered below.

Accounting for Revenues from Registration. The procedure described below is suggested in connection with registration. It assumes a centralized registration plan in which a large area, such as a gymnasium, auditorium, or library, is set up and equipped each term or semester for the registration process. Faculty advisors, representatives of the registrar, the business officer, deans of students, and other administrative officers are stationed in the area, and all students are required to carry out and complete their registration in that area. The payment of fees, or the making of suitable arrangements with the representative of the business office for their payment, is considered a part of the registration procedure, as follows:

1. Upon entering the registration room, the student receives a complete registration packet or folder containing personal information cards, subject and course cards, and other forms to be filled in.

2. The student meets with his faculty advisors, determines his course of study, and fills out the registration materials contained in the packet.

3. The student goes to the dean of men (or women) or to the director of student housing, where his registration packet is stamped DORMITORY or NONDORMITORY.

4. The student goes to the registrar's station, where all fees and charges are assessed. If the student intends to live in a dormitory, his assessment includes dormitory charges for the semester. Fee assessments are made on prenumbered assessment slips (Form 7.1). These slips are made in triplicate, the assessor keeping one copy and giving the original and the second copies to the student.

5. A checker verifies the footings and calculations on the student's assessment slip. At this point, the student indicates his intentions as to the complete or partial payment of his fees and other charges. If prepared to pay in full, he takes step 7. If, however, he can pay only part of his fees, he takes step 6.

6. The student arranges with the chief business officer or other official of the business office to pay his fees in deferred installments. If the deferment is granted, the student receives a written approval, then takes step 7.

7. At the business office station, the student presents to a cashier both copies of his assessment slip, along with his registration packet. He then either pays the amount indicated or presents the written permission to extend the time of payment. The cashier indicates on the assessment slips the amount paid or charged (if any), and stamps PAID on both copies of the assessment slip. One copy of the assessment slip is retained by the cashier. The other goes to the student as a receipt.

8. As a final step, the entire registration packet is taken up when

FORM 7.1

BLANK COLLEGE No. 0001

ASSESSMENT FEE SLIP

Name____________________ Date____________

Identification No.

Charges	Amount
Resident Tuition	
Nonresident Tuition	
Late Registration Fees	
Course Change Fee	
Deferred Test and Examination Fee	
Advanced Standing Examination Fee	
Music Fee	
Diploma Fee	
Thesis Fee	
Residence Hall	
Student Activity	
Summer Session	
University Extension	
Miscellaneous:	
Accounts Receivable--Students	
Net Cash Paid	

Official Cashier's Stamp

Assessor

the student presents the stamped receipt. In view of the fact that the student cannot leave the registration area without paying his fees and cannot officially complete his registration until his stamped registration packet is taken up, there is little possibility that a student will be officially registered without having paid or made provision for his fees.

Note that in the above procedure all assessments of fees and charges are made by representatives of the registrar's office and that the sole function of the business office is to collect the fees. This procedure, generally followed in colleges and universities, has much to commend it. The registrar's office is more familiar with courses of study and laboratory fees and, therefore, greater accuracy of assessment results. Similarly, the business office, by restricting its activities to collections, can proceed much faster and with less possibility of error. Since the registrar retains a duplicate copy of all assessment slips, an excellent means of internal check on the income from registration is provided by separating the duties of assessing and collecting fees. This method also serves as a check on the cashiers, who handle considerable sums of money during the short period of registration.

There are many variations of the registration procedures just described. Decentralized registration systems and the use of mechanical devices, such as the computer or tabulating machinery, result in different methods of handling registration materials. Preregistration, which a growing number of institutions use, may eliminate some or all of the steps just described. Prebilling permits the student to pay by mail or over an extended period, and it changes to some extent the procedures on registration day.

Regarding the accounting entries for registration income, the total amount collected at the end of each registration day is receipted in the usual manner and credited to undistributed revenues. Although some institutions distribute their receipts as a part of the registration process, it is generally not practicable to attempt distribution of the receipts among the various revenue accounts until some time after the registration period. However, as soon as possible after registration, a detailed distribution of the registration income should be made by the accounting office. The use of mechanical equipment greatly simplifies the distribution procedure. In a manual system, columnar working pads can be used, the columns being headed, as follows: name of student, assessment slip number, total fees, exemptions (for scholarships), accounts receivable, cash paid, resident tuition, nonresident tuition, and so on, with a column for each source of revenue. As the assessment slips are distributed on the worksheet, the mathematical correctness of each assessment is verified. After checking and balancing, the following journal entry is prepared from the columnar worksheet distribution:

Accounts receivable—students (debit individual detailed accounts in accounts receivable ledger)

Expenditures (the scholarship exemptions are charged as expenditures against the student aid budget)

Undistributed revenues
  Revenues (credit individual revenue accounts in the revenues ledger)
  Due to other funds (for money collected during registration on behalf of other funds, such as student loan funds)

The last phase of the registration process, as it concerns the business office, is the additional auditing of the assessment slips. The first step in the audit is to account for each assessment slip by number. If an assessment slip is spoiled during the process of registration, the assessor voids the slip and sends it to the accounting office. Thus, a missing slip would be the result of either the failure of a student to complete his registration or the withholding of a receipt by a cashier to cover a fraud. In addition to accounting for the assessment slips by number, a further verification is accomplished by comparing the slips in the accounting office with the records in the registrar's office.

Another phase of the auditing process consists of the verification of certain types of registration income. For example, the business office must make a reasonable effort to check further the assessment or nonassessment of the nonresident tuition. Laboratory fees should be verified by obtaining from instructors lists of students attending each laboratory class, but these lists cannot be obtained until several weeks after school has begun. Dormitory and dining hall revenues should be verified from lists or registers provided by the dormitory and dining hall managers, respectively. All fee exemptions, such as those for academic and athletic scholarships, should be verified (from some independent source).

After the registration period is over, late fees should be assessed by the registrar's office. A supplementary charge slip (Form 7.2) is used for this purpose. This form is prepared in duplicate by the registrar, who retains one copy. The other copy is presented to the cashier by the student when he pays his fees. The student, in turn, receives a cashier's receipt, which he takes back to the registrar's office to complete the process. Examples of supplementary fees are diploma fees, transcript fees, and special examination fees. In general, cash should not be collected in the registrar's office, but fees should be assessed only in that office by representatives of the registrar.

Forms 7.3 and 7.4 are used in connection with student accounts and other accounts receivable. Deferred assessments or sales on

FORM 7.2

No. 1

BLANK COLLEGE
Business Office

SUPPLEMENTARY CHARGE SLIP

Date__________

Charge:__________ $__________

For__________

Accounts To Be Credited:

__________ Signed__________

____

FORM 7.3

BLANK COLLEGE
Business Office

ACCOUNTS RECEIVABLE

Name__________ Month__________

Address__________

Date	Description	Reference	Charges	Credits	Balance

FORM 7.4

BLANK COLLEGE
Business Office

STATEMENT OF ACCOUNT

Name__________ Month of__________

Address__________

____

Detach here and return top portion with remittance

Date	Description	Reference	Charges	Credits	Balance

account are charged to individual accounts in the accounts receivable ledger (Form 7.3). The statement of account (Form 7.4) can be produced as a by-product of posting the individual account and necessitates no additional preparation. The sum of the individual

FORM 7.5
(Envelope)

BLANK COLLEGE

DAILY CASH RECEIPTS REPORT

____
Name of Unit

Date_______________

CHARGE		
Cash		
Cash Short or Over		
Total		
CREDIT		
Sales		
Cash over and Short		
Total		

Place in this envelope all evidence concerning the receipts, including cash register tapes, coupons, and sales tickets.

Signed_______________________
Manager of Unit

Received and Checked_______________________
Cashier

FORM 7.6

No. 1

BLANK COLLEGE
Business Office

CASH RECEIPT

Date________________

Received From________________________________ $__________

Credit Account	No.	Amount

Signed________________________
Cashier

accounts in the accounts receivable ledger must always balance with the accounts receivable control account in the general ledger.

Accounting for Daily Receipts. The usual sources of daily receipts are sales of auxiliary enterprises, collections of accounts receivable, receipt of state appropriations and federal grants, revenues from endowment investments, private gifts and grants, and collection of miscellaneous fees, such as diploma and transcript. The receipts of auxiliary enterprises, such as the college bookstore and cafeteria, are deposited daily with the cashier, with cash register tapes, sales tickets, and any other original documents supporting the cash. A small envelope prepared by the auxiliary enterprise, such as the one illustrated in Form 7.5, serves as a daily report and is also a convenient method of filing the sales tickets and other documents.

Neither the collection of accounts receivable nor the receipt of state appropriations, endowment income, or miscellaneous revenues gives rise to any particular accounting problem. The primary points to emphasize in connection with the accounting for receipts are, first, that all receipts, regardless of source or amount, should be received by the college cashier, and, second, that the receipts of each day should be deposited intact in the bank. Form 7.6 is a type of cash receipt. This form is prepared in duplicate.

At the end of the day, the cashier prepares three different re-

FORM 7.7

BLANK COLLEGE

DAILY CASH REPORT

Date________________

Rec.________Through________

Items		No.	Amount	Total
Checks (attach adding machine tape)				
Currency	$20			
"	10			
"	5			
"	1			xxx
Coins	$ 1.00			
"	.50			
"	.25			
"	.10			
"	.05			
"	.01			xxx
Other (itemize)				xxx
Total Cash in Drawer				xxx
Add: Cash Items				xxx
				xxx
Deduct: Advances for Change				xxx
				xxx
Cash Short or Over				xxx
Total Per Cash Receipts				xxx

Correct________________ Signed________________

Auditor Cashier

ports: the daily cash report (Form 7.7), the distribution of revenue form (Form 7.8), and the cash receipts voucher (Form 7.9). The daily cash report, in which the composition of the cash is analyzed, assists the auditor in verifying the day's receipts. The distribution of revenue form is a convenient method of posting to the detailed

FORM 7.8

BLANK COLLEGE

REVENUES DISTRIBUTION SHEET

Date____________

C.R.V. No.____________

Acct. No.	Account Name	Amount
500	Student Fees:	
501	Resident Tuition	
502	Nonresident Tuition	
503	Course Change Fee	
504	Advanced Standing Exam Fee	
505	Diploma	
700	Other Sources:	
731	Library Fines	
732	Int. on Temp. Investments	
733	Transcripts	
734	News Service	
735	Swimming Pool	
	Total for Day	

revenues ledger and is prepared from the cash receipts. An alternative method of posting the revenues ledger is to post from the individual receipts. The first method is preferable, however, in that posting from a summary considerably reduces the amount of detail posting necessary. After the cashier balances the cash received for the day with the cash receipts, the daily cash receipts voucher (printed envelope) is prepared. This voucher is then audited by some employee of the accounting division other than the cashier and is entered in the cash receipts journal (Form 7.10). At the end of the month, the cash receipts journal is summarized to provide a posting source to the general ledger. Since the receipts of all funds are entered in the cash receipts journal, the summary is divided into balanced fund groups. Following is an illustration of the monthly posting summary for the cash receipts journal:

1. UNRESTRICTED CURRENT FUNDS
   First National Bank—general account
   Second National Bank—salary payroll account
   Third National Bank—wage payroll account

FORM 7.9

BLANK COLLEGE

No. 0001

CASH RECEIPTS VOUCHER

Date______________

General Funds	Acct. No.	Amount	Other Funds	Acct. No	Amount
Debits:			Debits:		
Cash - First Nat. - Gen.	1001		Cash - F.N.B. - Restricted	1501	
Cash - Second Nat. - Sal.	1002		Cash - S.N.B. - Loan	2001	
Cash - Third Nat. - Wage	1003		Cash - F.N.B. - Endowment	3001	
Cash - Over and Short	1006		Cash - S.N.B. - Annuity	4001	
Other:			Cash - T.N.B. - Unexpended Plant Funds	5001	
			Cash - F.N.B. - R & R	5201	
			Cash - T.N.B. - R of Ind.	5401	
			Cash - F.N.B. - Agency	6001	
			Other:		
Total Debits			Total Debits		
Credits:			Credits:		
Bank Transfers	1005		Restricted Current Funds Balances	1851	
Accounts Receivable - Students	1015		Loan Funds Balances	2251	
Accounts Receivable - Other	1016		Endowment Fund Balances	3251	
Expenditures	1061		Unexpended Plant Fund Balances	5151	
Revenues	1251		R & R Plant Fund Bal.	5351	
Cash - Over and Short	1006		Deposit liabilities	6251	
Other:			Other:		
Total Credits			Total Credits		

POSTED

Accounts Receivable
Students__________ Other______________
Revenue Ledger______________
Expenditure Ledger______________
Cash Receipts Journal______________
Student Deposits______________
Other______________

Prepared By______________
(Cashier)

Approved By______________
(Auditor)

Receipt No.__________through No.________

FORM 7.10
(Left Side)

BLANK COLLEGE

CASH RECEIPTS JOURNAL

DEBITS

Date	Cash Receipts Voucher No.	General Funds			Restricted Funds	Loan Funds	Endowment Funds	Agency Funds	Other	
		General	Payroll	Wage					Account	Amount

FORM 7.10
(Right Side)

BLANK COLLEGE

CASH RECEIPTS JOURNAL

CREDITS

Unrestricted Current Funds				Restricted Funds		Loan Funds		Agency Funds		Other		
Revenues	Accounts Receivable	Miscellaneous		Account	Amount	Account	Amount	Account	Amount	Fund	Account	Amount
		Account	Amount									

Cash over and short
  Revenues
  Accounts receivable—students
  Accounts receivable—others
  Due to other funds
  Cash over and short
  Expenditures
  Due from other funds
  Bank transfers

2. RESTRICTED CURRENT FUNDS
   First National Bank—restricted funds
     Restricted funds balances

3. LOAN FUNDS
   First National Bank—loan funds
     Notes and interest receivable
     Income
     Loan funds balances

4. AGENCY FUNDS
   Third National Bank—agency funds
     Deposit liabilities

Accounting for Refunds. Usually the cashier is required to handle two types of refunds—refunds of expenditures and refunds of revenues. Refunds of expenditures, resulting from overpayments made by the institution, are entered on the cash receipts as a credit to expenditures (with the individual departmental allocation indicated). On the cash receipts voucher, the total of such refunds is credited to expenditures and is posted to the general ledger through the monthly summary. The proper subsidiary accounts in the allocations ledger are credited directly from the cash receipts.

Refunds of revenues, such as registration fees, board payments, and dormitory charges, are made by the cashier out of petty cash or in the accounting office by check. One important regulation concerning refunds of revenues is that such refunds should always be initiated by some office or department other than the business office. In other words, if a student is entitled to receive a refund of registration fees, the registrar's office should issue a refund order (Form 7.11), which authorizes the cashier or accounting office to make the refund to the student. The refund order also may be used

FORM 7.11

No. 1

BLANK COLLEGE
Business Office

REFUND ORDER

Date____________________

Refund:____ $______________

For____

____

Accounts To Be Charged

______________________________ Signed___________________________________

____

in case of a student's withdrawal from the dormitory or dining hall during a semester. In such cases, it should be issued by the dean of students or by the manager of the dining hall or dormitory. The refund order is prepared in duplicate, the originating office keeping a copy. The refund order serves as a permanent support to the petty cash voucher or other expenditure document. The detail revenues accounts affected are debited either directly from the expenditure vouchers or from a summary prepared at the end of the month.

Receipts of Funds Other Than Current Funds. As explained, the receipts of all funds are accounted for through the same channels, are evidenced by the same documents (the cash receipt and the cash receipts voucher), and are posted from the same journal (the cash receipts journal). In the case of fund balances supported by subsidiary ledgers, the detail information is posted to these ledgers from the cash receipt. A detailed explanation of accounting for funds other than current is given in Chapters 10, 11, and 12.

Temporary Investment of Surplus Cash. Most institutions temporarily invest as much as possible of their cash balances (if permitted by law), applying the interest earned to operating budgets. In order to make these investments in an orderly manner, it is essential that a cash budget be prepared at least on an annual basis, and preferably on a monthly basis, so that the cash position at various times throughout the year is known. This can be accomplished by determining the book balances of cash over a period of several years and plotting these balances on a graph that clearly delineates high and low points. This graph serves as the basis of determining approximately how much surplus cash is potentially available at any time and for what periods it can be invested. The next step is to determine and plot the cash balances according to bank statements for the same time periods. The difference between the book cash balances and the bank balances is commonly known as the "float." The knowledge of the float will permit the institution to maximize its temporary investments since the float can be used to cover a cash position that may be low as shown on the books.

In addition to being used for investment purposes, cash budgets are needed also in connection with construction, major repairs, and other special projects. The officer coordinating the investment program of the institution must be knowledgeable of all projects that the institution is undertaking and the cash requirements for these projects.

8

Data Processing Systems

A DECISION TO INSTALL an electronic data processing system (EDP system) in a college or university entails the expenditure of substantial sums of money. In addition to the cost of renting or purchasing the computer and the required peripheral equipment, consideration must be given to staff, space, site preparation, furniture, equipment, and operating supplies.

It should first be ascertained that EDP equipment is actually needed, that its acquisition and operation will contribute to improved administration of the institution, and that the outlays of moneys and added costs will be justified by more complete financial records and reports than are being produced by present equipment and procedures. An extensive exploration should be made of all the possible uses of the computer and related equipment to determine its application to teaching and research, as well as to administrative purposes—for example, student records; budget preparation; accounting and financial reporting; payroll operations in all aspects; gifts and financial promotion programs; and personnel records, reports, and analyses. An accurate determination should be made of the cost of the initial installation and of the annual expenditures for rentals, salaries and wages, and other expenses associated with an EDP system. Finally, the decision as to make, style, quantity of equipment, and other factors should be made with great care.

A computer installation generally requires major changes in the accounting system. The exact nature of these modifications, the length of time it will take to achieve them, and the kinds of results to be expected after the EDP equipment is installed are points of special concern to the college and university business officer and should be determined in advance.

The purposes of this chapter are (1) to discuss the feasibility study that should be made prior to the installation of an EDP system, (2) to analyze the kind of organization required for the EDP center, (3) to examine the preinstallation planning required before the change to a computer system is made, and (4) to examine modifications to be made to the accounting and financial reporting systems in order to utilize the computer efficiently.

The Feasibility Study. In order to resolve the major problems which an institution faces in converting a conventional accounting system to an electronic data processing system, it is essential that an in-depth feasibility study be conducted.

The basic objective of this study should be to determine the economic desirability and technical feasibility of placing business, administrative, research, and teaching functions on a computer or computers. Specifically, the study should cover the following areas: (1) the business and administrative systems to be placed on the computer, (2) the economic implications of changing to computer systems, (3) the computer time required for both scientific and nonscientific applications, (4) the length of time required to convert the systems initially selected for change, (5) the qualifications and number of staff required to design the new system and perform the conversion, (6) the proper layout of physical facilities, (7) the selection of appropriate equipment, and (8) the organizational structure for the electronic data processing center and the number of persons required to operate it. Few educational institutions will find it possible to conduct such feasibility studies without the help of outside consultants.

Organizational Structure of the EDP Center. EDP installations may be organized along several different lines. One approach is to establish a centralized EDP center to handle all institutional data processing. A second approach is to establish a single EDP center that provides computer services and supplement it with a separate department that provides program development, program maintenance, production, and other services. A third possibility is to establish two EDP centers—one for teaching and research and the other for administrative purposes, *i. e.*, accounting, financial reporting, admissions, registration, development, student records, financial aid, and other noninstructional and nonresearch activities.

The first two organizations described might be under the direction of the chief academic officer. Under the third type of organization, one EDP center would function as an adjunct to teaching and research activities and would be directly responsible to the chief academic officer. The other EDP center would be established for administrative record keeping and computation and would be under the jurisdiction of the chief business officer.

There are several major problems inherent in the operation of a single, centralized computer center. Because the authority for processing all data is centralized in one office, established lines of authority may be disrupted. Also, the establishment of schedules of work may present problems. All users prefer prime time, as opposed to less desirable time such as the night shift. Moreover, it is possible that a major user might suffer because of lack of access to the computer at the time most beneficial to him. If a centralized center is established, its equipment should have sufficient speed and memory capacity to provide virtually instantaneous service to most users.

It should be pointed out that with the centralized system there will be a decrease in peripheral units, thus reducing equipment costs over dual systems. Furthermore, because of the greater sophistication demanded of a highly centralized computer center, a more technically oriented staff will be required. More highly skilled staff will be required to support instructional and research needs as well as those related to administrative applications.

Preinstallation Planning. Once the decision to install electronic data processing equipment has been made, a detailed plan for the installation must be prepared. This preinstallation planning is vital to a smooth and successful system and encompasses the following major areas: (1) determining the initial applications to be placed on the equipment; (2) establishing a time schedule; (3) establishing the organization; (4) defining the problems, programming, and testing procedures for each application; (5) planning the conversion to the computer; (6) determining the equipment requirements and delivery dates; (7) training the staff of the center; and (8) planning the installation of equipment. The foregoing steps can be handled adequately only if a high-level administrative officer is assigned full responsibility for preinstallation phases.

The initial accounting applications normally would include those related to accounts receivable, accounts payable, payroll, general ledger, budget preparation and control, cash receipts, and check writing. Other accounting-related applications readily adaptable to computer operations include gift records, student loans and other institutional financial aid programs, personnel records, and inventory systems.

Preinstallation activities require the establishment of target dates for each major phase of the program. Materials have been developed for the guidance of administrative officials responsible for the installation of data processing systems. One such publication by the International Business Machines Corporation is *Planning for an IBM Data Processing System* (4th ed.; New York; April, 1970).

As soon as the preinstallation planning has been completed, the next and most important part of the installation is that of establishing a competent organization to implement the installation, to manage the conversion, and to operate the center. In the final analysis, the success of the EDP center depends to a large extent on the quality of the training, knowledge, and skill of the personnel who will operate it. The competence of the director of the center is of utmost importance.

The first step in the process of converting to EDP accounting procedures is to design the new system. At this stage, the flow of work charts and formats for accomplishing each particular program must be established. Once the system is designed, the programmer can convert design steps into a machine-readable language that will permit the computer to accept the written program and produce results from input data taken from cards or tapes. Proper design is critical to the success of an EDP operation; a highly skilled staff at this point will help assure the success of the installation.

The preparation of programs should begin well in advance of the actual computer installation so that a number of applications can be programmed, tested, and "debugged" prior to the arrival of the computer and related equipment. This can be accomplished by renting computer time from an organization with similar equipment for the purpose of testing and "debugging." The actual conversion to the new system will require several weeks. It is generally considered desirable to run parallel operations on both the old and new systems for approximately thirty to sixty days.

Manufacturers of equipment usually are acquainted with the needs of institutions of comparable size and function and can give advice on a specific list of equipment. A survey of comparable institutions, including discussions with persons knowledgeable about equipment capabilities in those institutions, will help insure that equipment of proper size and capacity is selected. Factors to consider include determining that the equipment has the capacity and speed necessary to meet assumed needs and that it is compatible, without reprogramming, with higher speed and larger capacity machines that may be needed in the future. One needs to know what future applications will be computerized. Also, one must be certain that the new equipment has the capability of handling these future applications. Another method of selecting equipment is to employ a consulting firm to survey the needs of the institution and to give advice on the equipment list.

The education and training of staff is a major problem in most institutions; however, operators and keypunch personnel can be trained in a short time. With the advent of more sophisticated large-scale computer systems, the position of the operator is important. The director and systems personnel, or programmers, must be carefully selected. Occasionally, personnel are selected from within the institution and trained in systems analysis and computer techniques.

The physical installation for the modern computer may be accomplished by the modification of space to meet the requirements of the equipment manufacturer. In most cases, the physical plant department of the institution can modify space so that it meets a manufacturer's requirements, and the installation can be made without difficulty. In general, the following physical requirements must be met: (1) year-round cooling, (2) humidity control, and (3) supply of cold water needed for cooling units on certain types of equipment.

Accounting and Financial Reporting. The balance of the chapter is devoted to a discussion of the accounting and financial reporting applications involved in the EDP system.

The Chart of Accounts. The conversion from a conventional accounting and fiscal system to an EDP system usually requires changes in coding in the chart of accounts. In some cases, modifications in the chart itself may be necessary, although a college or university having a satisfactory chart of accounts as described in this volume probably will find it necessary to change only the code numbers as it converts to an EDP system. The code numbers in the chart of accounts are the key to an efficient accounting system on electronic data processing equipment. Each digit in the code must be significant in order to avoid needless punching of extra digits. Superfluous digits take up space, cause extra punching, use up computer memory, and waste both time and machine capacity. It is highly desirable to create an accounting code that is sufficiently flexible to allow for expansion but at the same time avoid the use of digits having no significance. If an institution has a well-organized chart of accounts, complete reorganization is not required; it is necessary only to modify the account code numbers.

Coding System for EDP. The use of an EDP system requires the assignment of account numbers in a coded arrangement so that budgetary and accounting transactions can be recorded and reported in a variety of classifications. Each digit or group of digits in the code number should identify the account as to fund, type of transaction, and budget unit. The EDP system is thus provided with a means of sorting the accounts into any of these classifications for summary financial reports.

The system illustrated here consists of a code comprising ten digits for the basic number, followed by three digits representing object codes. The total of thirteen digits is divided into six groups (XX-X-X-X-XXXXX-XXX). The first two digits identify the fund group to which the account belongs. The third digit provides the fiscal year designation. The fourth digit is a ledger designation, and the fifth digit designates the campus or branch. The next five digits are as follows: two for function, one for college or division, and the last two for budget accounts. The following illustration is presented to show how these digits might be assigned:

(A)		(B)		(C)		(D)		(E)		(F)
XX	-	X	-	X	-	X	-	XXXXX	-	XXX

(A) XX *Fund designation*

00	Unassigned
01	Unrestricted current
02	Restricted current
10	Loan
20	Endowment
21	Term endowment
22	Quasi-endowment
30	Annuity and life income
40	Unexpended plant
41	Renewals and replacements
42	Retirement of indebtedness
43	Investment in plant
44	Agency funds

(B) X *Fiscal year designation*

0	Fiscal year 1975–1976
1	Fiscal year 1976–1977
2	Fiscal year 1977–1978
3	Fiscal year 1978–1979
4	Fiscal year 1979–1980
5	Fiscal year 1980–1981
6	Fiscal year 1981–1982
7	Fiscal year 1982–1983
8	Fiscal year 1983–1984
9	Fiscal year 1984–1985

(C) X *Ledger designation*

0	Unassigned
1	General ledger
2	Revenues ledger
3	Allocations ledger

Others as needed

(D) X *Campus or branch designation*

0	Unassigned
1	General university
2	Branch 1
3	Branch 2
4	Veterinary medicine
5	Agricultural experiment station
6	Cooperative extension

Others as needed

(E) XX X XX
1 2 3

(1) XX *Function designation*

00	Unassigned
05	Revenues—tuition and fees
10	Revenues—federal appropriations
12	Revenues—state appropriations
14	Revenues—local appropriations
16	Revenues—federal grants and contracts
18	Revenues—state grants and contracts
20	Revenues—local grants and contracts
22	Revenues—private gifts, grants, and contracts
25	Endowment income—detail as needed
28	Sales and services of educational departments—detail as needed
30	Sales and services of auxiliary enterprises—detail as needed
35	Added revenue accounts as needed
40	Sales and services of hospitals, health clinics, etc.
45	Other sources
46	Independent operations
50	Expenditures—instruction
55	Expenditures—research
58	Expenditures—public service
60	Expenditures—academic support
62	Expenditures—student services
64	Expenditures—institutional support
66	Expenditures—operation and maintenance of physical plant
70	Expenditures—scholarships and fellowships
75	Transfers—mandatory
80	Transfers—nonmandatory
85	Expenditures—auxiliary enterprises
90	Expenditures—hospitals
95	Expenditures—independent operations

(2)	X	*College or division*	
		0	Unassigned
		1	Agriculture
		2	Arts and sciences
		3	Business
		4	Education
		5	Engineering
		6	Home economics
		7	Technical institute
		8	Graduate
		9	Unassigned
(3)	XX	*Budget accounts*	
		00	Unassigned
		01	Dean's office
		02	Biochemistry
		03	Agricultural economics
		04	Agricultural education
		05	Agricultural engineering
		06	Agronomy
		07	Animal sciences
		08	Other departments
(4)	XXX	*Object code* (can be further detailed, as desired)	
		000–119	Personnel compensation
		200–399	Supplies and expense
		400–699	Capital expenditures

To illustrate the use of the coding system, personnel compensation paid by the university in 1976–1977 for the College of Business, Dean's Office, would be coded as follows: 01-1-3-1-50301-110. The first two digits indicate that the transaction involves the unrestricted current funds group. The next digit, 1, designates the fiscal year 1976–1977. Digit 3 indicates that the allocations ledger is involved. The campus or branch code, 1, is the general university, as distinguished from branches or other campuses. The next two digits, 50, classify the expenditure as instruction. The College of Business is digit 3, followed by the account number 01, designating the Dean's Office. The last three digits, 110, identify the object of expenditure as personnel compensation.

Budget Preparation. Budget preparation can be successfully adapted to an electronic data processing system. The first step in automating the budget is to punch data cards or input from the remote terminals, using the coding system described above, for each item of revenue and expenditure involved in the current year's operation. This provides a starting point for the preparation of estimates for the budget of the succeeding year.

After preparation of data cards punched from revenue and expenditure estimates for the current year, the desired number of printouts is produced by the computer. Listings of revenue estimates are sent to the chief business officer to be used in the preparation of the revenue portion of the budget for the new year. The sections involving expenditures are sent to the budget heads so that they may indicate employees' compensation requested for the new year, requests for positions, and changes in outlay requirements for supplies and expense and capital expenditures, with appropriate justifications for each change. Subsequent to consideration and approval of departmental requests, data cards are again prepared reflecting the new figures for each budget account.

When the budget has finally been approved by the president and the governing board, a final, revised computer run is made in order to produce the official budget for the year for appropriate distribution. In the process of running the budget, other statistical data and/or calculations can be produced which may prove helpful in budgetary formulation. For example, one or more of the following items of information can be produced: tenure reports; personnel statistical reports, pre-payroll analyses; personnel master records; salary averages by ranks, colleges, and departments; and equal pay analyses.

Budget revisions to increase or decrease departmental appropriations should be handled in the same manner as approval of the original budget document. The approved budget revision forms become the source documents for the preparation of punched cards used to reflect changes in revenue and expenditure accounts. Personnel status forms are the source documents from which data cards are punched to reflect changes in personnel.

Monthly budget statements are produced for personnel compensation, supplies and expense, and capital expenditures; they show allocations, encumbrances, expenditures, and (uncommitted) allocations balances. These statements are prepared as the budget is updated each month from transactions previously punched into cards or recorded on tapes. As the transactions deck or tape is processed against the budget ledger deck of cards or tapes, all records are updated. Most EDP systems provide for the transfer of information to tape or disc, thereby speeding up the updating process.

Budget Control, Expenditures, and Disbursements. After the budget has been approved, control of expenditures must be exercised by the business office to prevent the overexpenditure of departmental allocations. Chapter 5 presented budgetary control principles which apply to most institutional accounting systems regardless of the equipment used, that is, manual, bookkeeping machine, punched card, or EDP systems. Briefly, the budget control system suggested is based on centralized purchasing and the encumbering of budget allocations with the estimated cost of materials, supplies, and equipment to be procured on approved purchase orders. The encumbrance system can be automated through the preparation of data cards and, subsequently, magnetic tape, to which information is transferred directly from the purchase orders. When materials are received and invoices obtained from vendors, data cards are punched from remittance advices to remove the encumbrance and simultaneously charge the expenditure to the budget allocation, updating the uncommitted balance in the budget document and accounting records. These same cards may also be used in preparing checks for payment to vendors.

The Payroll System. Payrolls normally are divided into the two major categories of monthly and hourly. Monthly payrolls are placed on the computer through the use of budget sheets, which provide complete details as to name and rank of each authorized individual to be paid, number of months he is to be paid during the fiscal period, monthly rate of compensation, annual amount of compensation, and accounts to be charged. The budget tape (or disc pack), showing all pertinent information such as name, rank, rate, and deductions information on personnel paid monthly, is used to prepare the check for each individual listed on the monthly payroll.

Hourly payrolls also require a master tape setting forth the pertinent details about each individual. In order to complete the payroll for personnel paid on an hourly basis, it is necessary to ascertain the number of hours each employee has worked during the payroll period. Payrolls of the previous period, provided by the computer, produce all the information required for the new payroll except the number of hours or days worked. The computer printouts are forwarded to the appropriate departments so that the number of days or hours worked can be inserted by the department head. The names of persons who may have left the employ of the institution are deleted and names of new employees are added. Any changes in hourly or daily wage rates are also noted. After certifying that the work for which pay is requested has been performed, the printouts are returned to the payroll office. The data are then sent to the computer center for processing and for the issuance of paychecks.

As a by-product of producing the monthly and hourly payrolls, several subsidiary records are automatically available from computer records—for example, totals-to-date for earnings. Federal and state income tax withholdings, Social Security (FICA) taxes, cumulative information relative to group life insurance and other insurance payments, retirement payments, and other deductions may be compiled as a result of computer processing. It is possible also to update the budget document to reflect personnel compensation expenditures as well as unexpended balances in the accounts.

Other Fund Groups. EDP equipment and systems are readily adaptable to accounting and reporting the financial transactions of fund groups other than current funds and should be utilized in these areas to the fullest extent. In the Endowment and Similar Funds group, EDP systems are effective in recording investments, comparing market and book values of securities, and providing comparative and evaluative data on the growth of endowment funds and earnings from their investments. Amortization of premiums and discounts on bond transactions can be handled to advantage through the use of the computer.

Loan funds have increased considerably in recent years because of the vast expansion of federal, state, and private funds available for loans to students. The computer can be of great assistance in the collection of student loans by preparing statements both for the institution and for students, indicating due dates, amounts of periodic payments, amounts of interest due, and other pertinent data about the loans.

The operations and transactions of the various subgroups of plant funds can be computerized with great effectiveness, especially those relating to building and construction projects. Reports of costs, comparisons of costs with estimates or budgets, and construction progress reports are examples of periodic reports on new buildings that can be prepared and updated expeditiously through the use of EDP equipment and systems. Agency funds, especially those involving student bank or deposit accounts, can also be computerized to advantage.

Financial Reporting. The computer can be used to prepare interim reports as well as the annual financial report. The annual report, at least in preliminary form, may be produced as a byproduct of recording transactions in the departmental allocations accounts and in the accounts for the other fund groups.

Management Information System. In recent years, the term "management information system" has come to be used more and more in colleges and universities. It is generally used in relation to computer-based management information systems and is referred to by the acronym CBMIS. The development of management information systems flows logically from computer-based data processing systems and can be thought of as a maturing of such systems.

Management information system may be defined as "an organized method of providing past, present, and projected information related to internal operations and external intelligence. It supports the planning, control, and operational functions of an organization by furnishing uniform information in the proper time frame to assist the decision process."[1] Another definition that applies to a computer-based management information system is "one employed to store, manipulate, and retrieve data for use in management, planning, and resource allocation. CBMIS differs from standard data processing applications (such as payroll or student records) in that it emphasizes the capability to rapidly integrate

1. Walter J. Kennenen, "Management Information System," *Data Management*, VIII (September, 1970), 60–62.

and display data from various sources, both current and historical and to assist in planning, resource allocation, and general management decisions. Technically, CBMIS is characterized by (1) an integrated data base, (2) commonly defined data elements, (3) a generalized information retrieval capability, and (4) the techniques required to assure the security and integrity of the data maintained in the data base."[2]

The need for MIS has been brought about from demands for data by numerous external agencies such as state coordinating boards, agencies, legislators, and governors, as well as various federal government agencies. These requests and demands, largely in the interest of accountability, have forced institutions to adjust their computer-based data processing operations, with applications designed for a given user (*e. g.*, the registrar's office), to systems that provide data to outside agencies. This change has forced increasing involvement by top management to be certain that the data could be quickly and accurately prepared and transmitted.

There is an increasing emphasis on cost data in higher education. Costing procedures require data that extend far beyond that which may be found in most college accounting systems. To meet these kinds of requirements, management will need to exert a greater effort to develop appropriate management information systems.

In a recent survey by the National Center for Higher Education Management Systems at WICHE, 69 percent of the responding institutions (of 442 colleges and universities) indicated they are planning or implementing CBMIS. Forty percent indicated that their CBMIS was in partial operation. Colleges and universities are moving toward CBMIS for three basic reasons: (1) to meet state reporting requirements, (2) to improve management techniques in the institution, and (3) to support other management tools such as cost procedures.

2. Ronald W. Brady *et al*, *Administrative Data Processing: A Case for Executive Management Involvement* (Boulder, Colo.: National Center for Higher Education Management Systems, 1975), 30–31.

9

Accounting for Current Funds: Illustration

THE PRECEDING CHAPTERS have presented a complete discussion of the various phases of the accounting system as it pertains to current or operating funds. In order to amplify and supplement the explanatory material covered in the foregoing chapters, a complete illustration of accounting for current funds is presented in this chapter. Transactions are presented in general journal form with explanations regarding the purpose of the entry and the journal or register in which the entries are recorded. To present a complete picture, the current funds section of the balance sheet at the beginning of a period is given. Then, transactions involving typical operations are entered in journal form and are posted to general ledger accounts. A balance sheet before closing entries are made is presented. Finally, closing entries are entered and posted, and a balance sheet and a statement of changes in fund balances at the end of the period are prepared. The illustration treats separately the two groups of current funds—that is, unrestricted current and restricted current funds.

ACCOUNTING FOR CURRENT FUNDS

ACCOUNTING FOR UNRESTRICTED CURRENT FUNDS

A. Balance Sheet at Beginning of Period

BLANK COLLEGE

Balance Sheet
(Beginning of Period)

ASSETS		LIABILITIES AND FUND BALANCES	
CURRENT FUNDS:		CURRENT FUNDS:	
Unrestricted:		Unrestricted:	
Cash	$ 186,000	Accounts payable	$ 212,000
Investments, at cost (market $205,000)	200,000	Deferred revenues	490,000
Accounts receivable--students, less allowance for doubtful accounts of $4,000	325,000	Fund balances	617,200
Accounts receivable--others, less allowance for doubtful accounts of $2,000	311,000		
Inventories, at cost	290,000		
Prepaid expenses	7,200		
Total unrestricted current funds	$1,319,200	Total unrestricted current funds	$1,319,200

B. Recording of Typical Transactions

	GENERAL LEDGER Dr.	GENERAL LEDGER Cr.	SUBSIDIARY LEDGER Dr.	SUBSIDIARY LEDGER Cr.
1. Entry to record the unrestricted current funds budget (journal voucher):				
Estimated revenues	6,000,000			
Departmental allocations		5,983,940		
Unallocated budget Balances		16,060		
In revenue ledger (posted from budget):				
Resident tuition and fees			1,000,000	
Nonresident tuition and fees			360,000	
Governmental appropriations			1,500,000	
Residence halls			700,000	
All other revenue accounts			2,423,940	
			5,983,940	
In allocations ledger (posted from budget):				
President's office:				
Personnel compensation--salaries				90,000
Personnel compensation--wages				5,000
Supplies and expense				24,500
Capital expenditures				6,000
Art department:				
Personnel compensation--salaries				76,400
Personnel compensation--wages				4,000
Supplies and expense				2,250
Capital expenditures				600
All other allocations accounts				5,775,190
				5,983,940
2. Entry to record the issuance of purchase orders (orders placed and liquidated journal, in summary):				
Encumbrances	630,000			
Provision for encumbrances--current year		630,000		
In allocations ledger (purchase orders):				
Departmental allocations accounts			630,000	

	General Ledger Dr.	General Ledger Cr.	Subsidiary Ledger Dr.	Subsidiary Ledger Cr.
3. Entries to record payment of invoices covered by purchase orders:				
a. To liquidate encumbrances (orders placed and liquidated journal, in summary):				
Provision for encumbrances--current year	600,000			
Encumbrances		600,000		
In allocations ledger (purchase orders):				
Departmental allocations accounts				600,000
b. To charge expenditures (voucher register, in summary):				
Expenditures	605,000			
Vouchers payable		605,000		
In allocations ledger (invoices):				
Departmental allocations accounts			605,000	
4. Entry to record issuance of checks (check register):				
Vouchers payable	905,000			
Cash		905,000		
5. Entries to record transfer from general to payroll bank account:				
a. In voucher register:				
Bank transfers	140,000			
Vouchers payable		140,000		
b. In check register:				
Vouchers payable	140,000			
Cash		140,000		
c. In cash receipts journal:				
Payroll bank account	140,000			
Bank transfers		140,000		
6. Entry to record payroll (payroll register):				
Expenditures	189,600			
Retirement system deductions		9,600		
Withholding tax deductions		30,000		
Social security deductions		10,000		
Payroll bank account		140,000		
In allocations ledger (payroll distribution):				
Departmental allocations accounts			189,600	
7. Entry to establish petty cash fund (voucher register):				
a. Petty cash	6,000			
Vouchers payable		6,000		
b. Vouchers payable	6,000			
Cash		6,000		
In petty cash subsidiary ledger (voucher register):				
Custodian of fund			6,000	
8. Entry to replenish petty cash--$3,600 expended (voucher register):				
a. Expenditures	3,600			
Vouchers payable		3,600		
b. Vouchers payable	3,600			
Cash		3,600		
In allocations ledger (petty cash vouchers):				
Departmental allocations accounts			3,600	
9. Entry to record unpaid portion of state appropriation (journal voucher):				
State appropriations receivable	300,000			
Revenues		300,000		

	General Ledger Dr.	General Ledger Cr.	Subsidiary Ledger Dr.	Subsidiary Ledger Cr.
In revenues ledger (journal voucher):				
Revenues accounts				300,000
10. Entry to record receipt of gift from alumnus (cash receipts journal):				
Cash	300			
Revenues		300		
In revenues ledger (cash receipts):				
Revenues accounts--gifts				300
11. Entry to record purchase of materials for storeroom (voucher register):				
Physical plant stores	292,000			
Vouchers payable		292,000		
12. Entry to record issuance of materials to departments (interdepartmental transfer journal):				
Expenditures	386,000			
Physical plant stores		386,000		
In allocations ledger (interdepartmental invoices):				
Departmental allocations accounts			386,000	
13. Entry to record sale of materials to outside agency (cash receipts journal):				
Cash	600			
Physical plant stores		600		
14. Entry to record issuance of materials to plant funds (interdepartmental invoice):				
Due from unexpended plant funds	3,000			
Physical plant stores		3,000		
(In unexpended plant funds, debit unexpended plant funds balances and credit due to unrestricted current funds.)				
15. Entry to adjust physical plant stores inventory at book value to physical inventory (journal voucher):				
Expenditures	600			
Physical plant stores inventory		600		
16. Entry to record sales of supplies by bookstore to departments (interdepartmental transfer journal):				
Expenditures	390,000			
Revenues		390,000		
In allocations ledger (interdepartmental invoices):				
Departmental allocations accounts			390,000	
In revenues ledger (interdepartmental invoices):				
Bookstore--sales				390,000
17. Entry to record collection of student tuition and fees (cash receipts journal):				
Cash	1,240,000			
Revenues		1,240,000		
In revenues ledger (summary of registration revenues):				
Revenues accounts				1,240,000
18. Entry to record issuance of student loans (voucher and check registers):				
a. Due from loan funds	12,000			
Vouchers payable		12,000		

	GENERAL LEDGER Dr.	GENERAL LEDGER Cr.	SUBSIDIARY LEDGER Dr.	SUBSIDIARY LEDGER Cr.
b. Vouchers payable	12,000			
Cash		12,000		
(In loan funds group, debit notes receivable and credit due to unrestricted current funds.)				
19. Entry to record collection of student loans (cash receipts journal):				
Cash	6,000			
Due from loan funds		6,000		
(In loan funds group, debit due to unrestricted current funds and credit notes receivable.)				
20. Entry to record charging student fees based on promissory notes (journal voucher):				
Accounts receivable--students	62,000			
Revenues		62,000		
In accounts receivable ledger (registration slips):				
Individual student accounts			62,000	
In revenues ledger (summary of registration slips):				
Revenues accounts				62,000
21. Entry to record collection of fees previously charged (cash receipts journal):				
Cash	255,000			
Accounts receivable--students		255,000		
In accounts receivable ledger (cash receipts):				
Individual student accounts				255,000
22. Entry to record increase in allowance for doubtful accounts (journal voucher):				
Expenditures	1,800			
Allowance for doubtful accounts		1,800		
In allocations ledger (journal voucher):				
Departmental allocations accounts--provision for doubtful accounts			1,800	
23. Entry to record charging off student accounts receivable as uncollectible (journal voucher):				
Allowance for doubtful accounts--students	300			
Accounts receivable--students		300		
In accounts receivable ledger (journal voucher):				
Individual student accounts				300
24. Entries to record receipt of student accounts receivable previously written off as uncollectible (journal voucher and cash receipts journal):				
a. Accounts receivable--students	120			
Allowance for doubtful accounts--students		120		
In accounts receivable ledger (journal voucher):				
Individual student accounts			120	
b. Cash	120			
Accounts receivable--students		120		
In accounts receivable ledger (cash receipts journal):				
Individual student accounts				120

	General Ledger		Subsidiary Ledger	
	Dr.	Cr.	Dr.	Cr.
25. Entry to record collection of sales of auxiliary enterprises (cash receipts journal):				
Cash	1,283,600			
Revenues		1,283,600		
In revenues ledger (cash receipts):				
Revenues accounts				1,283,600
26. Entries to record transfers to plant funds for plant additions (voucher register and check register):				
a. Transfers to unexpended plant funds	60,000			
Vouchers payable		60,000		
b. Vouchers payable	60,000			
Cash		60,000		
(In unexpended plant funds group, debit cash and credit unexpended plant funds balances.)				
27. Entry to record purchases of equipment for departments (voucher register):				
Expenditures	60,000			
Vouchers payable		60,000		
In allocations ledger (invoices):				
Departmental allocations accounts			60,000	
(In the investment in plant section of plant funds debit equipment and credit net investment in plant.)				
28. Entry to record allocation to renewal and replacement reserve for property of auxiliary enterprises (voucher register and check register):				
a. Expenditures	6,000			
Vouchers payable		6,000		
b. Vouchers payable	6,000			
Cash		6,000		
Departmental allocations accounts			6,000	
(In the funds for renewals and replacements group, debit cash and credit renewals and replacements funds balances.)				
29. Entry to record refund of expenditures (cash receipts journal):				
Cash	6,000			
Expenditures		6,000		
In allocations ledger (cash receipts):				
Departmental allocations accounts				6,000
30. Entry to record refund of revenues (voucher register and check register):				
a. Revenues	1,200			
Vouchers payable		1,200		
b. Vouchers payable	1,200			
Cash		1,200		
In revenues ledger (invoices):				
Revenues accounts			1,200	
31. Entry to record sales of used equipment originally purchased out of current funds at a cost of $3,000 (cash receipts journal):				
Cash	600			
Revenues		600		
In revenues ledger (cash receipts):				
Revenues account--sale of surplus property				600

	GENERAL LEDGER Dr.	GENERAL LEDGER Cr.	SUBSIDIARY LEDGER Dr.	SUBSIDIARY LEDGER Cr.
(In plant funds group--investment in plant section--debit net investment in plant and credit equipment $3,000.)				
32. Entry to record collection of revenues applicable to subsequent accounting period (cash receipts journal):				
Cash	160,000			
Deferred revenues		160,000		
33. Entry to transfer deferred revenues to revenues at beginning of accounting period (journal voucher):				
Deferred revenues	490,000			
Revenues		490,000		
In revenues ledger (journal voucher):				
Revenues accounts				490,000
34. Entries to record payment of restricted current funds expenditures from unrestricted current funds (voucher register and check register):				
a. Restricted expenditures	2,110,000			
Vouchers payable		2,110,000		
b. Vouchers payable	2,110,000			
Cash		2,110,000		
In allocations ledger:				
Restricted allocations accounts			2,110,000	
35. Entry to record receipt of reimbursement from restricted current funds to cover expenditures made from unrestricted current funds during period (cash receipts journal):				
Cash	2,110,000			
Restricted revenues		2,110,000		
In revenues ledger (cash receipts):				
Revenues accounts				2,100,000
(In restricted current funds, debit restricted current funds balances and credit cash.)				
36. Entry to record receipt of state appropriation (cash receipts journal):				
Cash	1,500,000			
Revenues		1,500,000		
In revenues ledger (cash receipts):				
Revenues accounts				1,500,000
37. Entry to record sundry expenditures chargeable against departmental allocations (voucher register):				
Expenditures	4,070,800			
Vouchers payable		4,070,800		
In allocations ledger (vouchers):				
Departmental allocations accounts			4,070,800	
38. Entry to record issuance of checks in payment of audited vouchers (check register):				
Vouchers payable	3,800,000			
Cash		3,800,000		
39. Entry to record insurance expired during period (journal voucher):				
Expenditures	1,800			
Prepaid insurance		1,800		

	General Ledger Dr.	General Ledger Cr.	Subsidiary Ledger Dr.	Subsidiary Ledger Cr.
In allocations ledger (journal voucher):				
Departmental allocations account--property insurance			1,800	
40. Entry to record approval of voucher covering payment of withholding tax deductions and social security taxes to federal government (voucher register):				
a. Expenditures	10,000			
Withholding tax deductions	30,000			
Social Security deductions	10,000			
Vouchers payable		50,000		
b. Vouchers payable	50,000			
Cash		50,000		
In allocations ledger (vouchers):				
Departmental allocations account--employer's contribution to Social Security			10,000	
41. Entry to record purchase of investments (voucher register and check register):				
a. Investments (cost)	60,000			
Vouchers payable		60,000		
b. Vouchers payable	60,000			
Cash		60,000		
In investment ledger (vouchers):				
Investment accounts			60,000	
42. Entry to record purchase of investments through trust department of bank--bank account charged by debit advices (journal voucher):				
Investments (cost)	60,000			
Cash		60,000		
In investment ledger (vouchers):				
Investment accounts			60,000	
43. Entry to record sale of investments costing $18,000 for $19,200 (cash receipts journal):				
Cash	19,200			
Investments		18,000		
Revenues		1,200		
In investment ledger (cash receipts):				
Investment accounts				18,000
In revenues ledger (cash receipts):				
Revenues account--interest and capital gains on investments				1,200
44. Entry to record sale of investments costing $6,000 for $4,800 (cash receipts journal):				
Cash	4,800			
Revenues	1,200			
Investments		6,000		
In revenues ledger (cash receipts):				
Revenues accounts--interest and capital gains on investments			1,200	
In investment ledger (cash receipts):				
Investment accounts				6,000
45. Entries to record adjustments to budget (journal voucher):				
a. Increase in revenues estimates allocated to departments:				
Estimated revenues	6,000			
Departmental allocations		6,000		

	GENERAL LEDGER Dr.	GENERAL LEDGER Cr.	SUBSIDIARY LEDGER Dr.	SUBSIDIARY LEDGER Cr.
In revenues ledger (journal voucher):				
Revenues accounts			6,000	
In allocations ledger (journal voucher):				
Departmental allocations accounts				6,000
b. Increase in one department, decrease in another:				
Departmental allocations	30,000			
Departmental allocations		30,000		
In allocations ledger:				
Departmental allocations accounts			30,000	30,000
c. Increase in departmental budget financed by transfer from contingency reserves:				
Unallocated budget balances	6,000			
Departmental allocations		6,000		
In allocations ledger:				
Departmental allocations accounts				6,000
46. Entry to record recovery of indirect costs--sponsored programs (cash receipts journal):				
Cash	115,000			
Revenues		115,000		
In revenues ledger (cash receipts):				
Revenues accounts				115,000
(In restricted current funds, debit restricted current funds balances and credit cash.)				
47. Entry to record transfer to plant funds of debt service on educational plant (voucher register and check register):				
a. Transfer to funds for retirement of indebtedness	50,000			
Vouchers payable		50,000		
b. Vouchers payable	50,000			
Cash		50,000		
(In plant funds for retirement of indebtedness, debit cash and credit retirement of indebtedness funds balances.)				
48. Entry to record transfer to plant funds for retirement of indebtedness for debt service on auxiliary enterprise plant (voucher register and check register):				
a. Transfer to funds for retirement of indebtedness	35,000			
Vouchers payable		35,000		
b. Vouchers payable	35,000			
Cash		35,000		
(In allocations ledger, debit auxiliary enterprises subsidiary accounts.)				
(In plant funds for retirement of indebtedness, debit cash and credit retirement of indebtedness funds balances.)				
49. Entry to record transfer of unrestricted income from endowment to unrestricted current funds (cash receipts journal):				
Cash	520,000			
Revenues		520,000		
In revenues ledger (cash receipts):				
Revenues account--endowment income--unrestricted				520,000
(In endowment and similar funds, debit income--control [or undistributed pool income] and credit cash.)				

	GENERAL LEDGER Dr.	GENERAL LEDGER Cr.	SUBSIDIARY LEDGER Dr.	SUBSIDIARY LEDGER Cr.
50. Entry to record closing of departmental allocations and estimated revenues (journal vouchers):				
Departmental allocations	5,995,940			
Unallocated budget balances	10,060			
Estimated revenues		6,006,000		
51. Entry to close encumbrances open at year-end, prior to setting up provision for encumbrances on which materials and/or services were received at year-end (see Entry 53).				
Provision for encumbrances--current year	30,000			
Encumbrances		30,000		
In allocations ledger:				
Departmental allocations accounts				30,000
52. Entry to record closing of expenditures, revenues, and transfer accounts (journal vouchers):				
Revenues	5,900,300			
Restricted revenues	2,110,000			
Transfers to unexpended plant funds		60,000		
Transfers to funds for retirement of indebtedness		85,000		
Expenditures		5,719,200		
Restricted expenditures		2,110,000		
Unrestricted current funds balances		36,100		
53. Entry to set up provision for balances carried forward to cover encumbrances on which materials and/or services were received but not paid for at year-end:				
Unrestricted current funds balances	20,000			
Provision for balances carried forward to cover encumbrances		20,000		
(In following fiscal year, increase current departmental budgets as illustrated below):				
Provision for balances carried forward to cover encumbrances	20,000			
Departmental allocations		20,000		
In allocations ledger:				
Departmental allocations accounts				20,000
54. Entry to record collection of advances made to other funds (cash receipts journal):				
Cash	9,000			
Due from loan funds		6,000		
Due from unexpended plant funds		3,000		

C. General Ledger--Unrestricted Current Funds Section

Cash

	Beginning balance	186,000	Entry 4	Remittances	905,000
Entry 10	Alumnus gift	300	Entry 5b	Transfer to payroll account	140,000
Entry 13	Sale of stores	600	Entry 7b	Petty cash	6,000
Entry 17	Collections	1,240,000	Entry 8b	Petty cash	3,600
Entry 19	Collections	6,000	Entry 18b	Student loans issued	12,000
Entry 21	Collections	255,000	Entry 26b	Transfer to plant funds	60,000
Entry 24b	Collections	120	Entry 28b	Remittances	6,000
Entry 25	Sales of auxiliaries	1,283,600	Entry 30b	Remittances	1,200
Entry 29	Refund of expenditures	6,000	Entry 34b	Remittances	2,110,000
Entry 31	Sale of used equipment	600	Entry 38	Remittances	3,800,000
Entry 32	Deferred revenues	160,000	Entry 40b	Remittances	50,000
Entry 35	Reimbursement of restricted expenditures	2,110,000	Entry 41b	Investments	60,000
			Entry 42	Investments	60,000

(Cash, continued)

Entry 36 State appropriations	1,500,000	Entry 47b Transfer of funds for retirement of indebtedness	50,000
Entry 43 Sale of investments	19,200	Entry 48b Debt service	35,000
Entry 44 Sale of investments	4,800		
Entry 46 Recovery of indirect costs	115,000		
Entry 49 Endowment income	520,000		
Entry 54 Due from other funds	9,000		
(117,420)			

Payroll Bank Account

Entry 5c Transfer from general account	140,000	Entry 6 Payroll checks	140,000

Petty Cash

Entry 7a Establish fund	6,000		
(6,000)			

Bank Transfers

Entry 5a Transfer to payroll bank account	140,000	Entry 5c Payroll bank account	140,000

Accounts Receivable--Students

Beginning balance	329,000	Entry 21 Collections	255,000
Entry 20 Student fees	62,000	Entry 23 Accounts written off	300
Entry 24a Reinstatement of accounts written off	120	Entry 24b Collections	120
(135,700)			

Accounts Receivable--Others

Beginning balance	313,000		
(313,000)			

State Appropriations Receivable

Entry 9 Unpaid appropriation	300,000		
(300,000)			

Due from Loan Funds

Entry 18a Student loans issued	12,000	Entry 19 Collections	6,000
		Entry 54 Repayment by loan funds	6,000
	12,000		12,000

Due from Unexpended Plant Funds

Entry 12 Issues to plant funds	3,000	Entry 54 Repayment by unexpended plant funds	3,000

Physical Plant Stores

	Beginning balance	290,000	Entry 12 Issues to departments	386,000
Entry 11	Purchases	292,000	Entry 13 Cash sales	600
			Entry 14 Issues to departments	3,000
	(191,800)		Entry 15 Adjustment to physical inventory	600

Investments

	Beginning balance	200,000	Entry 43 Sales	18,000
Entry 41a	Purchases	60,000	Entry 44 Sales	6,000
Entry 42	Purchases	60,000		
	(296,000)			

Prepaid Insurance

	Beginning balance	7,200	Entry 39 Expired insurance	1,800
	(5,400)			

Transfers to Unexpended Plant Funds

Entry 26a	Plant additions	60,000	Entry 52 Closing	60,000

Transfers to Funds for Retirement of Indebtedness

Entry 47a	Debt service	50,000	Entry 52 Closing	
Entry 48a	Debt service	35,000		
		85,000		85,000

Expenditures

Entry 3b	Invoices	605,000	Entry 29 Refund of expenditures	6,000
Entry 6	Payroll	189,600	Entry 52 Closing	5,719,200
Entry 8	Petty cash expenditures	3,600		
Entry 12	Stores issues	386,000		
Entry 15	Adjust inventory	600		
Entry 16	Bookstores sales to departments	390,000		
Entry 22	Allowance for doubtful accounts	1,800		
Entry 27	Invoices	60,000		
Entry 28a	Replacement reserve	6,000		
Entry 37	Invoices	4,070,800		
Entry 39	Expired insurance	1,800		
Entry 40a	Social security taxes	10,000		
		5,725,200		5,725,200

Restricted Expenditures

Entry 34a		2,110,000	Entry 52 Closing	2,110,000

Encumbrances

Entry 2	Orders placed	630,000	Entry 3a Orders liquidated	600,000
			Entry 51 Closing	30,000
		630,000		630,000

Estimated Revenues

Entry 1 Record budget	6,000,000	Entry 50 Closing	6,006,000
Entry 45a Budget adjustments	6,000		
	6,006,000		6,006,000

Vouchers Payable

Entry 4 Checks issued	905,000	Beginning balance	212,000
Entry 5b Checks issued	140,000	Entry 3b Audited vouchers	605,000
Entry 7b Checks issued	6,000	Entry 5a Audited vouchers	140,000
Entry 8b Checks issued	3,600	Entry 7a Audited vouchers	6,000
Entry 18b Checks issued	12,000	Entry 8 Audited vouchers	3,600
Entry 26b Checks issued	60,000	Entry 11 Audited vouchers	292,000
Entry 28b Checks issued	6,000	Entry 18a Audited vouchers	12,000
Entry 30b Checks issued	1,200	Entry 26a Audited vouchers	60,000
Entry 34b Checks issued	2,110,000	Entry 27 Audited vouchers	60,000
Entry 38 Checks issued	3,800,000	Entry 28a Audited vouchers	6,000
Entry 40b Checks issued	50,000	Entry 30a Audited vouchers	1,200
Entry 41b Checks issued	60,000	Entry 34a Audited vouchers	2,110,000
Entry 47b Checks issued	50,000	Entry 37 Audited vouchers	4,070,800
Entry 48b Checks issued	35,000	Entry 40a Audited vouchers	50,000
		Entry 41a Audited vouchers	60,000
		Entry 47a Audited vouchers	50,000
		Entry 48a Audited vouchers	35,000
		(534,800)	

Withholding Tax Deductions

Entry 40a Remittance	30,000	Entry 6 Payroll deductions	30,000

Social Security Deductions

Entry 40a Remittance	10,000	Entry 6 Payroll deductions	10,000

Retirement System Deductions

		Entry 6 Payroll deductions	9,600
		(9,600)	

Deferred Revenues

Entry 33 Transfer to revenues	490,000	Beginning balance	490,000
		Entry 32 Revenues collected in advance	160,000
		(160,000)	

Revenues

Entry 30a Refund of revenues	1,200	Entry 9 Unpaid state appropriation	300,000
Entry 44 Loss on sale of investments	1,200	Entry 10 Alumnus gift	300
Entry 52 Closing	5,900,300	Entry 16 Bookstores sales to departments	390,000
		Entry 17 Student fees--cash	1,240,000
		Entry 20 Student fees--charge	62,000
		Entry 25 Sales of auxiliaries	1,283,600
		Entry 31 Sales of used equipment	600
		Entry 33 Transfer deferred revenues	490,000
		Entry 36 State appropriation	1,500,000
		Entry 43 Profit on sale of investments	1,200
		Entry 46 Recovery of indirect costs	115,000
		Entry 49 Endowment income	520,000
	5,902,700		5,902,700

Restricted Revenues

Entry 52 Closing	2,110,000	Entry 35 Reimbursement of restricted expenditures	2,110,000
	2,110,000		2,110,000

Departmental Allocations

Entry 45b Budget adjustment	30,000	Entry 1 Record budget	5,983,940
Entry 50 Closing	5,995,940	Entry 45a Budget adjustments	6,000
		Entry 45b Budget adjustments	30,000
		Entry 45c Budget adjustments	6,000
	6,025,940		6,025,940

Provision for Encumbrances--Current Year

Entry 3a Orders liquidated	600,000	Entry 2 Orders placed	630,000
Entry 51 Closing	30,000		
	630,000		630,000

Allowance for Doubtful Accounts--Students

Entry 23 Accounts written off	300	Beginning balance	4,000
		Entry 22 Increase allowance	1,800
		Entry 24a Reinstatement of account written off	120
		(5,620)	

Allowance for Doubtful Accounts--Other

		Beginning balance	2,000
		(2,000)	

Unallocated Budget Balances

Entry 45c Budget adjustment	6,000	Entry 1 Record budget	16,060
Entry 50 Closing	10,060		
	16,060		16,060

Provision for Balances Carried Forward to Cover Encumbrances

		Entry 53 Set up provision	20,000
		(20,000)	

Unrestricted Current Funds Balances

Entry 53 Set up provision	20,000	Beginning balance	617,200
		Entry 52 Closing	36,100
		(633,300)	

D. Balance Sheet Before Closing

BLANK COLLEGE

Balance Sheet
(Before Closing)

ASSETS

CURRENT FUNDS:		
Unrestricted		
Cash		114,420
Investments, at cost (approximate market $310,000)		296,000
Accounts receivable:		
Students, less allowance for doubtful accounts of $5,620	130,080	
Other, less allowance for doubtful accounts of $2,000	311,000	441,080
State appropriations receivable		300,000
Inventories, at cost		191,800
Prepaid expenses		5,400
Due from other funds		9,000
Transfers to other funds:		
Unexpended plant funds	60,000	
Retirement of indebtedness	85,000	145,000
Estimated revenues	6,006,000	
Less: Realized revenues	5,900,300	105,700
Total unrestricted current funds		1,608,400

LIABILITIES AND FUND BALANCES

CURRENT FUNDS:			
Unrestricted:			
Accounts payable			534,800
Retirement system deductions			9,600
Deferred revenues			160,000
Provision for encumbrances--current year			30,000
Departmental allocations		5,995,940	
Less:			
Expenditures	5,719,200		
Encumbrances	30,000	5,749,200	246,740
Unallocated budget balances			10,060
Fund balances			617,200
Total unrestricted current funds			1,608,400

E. Balance Sheet After Closing

BLANK COLLEGE

Balance Sheet
(After Closing)

ASSETS

CURRENT FUNDS:		
Unrestricted:		
Cash		123,420
Investments, at cost (approximate market $310,000)		296,000
Accounts receivable:		
Students, less allowance for doubtful accounts of $5,620	130,080	
Others, less allowance for doubtful accounts of $2,000	311,000	441,080
State appropriations receivable		300,000
Inventories, at cost		191,800
Prepaid expenses		5,400
Total unrestricted current funds		1,357,700

LIABILITIES AND FUND BALANCES

CURRENT FUNDS:	
Unrestricted:	
Accounts payable	534,800
Retirement system deductions	9,600
Deferred revenues	160,000
Fund balances:	
Provision for encumbrances	20,000
Unrestricted	633,300
Total unrestricted current funds	1,357,700

ACCOUNTING FOR RESTRICTED CURRENT FUNDS

A. Balance Sheet at Beginning of Period

BLANK COLLEGE
Balance Sheet
(Beginning of Period)

ASSETS		LIABILITIES AND FUND BALANCES	
CURRENT FUNDS:		CURRENT FUNDS:	
Restricted:		Restricted:	
Cash	195,200	Accounts payable	176,000
Investments, at cost (market $468,000)	452,000	Fund balances	1,358,700
Accounts receivable--principally agencies of the U.S. government	887,500		
Total restricted current funds	1,534,700	Total restricted current funds	1,534,700

B. Recording of Typical Transactions

	GENERAL LEDGER Dr.	GENERAL LEDGER Cr.	SUBSIDIARY LEDGER Dr.	SUBSIDIARY LEDGER Cr.
1. Entry to record receipt of restricted donations for specific purposes (cash receipts journal):				
Cash	2,417,000			
Restricted current funds balances		2,417,000		
In restricted current funds ledger (cash receipts):				
Individual fund accounts				2,417,000
2. Entry to record recovery of indirect costs--sponsored programs (voucher register and check register):				
a. Restricted current funds balances	115,000			
Vouchers payable		115,000		
b. Vouchers payable	115,000			
Cash		115,000		
(In unrestricted current funds, debit cash and credit revenues.)				
3. Entry to record reimbursement by restricted current funds to unrestricted current funds for expenditures made out of unrestricted current funds (voucher register and check register):				
a. Restricted current funds balances	2,110,000			
Vouchers payable		2,110,000		
b. Vouchers payable	2,110,000			
Cash		2,110,000		
In restricted current funds ledger (vouchers):				
Individual restricted fund accounts			2,110,000	
(In unrestricted current funds, debit cash and credit restricted revenues--individual revenues accounts.)				
4. Entry to record refund to grantor of restricted donation (voucher register):				
a. Restricted current funds balances	12,000			
Vouchers payable		12,000		
(In subsequent accounting period, vouchers payable is to be debited and cash credited.)				
In restricted current funds ledger (vouchers):				
Individual restricted fund accounts			12,000	

C. General Ledger--Restricted Current Funds Section

Cash

Beginning balance	195,200	Entry 2b Remittances	115,000
Entry 1 Receipt of donations	2,417,000	Entry 3b Remittances	2,110,000
(387,200)			

Accounts Receivable

Beginning balance	887,500		
(887,500)			

Investments

Beginning balance	452,000		
(452,000)			

Vouchers Payable

Entry 2b Checks issued	115,000	Beginning balance	176,000
Entry 3b Checks issued	2,110,000	Entry 2a Audited vouchers	115,000
		Entry 3a Audited vouchers	2,110,000
		Entry 4a Audited vouchers	12,000
		(188,000)	

Restricted Current Funds Balances

Entry 2a Recovery of indirect costs	115,000	Beginning balance	1,358,700
Entry 3a Reimbursement to unrestricted current funds	2,110,000	Entry 1 Donation	2,417,000
Entry 4a Refund to grantor	12,000	(1,538,700)	

D. Final Balance Sheet--Restricted Current Funds

BLANK COLLEGE
Balance Sheet
(End of Period)

ASSETS		LIABILITIES AND FUND BALANCES	
CURRENT FUNDS:		CURRENT FUNDS:	
Restricted:		Restricted:	
Cash	387,200	Accounts payable	188,000
Investments, at cost (market $460,000)	452,000	Fund balances	1,538,700
Accounts receivable--principally agencies of the U.S. government	887,500		
Total restricted current funds	1,726,700	Total restricted current funds	1,726,700

E. Statement of Changes in Fund Balances

BLANK COLLEGE

Statement of Changes in Fund Balances
For the Year Ended June 30, 19__

	CURRENT FUNDS	
	UNRESTRICTED	RESTRICTED
REVENUES AND OTHER ADDITIONS:		
Unrestricted current funds revenues	5,900,300	
Gifts and grants		2,417,000
	5,900,300	2,417,000
EXPENDITURES AND OTHER DEDUCTIONS:		
Educational and general expenditures	4,513,200	2,110,000
Auxiliary enterprises expenditures	1,200,000	
Indirect costs allowances		115,000
Refunded to grantors		12,000
	5,713,200	2,237,000
INTERFUND TRANSFERS--ADDITIONS (DEDUCTIONS):		
Mandatory debt service:		
Principal and interest	(85,000)	
Renewals and replacements	(6,000)	
Nonmandatory:		
Plant additions	(60,000)	
Total	(151,000)	
Net increase (decrease) for year	36,100	180,000
Balance at beginning of year	617,200	1,358,700
Fund balance, June 30, 19__	653,300	1,538,700

10

Accounting for Endowment and Similar Funds, and Annuity and Life Income Funds

Endowment and Similar Funds. Principle Five in *College and University Business Administration* (1968), states: "The Endowment and Similar Funds group includes those funds whose principal is nonexpendable as of the date of reporting and is invested, or is available for investment, for the purpose of producing income."[1] Three types of funds are included in this group:

(a) *Endowment funds* are those in which the donors have stipulated that the principal must remain inviolate and in perpetuity with only the income from the investment of the funds being available for expenditure. If the income can be used for general operating purposes, the funds are classed as unrestricted and the income is transferred to and accounted for in the unrestricted current funds group. If the income is restricted by donors to designated uses, the funds are classed as restricted and the income is transferred to and accounted for in the appropriate fund group. Examples of restricted endowment funds are those whose income is designated for the support of a particular instructional position or department, for maintenance and operation of certain buildings, for research projects, for scholarships or fellowships, and for loan funds. One institution classifies its restricted endowment funds in the following manner:

1. Professorships and chairs
2. Library
3. Research
4. Fellowships and scholarships
5. Prizes and awards
6. Loans

1. *College and University Business Administration* (2nd Rev. ed.; Washington, D.C.: American Council on Education, 1968), 144.

7. Building maintenance
8. Equipment
9. Lectures
10. Miscellaneous

The terms of an endowment fund may require that the income be added to the principal annually until a given amount has been accumulated. Then, the income may be used for designated purposes.

Occasionally, gifts for endowment purposes are not turned over directly to an institution but instead are placed by the donor in the hands of a trustee. The trustee invests the funds, turning over the income to the institution for use in accordance with the terms of the gift. Since such funds are not actually in the possession of the institution or under its control, they preferably should not be reported in the balance sheet as belonging to an institution. Instead, they should be disclosed parenthetically in the endowment and similar funds section of the balance sheet or in the notes accompanying the financial statements. However, if the institution has legally enforceable rights to the funds, including those as to income, such funds may be reported as assets in the financial statements and described as funds held in trust by others.

If funds were established under irrevocable trusts, with the trustees having no discretionary powers as to income, the income should be reported as endowment income or should be separately stated. If the funds were established under revocable trusts, or if the trustees have discretionary powers as to income distributions, such income is tantamount to a gift and should so be reported in the financial statements.

(b) *Term endowment funds* are those which donors have stipulated may be released from the status of endowment upon the happening of a particular event or the passage of a stated period of time. Examples are (1) a gift with the stipulation that a fund is to be held as endowment and the income is to be used for the maintenance of a building until the bonds used to finance the building are retired, and (2) a gift for endowment purposes which carries the stipulation that after twenty years the governing board may expend the principal at its discretion.

(c) *Quasi-endowment funds, or funds functioning as endowment*, are those determined by the governing board, rather than a donor, to be retained and invested as though they were endowment funds, at least for the present.

The three types of funds should be reported in the endowment and similar funds section of the balance sheet, with each group being reported separately in the equity section. All gifts and bequests and other receipts of funds in this group, all transfers to and from the group, as well as all forms of principal reductions, should be reported in the statement of changes in fund balances—endowment and similar funds.

Principles Governing Accounting and Reporting of Endowment Funds. From the point of view of college and university business officers, the more important considerations in handling endowment and other nonexpendable funds involve, first, an accurate and complete knowledge of all legal provisions pertaining to the funds and, second, an accurate distinction between the income and principal of the funds. The business officer must be thoroughly familiar with the terms of each gift and bequest. He must be prepared to safeguard the investment of endowment funds and the disbursement of income therefrom according to the conditions imposed by the gift. The maintenance of an accurate distinction between principal and income is extremely important. The institution is entitled to the exact net income from its endowment funds. To give it more would encroach upon the principal of the funds, and to give it less would be unfair to the purposes for which the funds are dedicated. Therefore, the accounts must always reflect an accurate and equitable separation of principal and income.

Chapter 14 in *College and University Business Administration* (1968) lists the following principles governing the management, recording, and reporting of endowment and other similar funds:[2]

(a) The total of each of the subgroups of funds should be identified separately in the accounts and in the equity section of the balance sheet.

(b) The funds may be classified further to show those for which the income is unrestricted in use and those for which the income is restricted by donors to specific uses.

2. *Ibid.*, 145.

(c) The funds in the endowment and similar funds group may be pooled for effective investment and management unless prohibited either by statute or by the terms of the instruments of gift. It is preferable not to merge assets of annuity and life income funds, unloaned balances of loan funds, and unexpended balances of current, plant, and agency funds groups with endowment and similar funds in the investment pool.

(d) If the assets of the funds in this group are pooled for investment purposes, only one control account need be maintained to reflect book values for each class of investments in the pool. For report purposes, the assets may be shown together in appropriate classes of investments, regardless of whether the investments are pooled.

(e) The operation of an investment pool necessitates adopting procedures that will provide for the equitable distribution of income and the assignment of capital appreciation to all funds participating in the pool. The market-value method is preferable to the book-value method in the operation of investment pools.

(f) In the event other funds are admitted to the endowment pool for investment purposes, special attention must be given to the accounting arrangements for admittance to and withdrawal from the pool. Proper arrangements will preclude crediting such funds with investment income and realized or unrealized net gains properly attributable to the permanently invested funds.

(g) Pooled investment income should be distributed to the income accounts of the participating funds without consideration of the gain or loss account. This will prevent dilution of the proper share of the various funds in the aggregate investment income of the pool.

(h) Realized gains and losses on investment transactions affect the principal of the invested funds either (1) by increasing or decreasing the individual fund balances or (2) by retaining as an undistributed accumulation the balances that are proportionately applicable to each fund. Such capital gains and losses are not operating revenues and expenditures, and they should not be treated differently from the amounts representing the original fund balances. They are subject to the same restrictions and limitations on investment, expenditure, and disposition as the funds from which they arose. *In some instances, realized gains and losses may be attributable to income as a matter of law—for example, when such treatment is required by a specific instrument or gift.*

(i) Investments purchased for the funds in this group should be recorded in the accounts and reported at cost. Gifts of securities and other donated assets should be recorded and reported at their market value or at an expertly appraised value as of the date of the gift.

(j) The book value of investments should not be changed to reflect fluctuations in market prices. However, market values based on appropriate periodic review of the investments should be disclosed in the balance sheet by means of a footnote or other reference. (The AICPA Audit Guide gives as a permissible alternative the reporting of investments at current market value or fair value, provided this basis is used for all investments of all funds.)

(k) In order to maintain unimpaired the principal of the funds in this group, provisions should be made for the depreciation of real properties that are the investment of funds in this group and for amortization of premiums on securities purchases. Provision may also be made for the accumulation of discounts.

(l) Endowment and term endowment funds should not be invested in institutional property.

(m) Endowment and term endowment funds should not be advanced for the use of other funds or fund groups.

(n) The principal of endowment and term endowment funds must not be hypothecated, and their investments must not be pledged for any purpose.

The Total Return Concept. Traditionally, educational institutions have considered as available for expenditure only the actual yield from the investments of endowment funds—dividends, interest, rents, and royalties. Realized capital gains, resulting from the sale of investments, have traditionally been considered not as expendable income but as additions to principal.

In recent years many institutions have adopted a "total return" concept in which they consider as available for expenditure not only yield but also capital gains and some portion of unrealized appreciation. Almost all of the total return arrangements provide for the protection of the endowment principal from its loss of purchasing power before appropriating or expending gains. Most total return approaches have been confined to appropriating only gains of quasi-endowment funds and not those generated from the investment of true endowment funds. Any institution wishing to adopt any of the total return concepts should rely on advice of counsel before proceeding. A number of states have adopted the Uniform Management of Institutional Funds Act, which under certain circumstances permits the expenditure of both realized and unrealized gains.

The total return concept causes accountants difficulty in that the current arrangements have produced few practical applications in which income can be objectively determined. This concern led the AICPA to conclude the following:

> Until a general practice evolves which is *objectively determinable*, the guide [AICPA Audit Guide] would do a disservice to higher education and the accounting profession to sanction as a permissible accounting treatment the inclusion in revenue of gains utilized under a total return approach. Therefore, any portion of gains utilized should be reported in the financial statements as a transfer. To the extent such a transfer is added to the current funds, it should be reported separately from traditional income yield of endowment and similar funds and should not be included in total current funds revenues.[3]

The following accounts are used in accounting for endowment and similar funds:

ASSETS
Cash
Due from other funds
Investments—securities (control)
Investments—real estate (control)
Reserve for depreciation on real estate
  (credit balance account)
Unamortized premiums on bonds

LIABILITIES AND FUND BALANCES
Vouchers payable
Due to other funds

3. *Audits of Colleges and Universities* (New York: American Institute of Certified Public Accountants, 1973), 40.

Mortgages payable
Income—control
Undistributed pool income
Reserve for accumulation of bond discounts
Net adjusted gains and losses
Endowment funds balances
Term endowment funds balances
Quasi-endowment funds balances
(or funds functioning as endowment funds balances)

Pledges for gifts for endowment funds normally are not recorded in the accounting records. They may be so recorded at their estimated net realizable value, however, if they represent legitimate, collectible obligations. Estimated net realizable value is defined in *Audits of Colleges and Universities* as "the present value of long-term pledges and reductions for any allowance for uncollectible pledges."[4] If pledges are entered in the accounts, a pledges receivable account would be set up in the asset accounts and credited to unrestricted revenues, deferred income, current restricted funds, endowment fund balances, or plant funds, as appropriate.

Accounting for the Investments of Endowment Funds. Endowment funds may be invested in bonds, preferred and common stocks, debentures, mutual fund shares, notes, mortgages, real estate, leases, oil and gas royalties, and even in business ownership. Investments should be recorded at total cost, including commissions, taxes, and all other costs of acquisition. Gifts of investments should be valued at market values as of the day on which title to the investments is transferred to the college or university. For listed securities, an appropriate valuation is the average of the high and low prices for the day; for unlisted securities and for real estate investments, valuations should be established by competent appraisers.

Expenses in connection with investment supervision, advice, counsel, and other expenses of endowment funds management may be charged against the income from the investments before the income is distributed to the appropriate funds. An alternative may be to show them as operating expenses of the institution, either as a separate item of institutional support or as part of the

4. *Ibid.*, 8.

expenses of the treasurer's office, comptroller's office, or business office.

Realized gains and losses on the sale of investments are credited or charged to an account for net adjusted gains and losses. The balance in this account is usually carried forward from year to year, although it may be distributed periodically to the funds involved. If the realized gains and losses are distributed to funds participating in an investment pool, the same method of distribution should be used in distributing the income from the pool to the participating funds, as described on pages 213–17, herein. For the majority of institutions, the accounting problems of endowment funds investments revolve around investments in bonds, stocks, mortgages, and real estate.

Accounting for Investments in Bonds. The more important accounting problems relating to bond investments include the handling of premiums and discounts, accrued interest, and profits and losses on the sale of these securities. Bonds generally are purchased at either a premium or a discount, seldom at par. If they are purchased at a premium, amortization of the premium is necessary in order to prevent a diminution of the principal of the funds for which the bonds were purchased. If purchased at a discount, the principal of the funds involved is not endangered, and for that reason most institutions do not amortize discounts. However, the Audit Guide states that "premiums paid on long term investments should be amortized and discounts accumulated ratably unless inappropriate because of default or quality of the bonds."[5]

Premiums and discounts may be accounted for in either of two ways. They may be included in the recorded cost of the bonds at the time of purchase, or they may be shown separately from the cost of the securities. In the former method, the total cost of the bonds is recorded in the investments-securities (control) account and in all subsidiary accounts for bond investments, and the sums representing the amortization of premiums and discounts are also recorded in these accounts. In the second method, the bond investments are recorded at par value in the investments-securities (control) account; premiums are set up as deferred charges in an account for unamortized premiums on bonds; and discounts are

5. *Ibid.*, 9.

shown as deferred credits in an account for reserve for accumulation of bond discounts.

There are three methods of amortizing premiums, each of which is used by educational institutions. The first is the straight line method, in which the premiums are written off over the life of the bonds in equal amounts at each interest date. The second, generally referred to as the scientific or actuarial method, involves the use of interest tables and is based on an amortization schedule. The amount of amortization at any interest date is represented by the difference between the nominal interest income (par value of the bonds × the contractual interest rate) and the actual or effective income (par value of the bonds + the unamortized premium × the yield rate of interest). The third method is termed the bonds outstanding method and is used in amortizing the premiums on serial bonds, in which case the first two methods are inapplicable. Under this method, the amount of par value of bonds owned at each interest date over the life of the issue is determined. The proportion that the amount of par value bonds outstanding at each interest date bears to the total par value of bonds outstanding is applied to the premium and determines the amount of periodic amortization.

In each of the methods of amortization, premiums are completely written off by the time the bonds mature. In the event the bonds are sold before their maturity, the unamortized premiums are included in the value of the bonds when determining the gain or loss on the sales.

Amortization of premiums is accomplished through periodic, usually annual, charges against the income from the bonds. If the bonds are assets of an investment pool, the charge is to the undistributed pool income account; if they are the investments of separately invested funds, the charge is to the income-control account. If premiums are recorded in the unamortized premiums on bonds account, the credit for the amortization is to this account. If premiums are included as part of the cost of the bonds, the credit is to the investments-securities (control) account and to the appropriate bond investment accounts in the subsidiary ledger. The following entries, all in the endowment and similar funds accounts, illustrate the methods of recording amortization of premiums on bonds under various conditions:

1. Bonds are part of pooled investments, and premiums are recorded separately from the investment account:
   Undistributed pool income
      Unamortized premiums on bonds
2. Bonds are part of pooled investments, and premiums are recorded as part of the cost of the bonds:
   Undistributed pool income
      Investments-securities (control)
3. Bonds are investments of separately invested funds, and premiums are recorded separately from the investment account:
   Income-control
      Unamortized premiums on bonds
4. Bonds are investments of separately invested funds, and premiums are recorded as part of the cost of the bonds:
   Income-control
      Investments-securities (control)

The amortization of discounts involves annual charges against either the reserve for accumulation of bond discounts account or the investments-securities (control) account (depending on the method used in accounting for the discounts) and credits to the income accounts of the funds involved. This procedure might call for the actual transfer of cash from the endowment and similar funds group to another fund group; and this, conceivably, could necessitate the sale of investments or a disruption of the investment program. The following entries, all in the endowment and similar funds accounts, illustrate the accounting for amortization of discounts under various conditions:

1. Bonds are part of pooled investments, and discounts are recorded separately from the investment account:
   Reserve for accumulation of bond discounts
      Undistributed pool income
2. Bonds are part of pooled investments, and discounts are recorded as part of the cost of the bonds:
   Investments-securities (control)
      Undistributed pool income
3. Bonds are investments of separately invested funds, and discounts are recorded separately from the investment account:
   Reserve for accumulation of bond discounts
      Income-control
4. Bonds are investments of separately invested funds, and discounts are recorded as part of the cost of the bonds:
   Investments-securities (control)
      Income-control

Bonds ordinarily are bought and sold between regular interest-paying dates. Since bond indentures call for the paying of interest to bondholders only on stipulated dates, the problem arises of accounting for the interest accrued between the last date on which interest was paid and the date of purchase or sale. The end result in accounting for accrued interest is that the income of the fund group to which the income is dedicated is charged when bonds are purchased and is credited when they are sold. If the bonds are in an investment pool, accrued interest items are first recorded in the account for undistributed pool income; if they are the investments of separately invested funds, accrued interest is first shown in the income-control account. The following entries, all in the endowment and similar funds accounts, illustrate the handling of transactions involving accrued interest under various conditions:

1. Entry to record purchase of bonds plus accrued interest:
   Investments-securities (control)
   Undistributed pool income (if bonds are in the investment pool), or income-control (if bonds are for separately invested funds)
   Cash
2. Entry to record collection of income:
   Cash
   Undistributed pool income (if bonds are in the investment pool), or income-control (if bonds are for separately invested funds)
3. Entry to record sale of bonds plus accrued interest:
   Cash
   Investments-securities (control)
   Undistributed pool income (if bonds are in the investment pool), or income-control (if bonds are for separately invested funds)

No entries for accrued interest are needed in other fund groups at the time of purchase or sale of bonds because accrued interest items are reflected in the income accounts in the endowment and similar funds group before the income is distributed to the other fund groups.

When bonds are sold before maturity, it is necessary to account for the gains or losses on the sale. Such gains or losses generally are credited or charged to the net adjusted gains and losses account, although they may be carried directly to the accounts for the principal or balances of the funds involved. The gain or loss is the difference between the book value of the bonds (par plus unamortized premiums, or less accumulated discounts) and the proceeds from the sale. The following entries, all in the endowment and similar funds accounts, illustrate the handling of transactions involving the sale of bonds at a profit and at a loss:

1. Bonds sold at a profit:
   Cash
       Investments-securities (control)
       Unamortized premiums on bonds (if bond premiums are recorded in this account)
       Net adjusted gains and losses, for amount of gain (or, to principal or balance of the fund involved)
2. Bonds sold at a loss:
   Cash
   Net adjusted gains and losses, for amount of loss (or, to principal or balance of fund involved)
       Investments-securities (control)
       Unamortized premiums on bonds (if bond premiums are recorded in this account)

Accounting for Investments in Stocks. Accounting for investments of endowment funds in stocks does not present serious problems. Stock purchases should be recorded in the accounts at cost and include brokerage fees, taxes, and other costs. Fluctuations in the market value should be ignored in the accounting records, though noted appropriately in financial reports. Information relative to market value of securities is essential to the proper management of the portfolio. However, such data should be gathered in memorandum accounts and not reflected in basic accounting records. Stocks may be held in an investment pool or may represent investments of specific endowment funds. A complete discussion of pooled investments appears later in this chapter.

Profits and losses on the sale of stock rights should be treated as additions to or deductions from the principal accounts involved. Stock dividends are not income and do not increase the value of the investment account. Such dividends should be recorded only as an increase in number of shares owned. If stock rights are sold, the chief problem presented is a determination of the profit or loss on the sale of the rights. The cost of the rights is found by apportioning the cost of the old stock between the rights and the stock on the basis of the relative market value of each at date of issuance of rights. Assuming the rights of a stock are selling at $20, the cost of the old stock is $84, and the market value of the stock ex-rights is $100, the assigned cost of each right is $\frac{20}{120} \times \$84$ or $14. The profit on the sale of one right is $6. The following entry should be made to record the sale of one right:

IN ENDOWMENT FUNDS:		
Cash	20	
Investments-securities (control)		14
Endowment funds balances		6

If an institution avails itself of the opportunity to purchase new shares through stock rights, the cost of the new shares should be charged to the investment account.

The following entries illustrate the accounting for various transactions in the endowment funds because of investments in stocks:

1. Entry to record purchase of stocks (recorded at cost):
   Investments-securities (control)
      Cash
2. Entry to record receipt of cash dividend:
   Cash
      Income-control, or undistributed pool income
3. Notification of receipt of stock dividend: No entry required, only notation in investment ledger increasing number of shares held.
4. Entry to record payment of fees to security consultant:
   Income-control, or undistributed pool income
      Cash
5. Entry to record sale of stocks at a profit:
   Cash
      Investments-securities (control)
      Net adjusted gains and losses, or endowment funds balances
6. Entry to record sale of stocks at a loss:
   Cash
   Net adjusted gains and losses, or endowment funds balances
      Investments-securities (control)

Accounting for Investments in Real Estate. The chief accounting problems in connection with the investment of endowment funds in real estate are (1) valuation of real estate acquired; (2) accounting for income, expenses, and the net operating income from each property; and (3) depreciation or depletion. Real estate may be acquired by gift, by purchase, or by mortgage foreclosure. If acquired by gift, it should be recorded at market value or, if there is not a readily determinable market value, at fair appraisal value. Property acquired by purchase should be recorded at full cost, including commissions, brokerage fees, costs of appraisals, fees for examining and recording title, delinquent taxes, if any, and all costs necessary to put the property into revenue-producing condition.

Property acquired as a result of foreclosure of mortgages should be recorded at cost, as described above, and include the unpaid balance of the mortgage, all expenses in connection with foreclosure, taxes and insurance unpaid at date of foreclosure, and extraordinary repairs. If foreclosed property is sold or if a deficiency judgment is obtained, the proceeds should be credited in full to the asset account for the mortgage. If the proceeds exceed the balance of the asset account, the net profit on the transaction should be credited to the endowment principal account or to net adjusted gains and losses. Any loss on the transaction should be charged in the same manner. Institutional property constructed or purchased as an investment of quasi-endowment funds should be accounted for in the same manner as outside property.

All items of income and expense related to real estate investments should be reflected in the income-control account. The determination of net income on each parcel of real estate is best handled by establishing an account for each property in a subsidiary ledger to which expenses are charged and income is credited. The more usual expenses chargeable against income from real estate consist of management fees and commissions, taxes, expenses for repair and maintenance of the properties, and insurance. Any disbursements which add to the value of the investment, such as improvements and special assessments, should be charged to the investment account.

At the end of the year the net income from each real estate investment is transferred to the appropriate fund group. As a general rule, real estate investments are not included in investment pools and would be considered the investments of separately invested funds. If the endowment funds so invested are restricted, the net income is transferred to the restricted current funds balances (control) account (and to the appropriate account in the subsidiary ledger) and is expended in accordance with the terms of the gift.

If the endowment funds invested in real estate are unrestricted, the net income is transferred to the revenues (control) account in the unrestricted current funds group and may be used for any operating purpose.

Following is an illustration of the accounting for income and expenses of endowment funds real estate:

1. Entry to record receipt of rental income:

   IN ENDOWMENT FUNDS

   Cash

       Income-control

   In the subsidiary ledger, credit the account set up to record income and expenses of each real estate investment involved.

2. Entry to record payment of expenses such as taxes, insurance, and repairs:

   IN ENDOWMENT FUNDS

   Income-control

       Cash

   In the subsidiary ledger, debit the appropriate operating account for each real estate investment involved.

3. Entries to record transfer of net income to proper fund group:

   a. IN ENDOWMENT FUNDS

      Income-control

          Cash

   In subsidiary ledger debit individual operating accounts for all real estate investments involved.

   b. IN UNRESTRICTED CURRENT FUNDS, if endowment fund is unrestricted:

      Cash

          Revenues (control)

   In revenues ledger credit unrestricted endowment income.

   c. IN RESTRICTED CURRENT FUNDS, if endowment fund is restricted:

      Cash

          Restricted funds balances

   In restricted funds ledger credit appropriate restricted funds balance account.

Depreciation on Real Estate. In order to protect the principal of an endowment fund which has been invested in real estate, suitable provision must be made for depreciation or depletion. Land, not being subject to loss in value through use, is not depreciable and therefore is not included in depreciation computations.

Buildings and other structures, on the other hand, possess a limited income-producing life. Consequently, funds must be accumulated out of income from the properties or from other current funds revenues to make up for reductions in the original value of this type of investment. This end is accomplished by means of periodic charges—depreciation expense—against the real estate operating accounts and by credits to the reserve for depreciation carried in the endowment and similar funds group. Funds represented by the reserve for depreciation should be invested and the income received should be added to the reserve. Any acceptable method of depreciation may be used. The following entries illustrate the treatment of depreciation and the accumulation of the reserve for depreciation:

1. Entry to record depreciation:
   IN ENDOWMENT FUNDS
   Income-control
       Reserve for depreciation
   In the subsidiary ledger debit the appropriate operating account for each real estate investment involved.
2. Entry to record investment of depreciation reserve:
   IN ENDOWMENT FUNDS
   Investments-securities (control)
       Cash

Investment Pools. Each endowment fund constitutes a separate, inviolate fund, the principal of which must be maintained separate and distinct from all other funds. Ordinarily, however, institutions are permitted to pool or group the cash and other assets belonging to various endowment funds in order to effect better management of the funds. This procedure is highly advantageous to the institution for two reasons. First, it permits greater diversification of investments with respect to geographical location, type of security, and type of enterprise, and thus affords greater safety than is possible when individual endowment funds are invested separately. Second, it permits greater flexibility in the investment program in that an institution can more easily find suitable investments in the units required than would be possible if the small amounts of uninvested cash of each fund had to be invested separately. Of course, if the terms of a particular endowment fund specify that it shall be invested separately, then pooling of the fund in question would not be possible. The principal accounts of funds participating in a pool should reflect the extent to which each endowment participates.

Income from pooled investments is recorded in the endowment funds group by crediting an account called undistributed pool income. Periodically, the income reflected in this account should be distributed to the participating funds. For unrestricted funds participating in the pool the income is transferred to the unrestricted current funds group. For participating funds that are restricted, the income is transferred to the balance account in the appropriate fund group.

There are two principal methods of allocating income to participating funds. The preferred method is known as the market-value method; the other is known as the book-value method. Under the latter plan, income is allocated to participating funds on the basis of the balance in the principal of each fund. Balances may be those existing at the time of distribution or may represent the average of the beginning and ending balances. In some instances, balances are based on monthly averaging. If a fund is added to or taken out of the pool, the basis of entry or exit is the book value of the fund. The book-value method is unfair to funds that entered the pool when asset values were relatively low, as compared with those that entered at a time when asset values were relatively high.

As stated previously, the market-value method is more equitable to participating funds and is the preferred method of allocating income to funds participating in an investment pool. Under this method, income "is distributed to the various funds on the basis of the assignment to each fund of a number of shares that is calculated on the market value of the assets of the pool at the time of entry of the fund in the pool."[6] When the pool is established, an arbitrary value is assigned to each participating share in the pool. For example, a fund of $50,000 might have 5,000 shares valued at $10 per share. After the establishment of the pool, assets are revalued periodically—weekly, monthly, or quarterly—and a new share value is determined by dividing the number of shares outstanding into the new asset values of the investments at market.

6. *Ibid.*, 44.

Funds may be admitted to or withdrawn from the pool only on investment dates; or, alternatively, funds may enter or leave the pool at any time, shares being valued as of the latest valuation date.

To illustrate the operations of an investment pool, assume its establishment with shares valued arbitrarily at $10:

	Book Value	*Market Value*	*No. of Shares*	*Unit Value*
Fund A	$ 50,000	$ 50,000	5,000	$10
Fund B	25,000	25,000	2,500	10
	$ 75,000	$ 75,000	7,500	$10

Assume that Fund C is admitted to the pool six months later. At that time the unit share value is $12:

Fund A	$ 50,000		5,000	$12
Fund B	25,000		2,500	12
Total	75,000	90,000	7,500	12
Fund C	36,000	36,000	3,000	12
	$111,000	$126,000	10,500	$12

Assume that Fund B is withdrawn at the end of the year:

Fund A	$ 50,000		5,000	$13
Fund B	25,000		2,500	13
Fund C	36,000		3,000	13
	111,000	136,500	10,500	13
Fund B	(25,000)	(32,500)	(2,500)	13
Total	$ 86,000	$104,000	8,000	$13

In distributing income earned by the pool, total investment income is divided by total number of shares participating in the pool in order to determine the rate of income per share. Appropriate adjustment is made for shares held less than a full year. In the above illustration the number of shares to be used in the calculation is as follows:

Total shares at end of year	10,500
Less: Shares of Fund C, adjusted for ½ year	1,500
Result	9,000

Assuming income to be $5,250 for an entire year, that figure divided by the number of shares (9,000) equals a rate per share of .5833, and the distribution would be:

Fund A—5,000 shares @ .5833	$2,916.50
Fund B—2,500 shares @ .5833	1,458.50
Fund C—1,500 shares @ .5833	875.00
	$5,250.00

If the book-value basis were used instead of the market-value basis, assuming book value to be the mean of beginning and ending balances, the distribution would be as follows:

	Book Value	*Percent of Total*	*Income Distribution*
Fund A	$50,000	53.8	$2,824
Fund B	25,000	26.9	1,412
Fund C ($36,000 for ½ year)	18,000	19.3	1,014
	$93,000	100.0	$5,250

As stated previously, the book-value basis results in an inequitable distribution, favoring the most recently admitted fund—in this illustration, Fund C.

A revenue stabilization reserve may be established to stabilize and regularize the amount available for annual use from the pooled investment income. However, the AICPA Audit Guide authorizes the creation of revenue stabilization reserves only out of earnings of unrestricted endowment funds; these reserves are carried on the balance sheet as an allocation of unrestricted current funds balances.

Realized gains and losses on endowment funds investments are recorded in the account net adjusted gains and losses. The net amount in this account usually is accumulated from year to year, although it may be distributed annually to the participating funds. If an institution elects to distribute net gains and losses, the method described above for distributing income should be used. As stated previously, unrealized gains and losses are usually not reflected in the records.

The following entries illustrate accounting for pooled endowment funds:

1. Entry to record merger of several endowment funds into pool:
   IN ENDOWMENT FUNDS
   Only subsidiary entries needed, showing which endowment funds are being merged into the pool.
2. Entry to record receipt of income on pooled investments:
   IN ENDOWMENT FUNDS
   Cash
      Undistributed pool income
3. Entry to record distribution of pooled income:
   a. IN ENDOWMENT FUNDS
      Undistributed pool income
         Cash
   b. IN UNRESTRICTED CURRENT FUNDS—for income on unrestricted endowment funds
      Cash
         Revenues
   c. IN RESTRICTED CURRENT OR OTHER FUNDS—for income on restricted endowment funds
      Cash
         Appropriate funds balances

Subsidiary Ledger Records. The following subsidiary ledger records are used in accounting for the transactions of endowment and other nonexpendable funds:

1. Endowment Funds Ledger (Form 10.1). This ledger is used to record the principal of each separately invested endowment, life income, and annuity fund in possession of the institution. The ledger is subdivided to show balance of cash, unamortized premium or discount, and investments made, as well as the total principal of the fund. The sum of the fund principal columns in the subsidiary ledger should agree with the endowment funds balances control account in the general ledger. Postings to the subsidiary ledger are made daily from original documents such as cash receipts, invoice vouchers, and journal vouchers. For pooled endowment funds, the endowment funds ledger would be subdivided only to record additions to, deductions from, and balances of principal.

2. Investment Ledger (Form 10.2). This ledger is used to record pertinent information pertaining to investments in bonds, stocks, notes, mortgages, and real estate. The form is applicable also as a subsidiary ledger for temporary investments of all fund groups.

FORM 10.1

BLANK COLLEGE

ENDOWMENT FUNDS LEDGER

Name of Fund__________

Restrictions: As To Income__________

As To Principal__________

Date	Reference	Explanation	Cash			Premiums and Discounts			Investments			Fund Principal
			Receipts	Disburse-ments	Balance	Acquired	Amor-tized	Balance	Acquired	Disposed of	Balance	

FORM 10.2
(front)

BLANK COLLEGE

INVESTMENT LEDGER

Name of Investment__________ Fund Group__________

Class of Investment__________ Name of Endowment Fund__________

Date	Reference	Explanation	Principal			Premiums and Discounts on Investments or Reserve for Depreciation			Income		
			Debits	Credits	Balance	Debits	Credits	Balance	Debits	Credits	Balance

FORM 10.2
(back)

B O N D S

Date Purchased________________ Price__________

Date of Maturity________________ Callable__________

Interest: Rate______% Amount__________ Date__________

Serial Numbers________________________________

Type of Bond________________________________
(Registered or Coupon)

Remarks:________________________________

Date Sold________________ Price__________

S T O C K S

Date Purchased________________ Price__________

Callable________________ Convertible__________

Dividend: Rate______ Amount__________ Date__________

Type of Stock________________________________

No. of Shares__________ Par Value__________

Remarks:________________________________

Date Sold________________ Price__________

N O T E S A N D M O R T G A G E S

Date of Loan________________ Maturity__________

Description of Property________________________________

Interest: Rate______% Amount__________ Date__________

Remarks:________________________________

R E A L E S T A T E

Date of Acquisition__________ How Acquired__________

Price, If Purchased__________ Appraisal__________

Description of Property________________________________

Rental: Rate and When
Collected________________________________

Depreciation: Rate__________ Amount__________

Remarks:________________________________

Date Sold________________ Price__________

The investment ledger should be subdivided into fund groups, with a subcontrol account over each group. The sum of the balances of the principal columns in each fund group should agree with the general ledger control account for investments of that group. In the case of endowment and similar funds, there may be separate control accounts for pooled investments and for individual investments. If properly arranged, this ledger produces information not only by funds but also by types of investments. Entries in the investment ledger are made from original documents such as cash receipts, invoices, and journal vouchers.

Annuity and Life Income Funds. Annuity and life income funds are funds acquired by an institution and subject to agreements requiring payments to one or more designated beneficiaries during the life of those individuals. If the institution is obligated to pay a stipulated amount, the fund is classified as an annuity fund. If the institution binds itself to pay to the beneficiaries only the income earned by the assets of the fund, it is classified as a life income fund.

Upon the death of the beneficiary or at any other specified time, the principal of the annuity or life income fund becomes the property of the institution and may be used in accordance with the terms of the agreement. Such funds may be unrestricted or restricted as to use.

Annuity and life income funds, like endowment funds, may be invested in securities or real estate and may, if agreements permit, be pooled with other annuity and life income funds for investment purposes. *College and University Business Administration* (1968) suggests that "it is preferable not to merge assets of Annuity and Life Income funds . . . with Endowment and Similar Funds in the investment pool."[7]

Separate accounts must be maintained for the receipts, disbursements, and balances of each fund in this group. Separate accounts also must be established for recording income belonging to each fund and for disbursements to annuitants and life income beneficiaries. Form 10.1, illustrated on page 218, is suitable for use in accounting for the transactions of annuity and life income funds that are separately invested. A ledger form showing additions, deduc-

7. *College and University Business Administration*, 145.

tions, and balances may be used to account for the principal of annuity and life income funds that have pooled investments.

The AICPA Audit Guide prescribes the method of accounting for annuity funds. Assets are recorded at cost or fair market value. The equity side includes an account for the present value of the aggregate liability for annuities payable, based upon acceptable life expectancy tables, and an account for the fund balance or deficit. When a gift is received, the present value of the annuity gift is credited to the liability account and the remainder to the fund balance. Investment gains and income and annuity payments and investment losses are charged to the liability account. Periodically, an adjustment is made between the liability account and the fund balance account to record the actuarial gain or loss due to recomputation of the liability based upon the revised life expectancy.

The following accounts are used in accounting for annuity and life income funds:

ASSETS
Cash
Due from other funds
Investments—securities (control)
Investments—real estate (control)
Reserve for depreciation (credit balance account)

LIABILITIES AND FUND BALANCES
Vouchers payable
Annuities payable
Due to other funds
Undistributed income—annuity funds (control)
Undistributed income—life income funds (control)
Net adjusted gains and losses
Annuity funds balances (control)
Life income funds balances (control)

Accounting for the investments of annuity and life income funds presents no different problems from those of endowment funds; hence, no further discussion of this subject is needed.

Following is an illustration of the accounting for endowment and similar funds and for annuity and life income funds. It gives a beginning balance sheet, typical transactions during the fiscal year, a final balance sheet, and a statement of changes in fund balances.

ACCOUNTING FOR ENDOWMENT AND SIMILAR FUNDS
AND ANNUITY AND LIFE INCOME FUNDS

ACCOUNTING FOR ENDOWMENT AND SIMILAR FUNDS

A. Balance Sheet at Beginning of Period

BLANK COLLEGE

Balance Sheet
(Beginning of Period)

ASSETS		LIABILITIES AND FUND BALANCES	
ENDOWMENT AND SIMILAR FUNDS:		ENDOWMENT AND SIMILAR FUNDS:	
Cash	100,000	Mortgages payable on real estate	15,000
Investments--securities	1,500,000	Fund balances:	
Investments--real estate (less reserve for depreciation) (Funds held in trust by others--$100,000)	250,000	Endowment funds	1,525,000
		Term endowment funds	100,000
		Quasi-endowment funds	175,000
		Net adjusted gains and losses	35,000
Total endowment and similar funds	1,850,000	Total endowment and similar funds	1,850,000

B. Recording of Typical Transactions

	General Ledger Dr.	General Ledger Cr.	Subsidiary Ledger Dr.	Subsidiary Ledger Cr.
1. Entry to record receipt of gift in cash for endowment purposes (cash receipts journal):				
Cash	22,000			
Endowment funds balances		22,000		
In endowment funds ledger (cash receipts journal):				
Principal account				22,000
2. To note receipt of gift of $5,000 to be held in trust for institution:				
No entry required, only memorandum record in both the general ledger and the endowment funds subsidiary ledger.				
3. Entry to record receipt of gift of land for endowment purposes (journal voucher):				
Investments--real estate (at current market, or appraised, value)	10,000			
Endowment funds balances		10,000		
In investment ledger (journal voucher):				
Real estate account			10,000	
In endowment funds ledger (journal voucher):				
Principal account				10,000
4. Entry to record purchase of rental property as investment of a separately invested restricted endowment fund (check register):[8]				
Investments--real estate	8,000			
Cash		8,000		
In investment ledger (invoice):				
Real estate account			8,000	
5. Entry to record purchase of four bonds, face value $4,000, at 102, plus accrued interest of $60 for the investment pool (check register):				
Investments--securities	4,000			
Unamortized premiums on bonds	80			
Undistributed pool income	60			
Cash		4,140		

8. Entries involving vouchers payable are omitted for simplicity.

	General Ledger Dr.	General Ledger Cr.	Subsidiary Ledger Dr.	Subsidiary Ledger Cr.
In investment ledger:				
Bond account			4,080	
6. Entry to record purchase of three bonds, face value $3,000, at 102, plus accrued interest of $45 for a separately invested unrestricted endowment fund (check register):				
Investments--securities	3,000			
Unamortized premiums on bonds	60			
Income--control	45			
Cash		3,105		
In investment ledger (invoice):				
Bond account			3,060	
In endowment funds ledger (journal voucher):				
Income account for fund involved			45	
7. Entry to record purchase of two bonds, face value $2,000, at 102, plus accrued interest of $30 for a separately invested restricted endowment fund (check register):				
In endowment funds (check register):				
Investments--securities	2,000			
Unamortized premiums on bonds	40			
Income--control	30			
Cash		2,070		
In investment ledger (invoice):				
Bond account			2,040	
In endowment funds ledger (journal voucher):				
Income account for fund involved			30	
8. Entry to record purchase of five bonds, face value $5,000, at 98, plus accrued interest of $100 for the investment pool (check register):				
Investments--securities	5,000			
Undistributed pool income	100			
Cash		5,000		
Reserve for accumulation of bond discounts		100		
In investment ledger (invoice):				
Bond account			4,900	
If the bonds were purchased for a separately invested fund, the $100 of accrued interest would be debited to the income-control account rather than to the undistributed pool income account. Appropriate entries then would be made by journal voucher in the endowment funds subsidiary ledger by debiting the income account for the fund involved.				
9. Entry to record purchase of stocks for the investment pool (check register):				
Investments--securities	60,000			
Cash		60,000		
In investment ledger (invoice):				
Common stocks account			40,000	
Preferred stocks account			20,000	
10. Entry to record receipt of income from pooled investments (cash receipts journal):				
Cash	60,000			
Undistributed pool income		60,000		

	GENERAL LEDGER		SUBSIDIARY LEDGER	
	Dr.	Cr.	Dr.	Cr.
11. Entry to record receipt of income from investments of a separately invested endowment fund (cash receipts journal):				
Cash	5,000			
Income--control		5,000		
In endowment funds ledger (cash receipts journal):				
Income account for individual fund involved				5,000
12. Entry to record payment of expenses for management of investments in the investment pool (check register):				
Undistributed pool income	5,000			
Cash		5,000		
13. Entry to record annual depreciation charge on rental property--investment of a separately invested restricted endowment fund (journal voucher):				
Income--control	1,000			
Reserve for depreciation on real estate		1,000		
In endowment funds ledger (journal voucher):				
Income account for individual fund involved			1,000	
14. Entry to record amortization of premiums on bonds in the investment pool (journal voucher):				
Undistributed pool income	4			
Unamortized premiums on bonds		4		
In investment ledger (journal voucher):				
Bond account				4
15. Entry to record amortization of premiums on bonds of separately invested endowment funds (journal voucher):				
Income--control	6			
Unamortized premiums on bonds		6		
In endowment funds ledger (journal voucher):				
Income account for individual funds involved			6	
In investment ledger (journal voucher):				
Bond account				6
16. Entry to record sale of two bonds from investment pool at 103, plus accrued interest of $20 (cash receipts journal):				
Cash	2,080			
Investments--securities		2,000		
Net adjusted gains and losses		22		
Undistributed pool income		20		
Unamortized premium on bonds		38		
In investment ledger (cash receipts journal):				
Bond account				2,038
17. Entry to record distribution of net amount in undistributed pool income to participating funds (journal voucher):				
a. In endowment funds				
Undistributed pool income	54,856			
Cash		54,856		
b. In other fund groups				
Appropriate entries would be made in each fund group involved, debiting cash and crediting revenues, endowment income--unrestricted (for unrestricted current funds)--and the accounts for the balances or principal of other funds involved.				

	GENERAL LEDGER		SUBSIDIARY LEDGER	
	Dr.	Cr.	Dr.	Cr.
18. Entry to record distribution of net income from investments of separately invested endowment funds (journal voucher):				
a. In endowment funds				
Income--control	3,919			
Cash		3,919		
In endowment funds ledger:				
Income accounts for each fund which is separately invested and to which income has been credited as received, as in Entry 11, above.			3,919	
b. In other fund groups				
Appropriate entries would be made in each fund group involved as in Entry 17b, above.				
19. Entry to record sale of common stocks costing $5,000, at a profit of $100 (cash receipts journal):				
Cash	5,100			
Investments--securities		5,000		
Net adjusted gains and losses		100		
In investments ledger (cash receipts journal):				
Common stocks account				5,000
20. Entry to record sale of preferred stocks costing $5,000, at a loss of $500 (cash receipts journal):				
Cash	4,500			
Net adjusted gains and losses	500			
Investments--securities		5,000		
In investment ledger (cash receipts journal):				
Preferred stocks account				5,000
21. Entry to record transfer of unrestricted current funds for purpose of establishing a quasi-endowment fund (cash receipts journal):				
Cash	5,000			
Quasi-endowment funds balances		5,000		
In endowment funds ledger (cash receipts journal):				
Principal account				5,000
(In unrestricted current funds, debit transfers to endowment funds and credit cash.)				
22. Entry to record transfer of term endowment which, by passage of time, had become free of restrictions, to unexpended plant funds (cash receipts journal):				
Term endowment funds balances	20,000			
Cash		20,000		
In endowment funds ledger:				
Principal account			20,000	
(In unexpended plant funds, debit cash, credit unexpended plant funds balances.)				

C. General Ledger--Endowment Funds Section

Cash

	Beginning balance	100,000	Entry 4	Purchase of property	8,000
Entry 1	Gift received	22,000	Entry 5	Purchase of bonds	4,140
Entry 10	Pool income	60,000	Entry 6	Purchase of bonds	3,105
Entry 11	Income from separately invested funds	5,000	Entry 7	Purchase of bonds	2,070
			Entry 8	Purchase of bonds	5,000
Entry 16	Sale of bonds	2,080	Entry 9	Purchase of stocks	60,000
Entry 19	Sale of stocks	5,100	Entry 12	Investment management expenses	5,000
Entry 20	Sale of stocks	4,500			
Entry 21	Transfer from current funds	5,000	Entry 17	Transfer to other funds	54,856
			Entry 18	Transfer to other funds	3,919
			Entry 22	Transfer to plant funds	20,000
	(37,590)				

Investments--Securities

	Beginning balance	1,500,000	Entry 16	Sale of bonds	2,000
Entry 5	Bonds	4,000	Entry 19	Sale of stocks	5,000
Entry 6	Bonds, separate	3,000	Entry 20	Sale of stocks	5,000
Entry 7	Bonds, separate	2,000			
Entry 8	Bonds	5,000			
Entry 9	Stocks	60,000			
	(1,562,000)				

Investments--Real Estate

	Beginning balance	275,000			
Entry 3	Gift	10,000			
Entry 4	Rental property purchased	8,000			
	(293,000)				

Mortgages Payable on Real Estate

				Beginning balance	15,000

Reserve for Depreciation on Real Estate

				Beginning balance	25,000
			Entry 13	Depreciation	1,000
				(26,000)	

Unamortized Premiums on Bonds

Entry 5	Purchase of bonds	80	Entry 14	Amortization of premiums	4
Entry 5	Purchase of bonds	60	Entry 15	Amortization of premiums	6
Entry 7	Purchase of bonds	40	Entry 16	Sale of bonds	38
	(132)				

Endowment Funds Balances

				Beginning balance	1,525,000
			Entry 1	Gift	22,000
			Entry 3	Gift	10,000
				(1,557,000)	

Term Endowment Funds Balances

Entry 22	Transfer to plant funds	20,000		Beginning balance	100,000
				(80,000)	

Quasi-Endowment Funds Balances

				Beginning balance	175,000
			Entry 21	Transfer from current funds	5,000
				(180,000)	

Net Adjusted Gains and Losses

Entry 20	Sale of preferred stocks	500		Beginning balance	35,000
			Entry 16	Sale of bonds	22
			Entry 19	Sale of common stocks	100
				(34,622)	

Undistributed Pool Income

Entry 5	Accrued interest	60	Entry 10	Income	60,000
Entry 8	Accrued interest	100	Entry 16	Accrued interest on sale of bonds	20
Entry 12	Management expenses	5,000			
Entry 14	Amortization of premiums	4			
Entry 17	Distribution	54,856			
		60,020			60,020

Income--Control

Entry 6	Accrued interest	45	Entry 11	Income on separately invested fund	5,000
Entry 7	Accrued interest	30			
Entry 13	Depreciation on rental property	1,000			
Entry 15	Amortization of premiums	6			
Entry 18	Distribution	3,919			
		5,000			5,000

Reserve for Accumulation--Bond Discounts

			Entry 8	Purchase of bonds	100
				(100)	

D. Balance Sheet at End of Period

BLANK COLLEGE

Balance Sheet
(End of Period)

ASSETS		LIABILITIES AND FUND BALANCES	
ENDOWMENT AND SIMILAR FUNDS:		ENDOWMENT AND SIMILAR FUNDS:	
Cash	37,590	Mortgages payable on real estate	15,000
Investments--securities	1,562,000	Reserve for accumulation of bond discounts	100
Investments--real estate (less reserve for depreciation)	267,000	Fund balances:	
Unamortized premiums (funds held in trust by others--$105,000)	132	Endowment funds	1,557,000
		Term endowment funds	80,000
		Quasi-endowment funds	180,000
		Net adjusted gains and losses	34,622
Total endowment and similar funds	1,866,722	Total endowment and similar funds	1,866,722

E. Statement of Changes in Fund Balances
Endowment and Similar Funds
For the Year Ended 19__

	Total	Endowment Funds	Term Endowment Funds	Quasi-Endowment Funds	Net Adjusted Gains and Losses
Balances, beginning of year	1,835,000	1,525,000	100,000	175,000	35,000
Additions:					
Gifts	32,000	32,000			
Transfers from current funds	5,000			5,000	
	37,000	32,000		5,000	
Deductions:					
Expiration of term endowment	20,000		20,000		
Net losses on sales of securities	378				378
	20,378				
Balances, end of year	1,851,622	1,557,000	80,000	180,000	34,622

ACCOUNTING FOR ANNUITY AND LIFE INCOME FUNDS

A. Balance Sheet at Beginning of Period

BLANK COLLEGE

Balance Sheet
(Beginning of Period)

ASSETS		LIABILITIES AND FUND BALANCES	
ANNUITY AND LIFE INCOME FUNDS:		ANNUITY AND LIFE INCOME FUNDS:	
Cash	5,000	Annuities payable	20,000
Investments--securities	100,000	Undistributed income--life income funds	2,000
		Undistributed income--annuity funds	1,000
		Annuity funds balances	5,000
		Life income funds balances	77,000
Total annuity and life income funds	105,000	Total annuity and life income funds	105,000

B. Recording of Typical Transactions

	GENERAL LEDGER		SUBSIDIARY LEDGER	
	Dr.	Cr.	Dr.	Cr.
1. Entry to record receipt of $5,000 as gift subject to annuity agreement (cash receipts journal):				
Cash	5,000			
Annuities payable		4,500		
Annuity funds balances		500		
In annuity and life income funds ledger (cash receipts):				
Principal account				500
2. Entry to record investment of annuity funds in securities:				
Investments--securities	6,000			
Cash		6,000		
In investment ledger (invoices):				
Securities account			6,000	
3. Entry to record receipt of life income fund (cash receipts journal):				
Cash	10,000			
Life income funds balances		10,000		
In annuity and life income funds ledger (cash receipts):				
Principal account				10,000
4. Entry to record receipt of income on investments of annuity funds (cash receipts journal):				
Cash	1,250			
Undistributed income--annuity funds		1,250		
5. Entry to record payment to beneficiaries of annuity funds (check register):				
Undistributed income--annuity funds	1,150			
Annuities payable		1,150		
Annuities payable	1,150			
Cash		1,150		
6. Entry to record receipt of income on investments of life income funds (cash receipts journal):				
Cash	4,000			
Undistributed income--life income funds		4,000		
7. Entry to record payment to beneficiaries of life income funds (check register):				
Undistributed income--life income funds	3,800			
Cash		3,800		
8. Entry to record termination of life income fund upon death of beneficiary. Fund is unrestricted as to use. Trustees transfer to quasi-endowment funds (check register):				
Life income funds balances	3,000			
Cash		3,000		
In subsidiary annuity and life income funds ledger (invoice):				
Principal account			3,000	
(In endowment and similar funds group, debit cash and credit quasi-endowment funds balances.)				
9. Entry at end of year to actuarially adjust annuities payable (journal voucher):				
Annuities payable	100			
Annuities funds balances		100		
In subsidiary annuity and life income funds ledger:				
Principal account				100

C. General Ledger--Annuity and Life Income Funds

Cash

Beginning balance	5,000	Entry 2 Purchase of securities	6,000
Entry 1 Receipt of annuity	5,000	Entry 5 Payment to beneficiaries	1,150
Entry 3 Receipt of life income fund	10,000	Entry 7 Payment to beneficiaries	3,800
Entry 4 Receipt of income	1,250	Entry 8 Transfer to endowment	3,000
Entry 6 Receipt of income	4,000		
(11,300)			

Investments--Securities

Beginning balance	100,000		
Entry 2 Purchases	6,000		
(106,000)			

Annuities Payable

Entry 5 Payment to beneficiaries	1,150	Beginning balance	20,000
Entry 9 Actuarial adjustment	100	Entry 1 Receipt of gift	4,500
		Entry 5 Distribution of income	1,150
		(24,400)	

Undistributed Income--Annuity Funds

Entry 5 Payment to beneficiaries	1,150	Beginning balance	1,000
		Entry 4 Receipt of income	1,250
		(1,100)	

Undistributed Income--Life Income Funds

Entry 7 Payment to beneficiaries	3,800	Beginning balance	2,000
		Entry 6 Receipt of income	4,000
		(2,200)	

Annuity Funds Balances

		Beginning balance	5,000
		Entry 1 Receipt of annuity	500
		Entry 9 Actuarial adjustment	100
		(5,600)	

Life Income Funds Balances

Entry 8 Transfer to endowment	3,000	Beginning balance	77,000
		Entry 3 Receipt of life income fund	10,000
		(84,000)	

D. Balance Sheet at End of Period

BLANK COLLEGE

Balance Sheet
(End of Period)

ASSETS		LIABILITIES AND FUND BALANCES	
ANNUITY AND LIFE INCOME FUNDS:		ANNUITY AND LIFE INCOME FUNDS:	
Cash	11,300	Annuities payable	24,400
Investments--securities	106,000	Undistributed income--life income funds	2,200
		Undistributed income--annuity funds	1,100
		Life income funds balances	84,000
		Annuity funds balances	5,600
Total annuity and life income funds	117,300	Total annuity and life income funds	117,300

E. Statement of Changes in Fund Balances

BLANK COLLEGE

Statement of Changes in Fund Balances
Annuity and Life Income Funds
For the Year Ended 19__

	Total	Annuity Funds	Life Income Funds
Balances, beginning of year	82,000	5,000	77,000
Additions:			
Gifts	10,500	500	10,000
Actuarial adjustment	100	100	
	10,600	600	10,000
Deductions:			
Transfers to endowment upon death of beneficiary	3,000		3,000
Balances, end of year	89,600	5,600	84,000

11

Accounting for Loan and Agency Funds

Loan Funds. Loan funds are those funds available for loans to students, faculty, and staff. They are established primarily for the purpose of aiding needy students. Loan funds may be provided by unrestricted current funds, gifts and bequests, endowment income, governmental grants, and, on occasion, by student contributions or fees. Loan funds arising from these sources generally are operated on a revolving fund basis, with repayments of loans and interest payments, if any, remaining in the loan funds group for lending to other students. Frequently, gifts to an institution are made under terms which provide that only the income from the investments of the original gift may be used as loan funds. In such cases, the income from the investments is classified in the loan funds group, and the principal of the gift is accounted for in the endowment and similar funds group. The identity of each loan fund must be shown clearly in the accounting records at all times.

If loan funds are temporarily invested, income from the investments should be credited to the principal of the funds so invested. Any realized gains and losses on the sale of the investments should be added to or deducted from the principal of the funds involved.

The ledgers used in accounting for loan funds are the general ledger, the subsidiary notes and interest receivable ledger (Form 11.1), and the subsidiary loan funds ledger (Form 11.2). In addition to the three ledgers, a vouchers payable register and a check register for the loan funds should be used. No separate cash receipts journal is needed for loan funds, as the cash receipts journal (Form 7.10) used for recording current and other funds receipts should be used for loan fund receipts. In this connection, it should be noted that many institutions handle the transactions of the loan funds through the current funds journals, registers, ledgers, and

FORM 11.1

BLANK COLLEGE

NOTES AND INTEREST RECEIVABLE LEDGER

Name ______ Fund ______

Address ______ Date of Note ______ Number of Note ______

Maturity of Note ______

Date	Reference	Interest		Notes Receivable		Balance	
		Debit	Credit	Debit	Credit	Interest	Note

FORM 11.2

BLANK COLLEGE

LOAN FUNDS LEDGER

______
Name of Fund

Date	Explanation	Cash			Notes Receivable			Principal		
		Debit	Credit	Balance	Debit	Credit	Balance	Debit	Credit	Balance

the use of the due to and due from accounts in both the current funds and the loan funds groups.

The accounts usually found in the loans funds section of the general ledger include the following:

ASSET ACCOUNTS
Cash
Due from other funds
Notes receivable
Interest receivable
Investments
Allowance for doubtful loans (credit balance account)

LIABILITY AND FUNDS BALANCES ACCOUNTS
Due to other funds
National Direct Student Loan fund—repayable to government
National Direct Student Loan fund—institutional share
Loan funds balances

If an institution possesses more than one loan fund, the accounts should be maintained in a manner that will segregate between funds the information pertaining to cash, notes receivable, investments, income and expenditures, and balances. Unless prohibited by the terms of the gifts or other instrument under which the loan funds arise, the assets of the funds may be pooled for lending purposes as well as for investment purposes. However, the principal of each loan fund must be identifiable in the accounting records.

The notes receivable account in the general ledger is the control account for the notes receivable columns in the subsidiary notes and interest receivable ledger. The interest receivable account in the general ledger is used only if interest is accrued on the notes receivable when it becomes due. If interest is not accrued, the interest receivable account will not be used.

Interest on loan fund notes receivable should be credited directly to the principal of the funds involved. Expenses for administration of the loan funds and other operating costs should also be charged directly to the principal of the funds involved. The degree of detailing in the accounts will be governed by the number and size of the funds in this group and the administrative needs with respect to day-by-day controls and periodic financial reporting. The income and expenditures of loan funds do not affect the current funds operations; therefore, the accounts for recording the transactions of loan funds should not be mingled with the revenue and expenditure accounts pertaining to current funds.

The accounting records should show separately the balances of governmental advances for loan funds, institutional contributions required to supplement such advances, other refundable loan funds, and funds available for loans to faculty and staff. In the event a governing board designates funds of other groups to function temporarily as loan funds, these should be identified separately because the board may choose, at some future time, to transfer the funds to other fund groups or return them to the groups from which they were temporarily transferred.

Some institutions set aside out of loan funds income an allowance to cover possible losses from uncollectible loans. If this procedure is followed, the allowance should be shown as an account carrying a credit balance but reported as a deduction from the notes receivable account on the asset side of the balance sheet.

Following is an illustration of the accounting entries for loan funds. A beginning balance sheet, transactions during the fiscal year, a final balance sheet, and a statement of changes in fund balances are presented.

ACCOUNTING FOR LOAN FUNDS

A. Balance Sheet at Beginning of Period

BLANK COLLEGE

Balance Sheet
(Beginning of Period)

ASSETS		LIABILITIES AND FUND BALANCES	
LOAN FUNDS:		LOAN FUNDS:	
Cash	25,000	National Direct Student Loan fund--repayable to federal government	550,000
Notes receivable	700,000	National Direct Student Loan fund--institutional share	61,000
Investments	30,000	Interest on National Direct Student Loans	19,000
		Loan funds balances	125,000
Total loan funds	755,000	Total loan funds	755,000

B. Recording of Typical Transactions

	GENERAL LEDGER Dr.	GENERAL LEDGER Cr.	SUBSIDIARY LEDGER Dr.	SUBSIDIARY LEDGER Cr.
1. Entry to record receipt of gift to create new loan fund (cash receipts journal):				
Cash	10,000			
Loan funds balances		10,000		
Loan funds ledger (cash receipts):				
Individual loan funds accounts				10,000

	GENERAL LEDGER Dr.	GENERAL LEDGER Cr.	SUBSIDIARY LEDGER Dr.	SUBSIDIARY LEDGER Cr.
2. Entry to record granting of loans other than N.D.S.L. loans (check register):				
Notes receivable	10,000			
Cash		10,000		
In notes and interest receivable ledger (vouchers):				
Individual accounts			10,000	
3. Entry to record receipt of interest of temporary investments (cash receipts journal):				
Cash	1,000			
Loan funds balances		1,000		
In loan funds ledger (cash receipts):				
Individual loan funds accounts				1,000
4. Entry to record collection of notes plus interest (cash receipts journal):				
Cash	5,150			
Notes receivable		5,000		
Loan funds balances		150		
In loan funds ledger (cash receipts):				
Individual loan funds accounts				150
In notes and interest receivable ledger (cash receipts):				
Individual accounts				5,000
5. Entry to record expenses of administration (check register):				
Loan funds balances	8,000			
Cash		8,000		
In loan funds ledger (vouchers):				
Individual loan funds accounts			8,000	
6. Entry to record writing off uncollectible notes (journal voucher):				
Loan funds balances	1,000			
Notes receivable		1,000		
In loan funds ledger (journal voucher):				
Individual loan funds accounts			1,000	
7. Entry to record receipt of funds from U.S. government for N.D.S.L. loans (cash receipts):				
Cash	100,000			
National Direct Student Loan funds--repayable to U.S. government		100,000		
8. Entry to record transfer of institutional contribution to N.D.S.L. funds (cash receipts):				
Cash	11,000			
National Direct Student Loan funds--institutional share		11,000		
(In unrestricted current funds, debit transfers to loan funds and credit cash.)				
9. Entry to record granting of N.D.S.L. loans (check register):				
Notes receivable	70,000			
Cash		70,000		
In notes and interest receivable ledger (vouchers):				
Individual accounts			70,000	

	General Ledger Dr.	General Ledger Cr.	Subsidiary Ledger Dr.	Subsidiary Ledger Cr.
10. Entry to record repayments of N.D.S.L. loans (cash receipts):				
Cash	10,200			
Notes receivable		10,000		
Interest on National Direct Student Loans		200		
In notes and interest receivable ledger (cash receipts):				
Individual accounts				10,000
(Note: Interest received on National Direct Student Loans is accumulated and is considered as cash on hand in subsequent funds applications to the U.S. government.)				
11. Entry to write off National Direct Student Loan receivable due to death of student borrower (journal voucher):				
National Direct Student Loans funds--repayable to U.S. government	765			
National Direct Student Loans funds--institutional share	85			
Notes receivable		850		
In notes and interest receivable ledger (journal voucher):				
Individual account				850

C. General Ledger--Loan Funds Section

Cash

	Beginning balance	25,000	Entry 2	Granting of loans	10,000
Entry 1	Gift	10,000	Entry 5	Expenses	8,000
Entry 3	Interest on investments	1,000	Entry 9	Granting of loans	70,000
Entry 4	Collection of notes	5,150			
Entry 7	Receipt of N.D.S.L. funds	100,000			
Entry 8	Receipt of institutional share	11,000			
Entry 10	Collection of notes	10,200			
	(74,350)				

Notes Receivable

	Beginning balance	700,000	Entry 4	Collection of notes	5,000
Entry 2	Granting of loans	10,000	Entry 6	Notes written off	1,000
Entry 9	Granting of loans	70,000	Entry 10	Collection of notes	10,000
			Entry 11	Notes written off	850
	(763,150)				

Investments

	Beginning balance	30,000			
	(30,000)				

National Direct Student Loan Fund--Repayable to Federal Government

Entry 11	Notes written off	765		Beginning balance	550,000
			Entry 7	Receipt of funds	100,000
				(649,235)	

National Direct Student Loan Fund--Institutional Share

Entry 11 Notes written off	85	Beginning balance	61,000
		Entry 8 Transfer from current funds	11,000
		(71,915)	

Interest on National Direct Student Loan Funds

		Beginning balance	19,000
		Entry 10 Collection of interest	200
		(19,200)	

Loan Funds Balances

Entry 5 Expenses	8,000	Beginning balance	125,000
Entry 6 Notes written off	1,000	Entry 1 Gift	10,000
		Entry 3 Interest on investments	1,000
		Entry 4 Interest on loans	150
		(127,150)	

D. Balance Sheet--End of Period

BLANK COLLEGE

Balance Sheet
(End of Period)

ASSETS		LIABILITIES AND LOAN FUNDS	
LOAN FUNDS:		LOAN FUNDS:	
Cash	74,350	National Direct Student Loan fund--repayable to federal government	649,235
Notes receivable	763,150	National Direct Student Loan fund--institutional share	71,915
Investments	30,000	Interest on National Direct Student Loan fund	19,200
		Loan funds balances	127,150
Total loan funds	867,500	Total loan funds	867,500

E. Statement of Changes in Fund Balances

BLANK COLLEGE

Statement of Changes in Fund Balances--Loan Funds
(End of Period)

Balance, beginning of period		755,000
Additions:		
Federal grant		100,000
Gifts		10,000
Interest income		350
Investment income		1,000
Transfers from current fund		11,000
		122,350
Deductions:		
Uncollectible notes charged off		1,850
Expenses		8,000
		9,850
Balances, end of period		
U.S. government grants, refundable	649,235	
Interest on N.D.S.L. funds	19,200	
Institutional loan funds:		
Established by donors	127,150	
Established by governing board	71,915	867,500

Agency Funds. Agency funds are those funds in the possession of an institution for which it is custodian or fiscal agent but not owner. They are funds deposited with the institution for safekeeping, to be used or withdrawn by the depositor at will, the institution exercising no control over such withdrawals. The typical example of agency funds is deposits by students and student organizations. Receipts and disbursements of agency funds should not be included in current funds operating statements, for they do not constitute current funds revenues and expenditures.

The ledgers used in accounting for agency funds are the general ledger and the subsidiary deposit ledger, the latter containing an individual account with each depositor. The journals employed include the vouchers payable register and the check register. Cash receipts are entered in the cash receipts journal used for current and other funds.

Accounting for these funds is not complicated. When funds are deposited, they are posted to the credit of the individual depositor. Form 11.3 is a type of deposit ledger card. When funds are withdrawn in accordance with specified rules and regulations, the individual withdrawing the fund is required to sign a withdrawal slip (Form 11.4). Later, this slip is used to charge the appropriate account in the deposit ledger. Many colleges employ mechanical cash registers that automatically post the deposit ledger and simultaneously produce a copy for the student or organization to use as a bank record.

FORM 11.3

BLANK COLLEGE

AGENCY FUNDS DEPOSIT LEDGER

Name____

Address______________________________________

Date	Description	Ref.	Charges	Credits	Balance

FORM 11.4

BLANK COLLEGE — No. 1

A G E N C Y   F U N D S   W I T H D R A W A L   S L I P

Date________________

Charge Account of____________________________
Name of Depositor

____________________________ $__________

For Withdrawal of Funds

____
Signature of Depositor

An account in the general ledger, deposit liabilities, is the control account for all the accounts in the subsidiary deposit ledger. The subsidiary ledger should be balanced monthly with the general ledger control account.

The general ledger accounts needed to record agency fund transactions are the following:

ASSETS
Cash
Due from other funds
Investments (if authorized by the depositor)

LIABILITIES
Due to other funds
Deposit liabilities

If agency funds assets are immaterial in amount, the assets and liabilities may be reported as assets and liabilities of the current funds group and need not be accounted for in a separate fund group.

The following is an illustration of the accounting for agency funds. A beginning balance sheet, transactions during the fiscal year, and a final balance sheet are shown. Since the balances in each agency fund are liabilities, not fund balances, a statement of changes in fund balances is not appropriate for this group.

ACCOUNTING FOR AGENCY FUNDS

A. Balance Sheet at Beginning of Period

BLANK COLLEGE

Balance Sheet
(Beginning of Period)

ASSETS		LIABILITIES	
AGENCY FUNDS:		AGENCY FUNDS:	
Cash	20,000	Deposit liabilities	20,000
		Subsidiary funds:	
		Student deposits	15,000
		Organization deposits	5,000
			20,000

B. Recording of Typical Transactions

	General Ledger Dr.	General Ledger Cr.	Subsidiary Ledger Dr.	Subsidiary Ledger Cr.
1. Entry to record receipt of deposits (cash receipts journal):				
Cash	10,000			
Deposit liabilities		10,000		
In deposit ledger (cash receipts):				
Student deposits accounts				9,000
Organization deposits accounts				1,000
2. Entry to record breakage deposits collected at beginning of year (cash receipts journal):				
Cash	2,000			
Deposit liabilities		2,000		
In deposit ledger (cash receipts):				
Breakage deposit accounts				2,000
3. Entry to record refund of breakage deposits at end of year (check register):				
Deposit liabilities	1,800			
Cash		1,800		
In deposit ledger (vouchers):				
Breakage deposit accounts			1,800	
4. Entry to record transfer of balances of breakage deposits, representing breakage charges, to general current funds (check register):				
Deposit liabilities	200			
Cash		200		
In deposit ledger:				
Breakage deposit accounts			200	
(In unrestricted current funds debit cash and credit miscellaneous income or appropriation expenditures.)				
5. Entry to record withdrawal of deposits (check register):				
Deposit liabilities	12,000			
Cash		12,000		
In deposit ledger (withdrawal slips):				
Student deposits accounts			10,000	
Organization deposits accounts			2,000	

C. General Ledger--Agency Funds Section

Cash

	Beginning balance	20,000	Entry 3	Refund of breakage deposits	1,800
Entry 1	Deposits	10,000	Entry 4	Transfer to general current funds	200
Entry 2	Breakage deposits	2,000	Entry 5	Withdrawal of deposits	12,000
	(18,000)				

Deposit Liabilities

Entry 3	Refund of breakage deposits	1,800		Beginning balance	20,000
Entry 4	Transfer to general funds	200	Entry 1	Deposits	10,000
Entry 5	Withdrawal of deposits	12,000	Entry 2	Breakage deposits	2,000
				(18,000)	

D. Balance Sheet at End of Period

BLANK COLLEGE

Balance Sheet
(End of Period)

ASSETS		LIABILITIES	
AGENCY FUNDS:		AGENCY FUNDS:	
Cash	18,000	Deposit liabilities	18,000

12

Accounting for Plant Funds

PLANT FUNDS CONSIST of those funds to be used for acquisition, rehabilitation, and construction of physical properties for institutional purposes; funds set up and available for renewals and replacements; funds accumulated and available for debt retirement; and funds previously expended for plant properties, and their associated liabilities. The plant funds section of the balance sheet is divided into four self-balancing subgroups as follows:

Unexpended Plant Funds. Funds available for the acquisition of long-lived assets for institutional purposes.

Funds for Renewals and Replacements. Funds set aside for the renewal and replacement of institutional properties.

Funds for the Retirement of Indebtedness. Funds set aside for debt service charges and for the retirement of indebtedness on institutional plant.

Investment in Plant. Funds reflecting the cost (or fair value at time of donation) of long-lived assets (other than those of endowment and similar funds) and the sources from which the cost is funded, including associated liabilities.

An institution may, at its option, consolidate the plant funds group into two major subsections—unexpended plant funds and investment in plant. In such cases, retirement of indebtedness and renewals and replacement funds are carried as equity accounts in the unexpended plant funds subgroup. The problems involved in accounting for the four types of plant funds are discussed in this chapter.

Unexpended Plant Funds. The routine of accounting for the transactions of unexpended plant funds is no different from that relating to current funds. The same requisition forms, purchase orders, and invoices are used; and documents are prepared in the same manner, except that they are identified as unexpended plant funds or are coded appropriately. These documents are recorded in a separate set of journals, including a cash receipts journal, a voucher register, an orders placed and liquidated journal, a check register, and a general journal. In addition, a subsidiary ledger account is maintained for each unexpended plant fund. The regular allocations ledger form, with some adaptation, is suitable for this purpose.

Additions to unexpended plant funds include gifts designated for plant use, governmental appropriations, proceeds from bond issues and other forms of financing, and income from and net realized gains on the sale of the temporary investments of funds belonging to this group. Deductions include disbursements for plant facilities and net realized losses on the sale of temporary investments. Encumbrances which are outstanding as of the reporting date may be reported as an allocation of fund balances. An alternative is to footnote the balance sheet. Following are the accounts customarily used in accounting for unexpended plant funds:

ASSETS
Cash
Investments
Accounts receivable
Due from other funds
State appropriations receivable
Construction in progress

LIABILITIES AND FUND BALANCES
Vouchers payable
Notes payable
Bonds payable
Mortgages payable
Due to other funds
Unexpended plant funds balances—restricted
Unexpended plant funds balances—unrestricted

The state appropriations receivable account represents balances due to a college or university from capital outlay appropriations made by a state legislature. Accounting for the state appropriation varies in accordance with the fiscal system of the state. Funds for building purposes in some states are sent to the institution for deposit and disbursement. In other states, the funds remain in the state treasury to the credit of the institution and are subject to withdrawal upon submission of audited vouchers or warrants of the institution. The following entry is made on the institution's records in the unexpended plant funds group to record the state appropriation for buildings or plant expansion:

State appropriations receivable
  Unexpended plant funds balances

If funds are sent to the college for deposit, the following entry is made:

Cash
  State appropriations receivable

If funds are retained in the state treasury, the following entries are made when such funds are used:

1. Upon the approval of a voucher or warrant for the payment of expenditures related to a building project

   Construction in progress
     State appropriations receivable

2. To transfer the value of the construction at the end of the fiscal period to the investment in plant section

   Unexpended plant funds balances
     Construction in progress

Unexpended plant funds balances is a control account representing the sum of the individual funds being held for purposes of financing plant additions. If an institution possesses only a few individual plant funds, separate accounts may be set up in the general ledger for each fund. If separate funds for plant additions are numerous, however, a subsidiary ledger for unexpended plant funds should be maintained. The regular allocations ledger form, illustrated on page 101, herein, will serve in this connection. Because the budget is not ordinarily posted to the accounts in the case of unexpended plant funds, the column in the allocations ledger headed allocations and other credits is used to record receipts instead of departmental budget allocations. The free balance column of the ledger form shows the unencumbered cash balance of each fund. The unexpended plant funds balances account will control all columns in the subsidiary ledger. Encumbering or charging purchase orders in the records is optional. If purchase orders are recorded, the usual procedure of encumbrance and liquidation is followed.

The entries to account for transactions pertaining to the expenditure of unexpended plant funds are as follows:

1. To record expenditure of funds for a building project in process of construction during the year

   Construction in progress
      Cash

2. To transfer the value of the construction at the end of the year to the investment in plant section

   Unexpended plant funds balances—restricted
      Construction in progress

3. To record the expenditure of funds for a plant asset item through outright purchase, or other transaction, which is completed within the fiscal period

   Unexpended plant funds balances—restricted
      Cash

Funds for Renewals and Replacements. According to *College and University Business Administration*, "the resources of this subgroup provide for the renewal and replacement of plant assets as distinguished from additions and improvement to plant. In some instances, there is a fine line of distinction between a renewal or replacement and an improvement. Some portions of renewals and replacements may be capitalized as additions to plant."[1] Accounting for depreciation on property used for institutional purposes is discussed in Chapter 13. Periodically, it is desirable, when permitted by applicable state law, to set aside portions of unrestricted current funds revenues for the renewal or replacement of physical properties. Bond issues on residence halls and other revenue-producing structures usually require that such reserves be created out of current revenues. The allocation of unrestricted current funds revenues for plant renewals on property used in the educational program is recorded as a mandatory transfer as follows:

1. *College and University Business Administration* (3rd Rev. ed.; Washington, D.C.: American Council on Education, 1974), 198.

IN UNRESTRICTED CURRENT FUNDS

Transfer to funds for renewals and replacements—restricted
    Cash

IN FUNDS FOR RENEWALS AND REPLACEMENTS—RESTRICTED

Cash
    Renewals and replacements funds balances—restricted
    (Separate subsidiary accounts established as required)

In current funds, the allocation is reported in the transfers section of the statement of current funds revenues, expenditures, and other changes.

To set up replacement reserves for auxiliary enterprise plant, charges are made annually against the operations of the respective auxiliary enterprises and are entered as transfers. In addition, there should be a transfer of cash from unrestricted current funds to funds for renewals and replacements. As they occur, actual replacements and renewals, including equipment and major repairs, should be charged against the funds thus created.

The entries to account for transactions pertaining to funds for renewals and replacements on auxiliary enterprise plant are as follows:

1. To record transfer of cash from unrestricted current funds to funds for renewals and replacements:
    a. In unrestricted current funds:
        Transfer to funds for renewals and replacements
            Cash
        In subsidiary allocations ledger:
        Debit expenditure accounts of appropriate auxiliary enterprises.
    b. In funds for renewals and replacements:
        Cash
            Renewals and replacements funds balances—restricted
2. To record expenditures for renewals and replacements:
    In funds for renewals and replacements:
    Renewals and replacements funds balances—restricted
        Cash

The accounts of replacement funds should be kept in such a manner that the balance applicable to each enterprise or activity is shown or can be determined. This recommendation can be carried out either by coding entries in the renewals and replacements funds balances account or, preferably, by using subsidiary accounts for each of the activities such as residence halls, cafeterias, and educational plant.

Costs of ordinary recurring repairs to buildings and equipment should be considered current expenses and paid out of current funds, but disbursements for extraordinary repairs, replacements, and renewals should not be reported as current expense. Disbursements of this nature should be made out of funds for renewals and replacements and reported as part of the transactions of that fund group.

The following accounts are used in recording the transactions of funds for renewals and replacements:

ASSETS
Cash
Investments
Deposits with others
Due from other funds
Construction in progress

LIABILITIES AND FUND BALANCES
Vouchers payable
Notes payable
Due to other funds
Renewals and replacements funds balances—restricted
Renewals and replacements funds balances—unrestricted

Funds for Retirement of Indebtedness. This subdivision of plant funds is used to record transactions pertaining to the payment of interest and the retirement of bonds, mortgages, or other forms of indebtedness on the plant assets used for institutional purposes. It does not apply to indebtedness on real estate properties which are the investment of endowment and similar funds. The retirement of indebtedness funds balances account is credited with funds received for the appropriate purpose and is charged with disbursements resulting in payment of interest and the retirement of debts. Transfers from unrestricted current funds, income realized on the temporary investments of the retirement funds, governmental appropriations, and special student fees are the usual sources of funds for debt retirement. Even in the case of serial bonds, in which it is not necessary to accumulate sinking funds, a transfer should be made from current funds to funds for retirement of indebtedness; and the payment of all debt service expenses should be recorded in the latter fund group. Entries in the fund balances account should differentiate between principal repayments and interest charges, since payments on the principal of the indebtedness must be reflected as adjustments in the net investment in plant account. Separate fund balance accounts must be maintained in order to distinguish between board-designated transactions and those restricted by donor agreements or other legal provisions.

Transfers from current funds to plant funds for covering debt service on bonds or mortgages acquired to finance construction of educational plant are recorded as follows:

IN UNRESTRICTED CURRENT FUNDS:

Transfers to funds for retirement of indebtedness—restricted
  Cash

IN FUNDS FOR RETIREMENT OF INDEBTEDNESS:

Cash
  Retirement of indebtedness funds balances—restricted
  (Separate subsidiary accounts established as required)

The following accounts are used in recording the transactions of funds for retirement of indebtedness:

ASSETS

Cash
Investments
Deposited with others
Accounts receivable
Due from other funds

LIABILITIES AND FUND BALANCES

Vouchers payable
Due to other funds
Retirement of indebtedness funds balances—restricted
Retirement of indebtedness funds balances—unrestricted

Investment in Plant. With the exception of long-lived assets held as investments in the endowment and similar funds and related liabilities, the investment in plant section of plant funds is used to account for fixed assets owned by the institution and used for institutional purposes including land, buildings, improvements other than buildings, and equipment. Additions to plant may be acquired and financed directly through unexpended plant funds or through current funds. In addition, they may be financed indirectly through current funds by transfer from those funds to unexpended plant funds. All items of physical plant owned by the institution are reported in the investment in plant section of the balance sheet. Real property that is the investment of endowment and similar funds is not included here. "Depreciation allowances on long-lived assets may be reported in the balance sheet and provision for depreciation in the statement of changes in fund balances in the Invested in Plant subgroup."[2]

The following general ledger accounts are found in the investment in plant section of plant funds:

ASSETS
Land
Buildings
Improvements other than buildings
Equipment
Library books
Due from other funds
Construction in progress

LIABILITIES AND FUND BALANCES
Vouchers payable
Notes payable
Mortgages payable
Bonds payable
Due to other funds
Net investment in plant

The construction in progress account, which may be carried either in the investment in plant section or as part of unexpended plant funds, is used to accumulate costs of construction while a project is under construction. As soon as construction is completed, this account is closed into a permanent property account, *i.e.*, buildings, or improvements other than buildings. As an alternative, it may be closed at the end of each fiscal year.

2. *Ibid.*, 199.

The other asset accounts represent the permanent property of the institution. They are control accounts, each controlling a section of the subsidiary plant ledger and containing a detailed record of individual items of plant such as parcels of land, individual buildings, and items of equipment. A complete discussion of the perpetual inventory system for fixed assets is found in Chapter 13.

The net investment in plant account represents the total equity of the institution in its physical plant assets. The assets should be valued at cost. If there are no bonds, mortgages, or notes outstanding, the total of the asset accounts for land, buildings, improvements, and equipment will equal the net investment in plant account. However, if the college has outstanding bonds, mortgages payable, or notes, the net investment in plant account will be less than the total of the assets by the amount of the outstanding debts. As the obligations are retired, the net investment in plant will increase to the point of equaling the value of the assets when all obligations have been liquidated. The net investment in plant account should be set up so as to provide information concerning the source of the funds invested in plant, which may be from state appropriations, from current funds, or from gifts. This end may be accomplished through the use of code symbols.

As stated before, all fixed assets owned by the college, except those held as a part of endowment funds investments, should be included in the investment in plant section of plant funds, regardless of the source of the funds or the manner in which the assets were acquired. Long-lived property is acquired in the following ways: (1) direct purchase out of current funds, (2) transfer of funds from current to unexpended plant funds, (3) direct purchase out of unexpended plant funds, (4) issuance of bonds, (5) purchase out of funds for renewals and replacements, and (6) gifts.

Equipment is usually purchased directly out of current funds. In making allocations to departments, equipment frequently is considered as a separate budget section coordinate with personnel compensation and supplies and expense. Periodically, usually once a year, the expenditures for equipment made from current funds should be brought into the investment in plant section of plant funds. Illustrative entries to account for equipment purchases are as follows:

1. To record purchase of equipment out of current funds:
   In unrestricted current funds:

   Expenditures
       Cash

   In the subsidiary allocations ledger, debit departmental accounts.

2. To record capitalization of equipment expenditures:
   In investment in plant funds:

   Equipment
       Net investment in plant

When current funds are used to finance additions to plant other than equipment, the correct procedure is to transfer cash to unexpended plant funds, from which the actual disbursement is made. The transfer of funds is recorded in unrestricted current funds and appears in the transfers section of the statement of current funds revenues, expenditures, and other changes. Expenditures for plant additions made from unexpended plant funds are capitalized by entry in the investment in plant section. The entries to account for these transactions are as follows:

1. Entries to record transfer of funds from unrestricted current to unexpended plant funds:
   a. In unrestricted current funds:
      Transfers to unexpended plant funds—restricted
          Cash
   b. In unexpended plant funds:

      Cash
          Unexpended plant funds balances—restricted

2. Entry to record the expenditure of funds for the construction of a building:
   In unexpended plant funds:

   Construction in progress
       Cash

3. Entries to record the transfer of the value of the building at the end of the fiscal period or upon completion of the project to the investment in plant section:
   a. In unexpended plant funds:

      Unexpended plant funds balances—restricted
          Construction in progress
   b. In investment in plant funds:

      Buildings
          Net investment in plant

If the expenditures were for the purchase of a building or other plant asset, and all the financial matters were completed within the fiscal period, the entries would be—

a. In unexpended plant funds:
   Unexpended plant funds balances—restricted
      Cash
b. In investment in plant funds:
   Buildings
      Net investment in plant

Bonds are sometimes issued to finance additions to plant. Frequently, so-called revenue bonds are sold to finance the purchase or construction of auxiliary plant; the bonds are to be retired out of the earnings of the auxiliary enterprise. The proceeds of the bond issue are accounted for through unexpended plant funds, as is the actual expenditure for the property being constructed or otherwise acquired. During the process of construction, the bond liability is carried temporarily in unexpended plant funds and is transferred periodically to investment in plant as the construction proceeds.

The entries to show the acquisition of plant funds from a bond issue, the expenditure of such funds for the construction of a building, the capitalization of the value of the building, the recording of the indebtedness, and the retirement of bonds are as follows:

1. Entry to record the receipt of proceeds from a bond issue:
   In unexpended plant funds:
   Cash
      Bonds payable
2. Entry to record payments to contractors:
   In unexpended plant funds:
   Construction in progress
      Cash
3. Entries to record the capitalization of construction in process:
   a. In unexpended plant funds:
      Bonds payable (for amount of construction accomplished during the year)
         Construction in progress
   b. In investment in plant funds:
      Construction in progress
         Bonds payable

4. Entry to record completion of project:
   In investment in plant funds:
   Buildings
   Construction in progress
5. Entries to record retirement of the bonds:
   a. In funds for retirement of indebtedness:
      Retirement of indebtedness funds balances—restricted
      Cash
   b. In investment in plant funds:
      Bonds payable
      Net investment in plant

Gifts furnish a frequent source of funds for plant expansions. If the gift is in cash, it is handled through unexpended plant funds, as already described. If the gift is in the form of property, it is entered in the investment in plant section as a debit to the appropriate asset account and as a credit to net investment in plant. The property representing the gift should be recorded at an appraised value, or if such is not obtainable, at a nominal value.

Following is an illustration of the accounting for the four subsections of plant funds. A beginning balance sheet, typical transactions during the fiscal year, closing entries, a final balance sheet, and a statement of changes in fund balances are presented.

ACCOUNTING FOR PLANT FUNDS

ACCOUNTING FOR UNEXPENDED PLANT FUNDS

A. Balance Sheet at Beginning of Period

BLANK COLLEGE

Balance Sheet
(Beginning of Period)

ASSETS		LIABILITIES AND FUND BALANCES	
UNEXPENDED PLANT FUNDS:		UNEXPENDED PLANT FUNDS:	
Cash	85,000	Notes payable	10,000
Investments	75,000	Bonds payable	100,000
Appropriations receivable	100,000	Fund balances--restricted	200,000
Construction in progress	50,000		
Total unexpended plant funds	310,000	Total unexpended plant funds	310,000

Subsidiary accounts:

Fund A--Green Hall	25,000
Fund B--Smith Hall	35,000
Fund C--science laboratory	140,000
	200,000

B. Recording of Typical Transactions

	GENERAL LEDGER Dr.	GENERAL LEDGER Cr.	SUBSIDIARY LEDGER Dr.	SUBSIDIARY LEDGER Cr.
1. Entry to record state appropriation for land ($5,500) and improvements ($11,000) (journal voucher):				
Appropriations receivable (state)	16,500			
Funds balance --restricted		16,500		
In unexpended plant funds ledger (journal voucher):				
Fund D--land				5,500
Fund E--improvements				11,000
2. Entry to record receipt of moneys from state for capital outlay appropriations granted in previous year (cash receipts journal):				
Cash	100,000			
Appropriations receivable (state)		100,000		
3. Entry to record receipt of gift to equip science laboratory (cash receipts journal):				
Cash	15,000			
Funds balances--restricted		15,000		
In unexpended plant funds ledger (cash receipts):				
Fund C--science laboratory equipment				15,000
4. Entry to record expenditures (check register):[3]				
Funds balance--restricted	16,000			
Cash		16,000		
In unexpended plant funds ledger (vouchers):				
Fund D--land			5,000	
Fund E--improvements			11,000	
(In investment in plant funds, debit land $5,000, improvements other than buildings $11,000, and credit net investment in plant $16,000.)				
5. Entry to record receipt of funds for construction of dormitory made available through issuance of bonds (cash receipts journal):				
Cash	100,000			
Bonds payable		100,000		
6. Entry to record transfer of funds for the construction of Green Hall from current funds (cash receipts journal):				
Cash	20,000			
Funds balance--restricted		20,000		
In unexpended plant funds ledger (cash receipts):				
Fund A--Green Hall				20,000
(In unrestricted current funds, debit transfers to unexpended plant funds and credit cash.)				
7. Entry to record investment of surplus funds in securities (check register):				
Investments	10,000			
Cash		10,000		
8. Entry to record sale of worn-out equipment. Proceeds credited by trustees to Fund X--undesignated (cash receipts journal):				
Cash	1,000			
Funds balance--unrestricted		1,000		
In unexpended plant funds ledger (cash receipts):				
Fund X--unallocated				1,000
(In investment in plant section of plant funds, debit net investment in plant and credit equipment.)				

3. Entries involving vouchers payable are omitted for simplicity.

	GENERAL LEDGER Dr.	GENERAL LEDGER Cr.	SUBSIDIARY LEDGER Dr.	SUBSIDIARY LEDGER Cr.
9. Entry to record return of unused state appropriation for land (check register):				
Funds balance--restricted	500			
Cash		500		
In unexpended plant funds ledger (voucher):				
Fund D--farmland			500	
10. Entry to record progress payment on dormitory under construction (check register):				
Construction in progress	50,000			
Cash		50,000		
11. Entry to record transfer of construction in progress to investment in plant (journal voucher):				
Bonds payable	50,000			
Construction in progress		50,000		
(In investment in plant funds, debit construction in progress and credit bonds payable.)				

C. General Ledger--Unexpended Plant Funds Section

Cash

Beginning balance		85,000	Entry 4	Plant additions	16,000
Entry 2	Appropriations	100,000	Entry 7	Investments	10,000
Entry 3	Gift	15,000	Entry 9	Return of state appropriation	500
Entry 5	Issuance of bonds	100,000	Entry 10	Construction	50,000
Entry 6	Transfer from current funds	20,000			
Entry 8	Sale of used equipment	1,000			
	(244,500)				

Investments

Beginning balance		75,000			
Entry 7	Investments	10,000			
	(85,000)				

Appropriations Receivable (State)

Beginning balance		100,000	Entry 2	Cash received	100,000
Entry 1	Appropriation	16,500			
	(16,500)				

Construction in Progress

Beginning balance		50,000	Entry 11	Transfer to investment in plant	50,000
Entry 10	Payments	50,000			
	(50,000)				

Notes Payable

			Beginning balance		10,000
				(10,000)	

Bonds Payable

Entry 11 Transfer to investment in plant	50,000	Beginning balance	100,000
		Entry 5 Issuance of bonds	100,000
		(150,000)	

Fund Balances--Restricted

Entry 4 Plant additions	16,000	Beginning balance	200,000
Entry 9 Return of state appropriation	500	Entry 1 State appropriations	16,500
		Entry 3 Gift	15,000
		Entry 6 Transfer from current funds	20,000
		(235,000)	

Fund Balances--Unrestricted

		Entry 8 Sale of used equipment	1,000
		(1,000)	

D. Balance Sheet at End of Period

BLANK COLLEGE

Balance Sheet
(End of Period)

ASSETS		LIABILITIES AND FUND BALANCES	
PLANT FUNDS:		PLANT FUNDS:	
Unexpended plant funds:		Unexpended plant funds:	
Cash	244,500	Notes payable	10,000
Temporary investments	85,000	Bonds payable	150,000
Appropriations receivable	16,500	Fund balances	
		Restricted	235,000
Construction in progress	50,000	Unrestricted	1,000
Total unexpended plant funds	396,000	Total unexpended plant funds	396,000

Subsidiary accounts:

Fund A--Green Hall	45,000
Fund B--Smith Hall	35,000
Fund C--science laboratory	155,000
Fund X--unrestricted	1,000
Total	236,000

E. Statement of Changes in Fund Balances

BLANK COLLEGE

Statement of Changes in Fund Balances
Unexpended Plant Funds
For the Year Ended 19__

Balances, beginning of year	200,000
Additions:	
Appropriations--state	16,500
Gifts	15,000
Transfers from current funds	20,000
Sale of used equipment	1,000
	252,500
Deductions:	
Expenditures for plant facilities	16,000
Return of unused state appropriation	500
	16,500
Balances, end of year	236,000

ACCOUNTING FOR RENEWAL AND REPLACEMENT FUNDS

A. Balance Sheet at Beginning of Period

BLANK COLLEGE

Balance Sheet
(Beginning of Period)

ASSETS		LIABILITIES AND FUND BALANCES	
PLANT FUNDS:		PLANT FUNDS:	
Funds for renewals and replacements:		Funds for renewals and replacements:	
Cash	10,000	Fund balances--restricted	100,000
Investments	90,000		
Total funds for renewals and replacements	100,000	Total funds for renewals and replacements	100,000

Subsidiary accounts:

Fund A--dormitory system	60,000
Fund B--food services equipment	10,000
Fund C--instructional equipment	30,000
Total	100,000

B. Recording of Typical Transactions

	GENERAL LEDGER		SUBSIDIARY LEDGER	
	Dr.	Cr.	Dr.	Cr.
1. Entry to record annual transfer from dormitory system and food services (cash receipts journal):				
Cash	25,000			
Fund balances--restricted		25,000		
In renewals and replacements funds ledger:				
Fund A--dormitory system				20,000
Fund B--food service equipment				5,000
(In unrestricted current funds, debit transfers and credit cash. Also, charge operating accounts of respective auxiliary enterprises.)				
2. Entry to record transfer from unrestricted current funds for replacement of instructional equipment (cash receipts journal):				
Cash	10,000			
Fund balances--restricted		10,000		
In renewals and replacements funds ledger:				
Fund C--instructional equipment				10,000
(In unrestricted current funds, debit transfers to funds for renewals and replacements and credit cash.)				
3. Entry to record disbursement of funds for renewals and replacements (check register):				
Fund balances--restricted	10,000			
Cash		10,000		
In renewals and replacements ledger:				
Fund A--dormitory system			8,000	
Fund B--food services			1,000	
Fund C--instructional equipment			1,000	

	GENERAL LEDGER Dr.	GENERAL LEDGER Cr.	SUBSIDIARY LEDGER Dr.	SUBSIDIARY LEDGER Cr.
4. Entry to record receipt of income from investments (cash receipts journal):				
Cash	4,500			
Fund balances--restricted		4,500		
In renewals and replacements funds ledger:				
Fund A--dormitory system				2,700
Fund B--food services				450
Fund C--instructional equipment				1,350
5. Entry to record sale of investments at profit (cash receipts journal):				
Cash	3,000			
Investments		2,800		
Fund balances--restricted		200		
In renewals and replacements funds ledger:				
Fund A--dormitory system				120
Fund B--food services				20
Fund C--instructional equipment				60

C. General Ledger--Renewals and Replacements Funds Section

Cash

Beginning balance	10,000		Entry 3 Payments	10,000
Entry 1 Transfer from auxiliaries	25,000			
Entry 2 Transfer from current funds	10,000			
Entry 4 Investment income	4,500			
Entry 5 Gain--sale of investments	3,000			
(42,500)				

Investments

Beginning balance	90,000		Entry 5 Sale of investments	2,800
(87,200)				

Fund Balances--Restricted

Entry 3 Payments	10,000		Beginning balance	100,000
			Entry 1 Transfer from auxiliaries	25,000
			Entry 2 Transfer from current funds	10,000
			Entry 4 Investment income	4,500
			Entry 5 Sale of investments	200
			(129,700)	

D. Balance Sheet at End of Period

BLANK COLLEGE

Balance Sheet
(End of Period)

ASSETS		LIABILITIES AND FUND BALANCES	
PLANT FUNDS:		PLANT FUNDS:	
Funds for renewals and replacements:		Funds for renewals and replacements:	
Cash	42,500	Fund balances--restricted	129,700
Investments	87,200		
Total funds for renewals and replacements	129,700	Total funds for renewals and replacements	129,700

Subsidiary accounts:

Fund A--dormitory system	74,820
Fund B--food services equipment	14,470
Fund C--instructional equipment	40,410
Total	129,700

E. Statement of Changes in Fund Balances

BLANK COLLEGE

Statement of Changes in Fund Balances
Funds for Renewals and Replacements
For the Year Ended 19__

Balances, beginning of year	100,000
Additions:	
Transfers from current funds	10,000
Transfers from auxiliary enterprises	25,000
Investment income	4,500
Net gain--sale of investments	200
	139,700
Deductions:	
Expenditures	10,000
Balances, end of year	129,700

ACCOUNTING FOR RETIREMENT OF INDEBTEDNESS FUNDS

A. Balance Sheet at Beginning of Period

BLANK COLLEGE

Balance Sheet
(Beginning of Period)

ASSETS		LIABILITIES AND FUND BALANCES	
PLANT FUNDS:		PLANT FUNDS:	
Funds for retirement of indebtedness:		Funds for retirement of indebtedness:	
Cash	50,000	Fund balances--restricted	250,000
Investments	200,000		
Total funds for retirement of indebtedness	250,000	Total funds for retirement of indebtedness	250,000

Subsidiary accounts:

Fund A-dormitory system	150,000
Fund B-science center	100,000
Total	250,000

B. Recording of Typical Transactions

	GENERAL LEDGER Dr.	GENERAL LEDGER Cr.	SUBSIDIARY LEDGER Dr.	SUBSIDIARY LEDGER Cr.
1. Entry to record receipt of debt service payment covering dormitory system bonds (cash receipts journal):				
Cash	8,000			
Fund balances--restricted		8,000		
In retirement of indebtedness funds ledger (cash receipts):				
Fund A--dormitory system				8,000
(In unrestricted current funds, debit transfers and credit cash. Also, debit dormitory system operating accounts.)				
2. Entry to record receipt of debt service payment covering science center bonds (cash receipts journal):				
Cash	6,000			
Fund balances--restricted		6,000		
In retirement of indebtedness funds ledger (cash receipts):				
Fund B--science center				6,000
(In unrestricted current funds, debit transfers to funds for retirement of indebtedness and credit cash.)				
3. Entry to record payment of debt service on bonds (interest $2,000; principal $10,000) (check register):				
Fund balances--restricted	12,000			
Cash		12,000		
In retirement of indebtedness funds ledger (vouchers):				
Fund A--dormitory system			7,000	
Fund B--science center			5,000	
(In investment in plant section, debit bonds payable and credit net investment in plant $10,000.)				

C. General Ledger--Funds for Retirement of Indebtedness Section

Cash

Beginning balance	50,000	Entry 3 Payment of debt service	12,000
Entry 1 Transfer from auxiliary enterprises	8,000		
Entry 2 Transfer from current funds	6,000		
(52,000)			

Investments

Beginning balance	200,000		
(200,000)			

Fund Balances--Restricted

Entry 3 Payment of debt service	12,000	Beginning balance	250,000
		Entry 1 Transfer from auxiliary enterprises	8,000
		Entry 2 Transfer from current funds	6,000
		(252,000)	

D. Balance Sheet at End of Period

BLANK COLLEGE

Balance Sheet
(End of Period)

ASSETS		LIABILITIES AND FUND BALANCES	
PLANT FUNDS:		PLANT FUNDS:	
Retirement of indebtedness funds:		Retirement of indebtedness funds:	
Cash	52,000	Fund balances--restricted	252,000
Investments	200,000		
Total retirement of indebtedness funds	252,000	Total retirement of indebtedness funds	252,000

Subsidiary accounts:

Fund A--dormitory system	151,000
Fund B--science center	101,000
Total	252,000

E. Statement of Changes in Fund Balances

BLANK COLLEGE

Statement of Changes in Fund Balances
Funds for Retirement of Indebtedness
For the Year 19__

Balances, beginning of year	250,000
Additions:	
Transfers from current funds	6,000
Transfers from auxiliary enterprises	8,000
	264,000
Deductions:	
Bonds retired	10,000
Bond interest paid	2,000
	12,000
Balances, end of year	252,000

ACCOUNTING FOR INVESTMENT IN PLANT

A. Balance Sheet at Beginning of Period

BLANK COLLEGE

Balance Sheet
(Beginning of Period)

ASSETS		LIABILITIES AND FUND BALANCES	
PLANT FUNDS:		PLANT FUNDS:	
Investment in plant:		Investment in plant:	
Land	100,000	Net investment in plant:	
Buildings	1,500,000	From state appropriations	1,700,000
Improvements other than buildings	150,000	From gifts	150,000
Equipment	250,000	From current funds	250,000
Library books	100,000		
Total invested in plant	2,100,000	Total invested in plant	2,100,000

B. Recording of Typical Transactions

	GENERAL LEDGER Dr.	GENERAL LEDGER Cr.	SUBSIDIARY LEDGER Dr.	SUBSIDIARY LEDGER Cr.
1. Entry to record receipt of parcel of land as a gift (journal voucher):				
Land (at appraised value)	1,000			
Net investment in plant		1,000		
In plant ledger (journal voucher):				
Individual asset account			1,000	
2. Entry to record receipt of used furniture as a gift (journal voucher):				
Equipment (at nominal value)	1			
Net investment in plant		1		
In plant ledger (journal voucher):				
Individual asset account			1	
3. Entry to record sale of bonds for construction of dormitory:				
(In unexpended plant funds, debit cash and credit bonds payable $100,000.)				
4. Entry to record transfer of construction in progress on building financed by bond issue:				
Construction in progress	50,000			
Bonds payable		50,000		
(In unexpended plant funds, debit bonds payable and credit construction in progress $50,000.)				
5. Entry to record sale of truck costing $3,000 for $1,000 (journal voucher):				
Net investment in plant	3,000			
Equipment		3,000		
In plant ledger (journal voucher):				
Individual asset account				3,000
(In unexpended plant funds, debit cash and credit fund balances--unrestricted $1,000.)				

	GENERAL LEDGER Dr.	GENERAL LEDGER Cr.	SUBSIDIARY LEDGER Dr.	SUBSIDIARY LEDGER Cr.
6. Entry to record abandonment of old building (journal voucher):				
Net investment in plant	50,000			
Buildings		50,000		
In plant ledger (journal voucher):				
Individual asset account				50,000
7. Entry to record value of equipment reported by department heads as being lost, destroyed, or otherwise disposed of:				
Net investment in plant	10,000			
Equipment		10,000		
In plant ledger (journal voucher):				
Individual asset account				10,000
8. Entries to record capitalization of expenditures made out of current funds, unexpended plant funds, and funds for renewals and replacements (journal voucher):				
a. From current funds:				
Equipment	60,000			
Net investment in plant		60,000		
In plant ledger:				
Individual asset accounts			60,000	
(In unrestricted current funds, debit expenditures and credit cash.)				
b. From unexpended plant funds:				
Land	5,000			
Improvements other than buildings	11,000			
Net investment in plant		16,000		
In plant ledger:				
Individual asset accounts			16,000	
(In unexpended plant funds, debit fund balances--restricted and credit cash.)				
c. Renewals and replacements funds:				
Equipment	10,000			
Net investment in plant		10,000		
In plant ledger:				
Individual asset accounts			10,000	
(In renewals and replacement funds, debit fund balances--restricted and credit cash.)				
9. Entry to record retirement of some of the bonds (journal voucher):				
Bonds payable	10,000			
Net investment in plant		10,000		
(In retirement of indebtedness funds, debit fund balances--restricted and credit cash.)				

C. General Ledger--Investment in Plant Section

Land

	Beginning balance	100,000	
Entry 1	Gift (at appraised value)	1,000	
Entry 8b	Purchased from plant funds	5,000	
	(106,000)		

Buildings

Debit		Credit	
Beginning balance	1,500,000	Entry 6 Abandonment of old building	50,000
(1,450,000)			

Improvements Other Than Buildings

Debit		Credit	
Beginning balance	150,000		
Entry 8b Purchased from plant funds	11,000		
(161,000)			

Equipment

Debit		Credit	
Beginning balance	250,000	Entry 5 Sale of truck	3,000
Entry 2 Gift (at nominal value)	1	Entry 7 Write off	10,000
Entry 8a Purchased from current funds	60,000		
Entry 8c Purchased from renewals and replacement funds	10,000		
(307,001)			

Library Books

Debit		Credit	
Beginning balance	100,000		

Construction in Progress

Debit		Credit	
Entry 4 Progress payment	50,000		
(50,000)			

Bonds Payable

Debit		Credit	
Entry 9 Bonds retired	10,000	Entry 4 Progress payment	50,000
		(40,000)	

Net Investment in Plant

Debit		Credit	
Entry 5 Sale of truck	3,000	Beginning balance	2,100,000
Entry 6 Abandonment of old building	50,000	Entry 1 Gift of land	1,000
Entry 7 Equipment written off	10,000	Entry 2 Gift of furniture	1
		Entry 8a Expenditures from current funds	60,000
		Entry 8b Expenditures from unexpended plant funds	16,000
		Entry 8c Expenditures from renewals and replacement funds	10,000
		Entry 9 Retirement of bonds	10,000
		(2,134,001)	

D. Balance Sheet at End of Period

BLANK COLLEGE

Balance Sheet
(End of Period)

ASSETS		LIABILITIES AND FUND BALANCES	
PLANT FUNDS:		PLANT FUNDS:	
Investment in plant:		Investment in plant:	
Land	106,000	Bonds payable	40,000
Buildings	1,450,000	Net investment in plant:	
Improvements other than buildings	161,000	From state appropriations	1,668,000
Equipment	307,001	From current funds	315,000
Library books	100,000	From gifts	151,001
Construction in progress	50,000		
Total investment in plant	2,174,001	Total investment in plant	2,174,001

E. Statement of Changes in Fund Balances

BLANK COLLEGE

Statement of Changes in Net Investment in Plant
For the Year Ended 19__

Balances, beginning of year	2,100,000
Additions:	
Gifts of plant assets	1,001
Amounts expended from:	
Unrestricted current funds	60,000
Unexpended plant funds	16,000
Funds for renewals and replacements	10,000
Funds for retirement of indebtedness	10,000
	2,197,001
Deductions:	
Disposal of plant assets	63,000
Balances, end of year	2,134,001

13

Physical Plant Inventory

MANY COLLEGES AND UNIVERSITIES having up-to-date accounting systems do not have perpetual inventory systems for the fixed assets of their plant funds. This neglect seems to stem from a tendency on the part of institutional organizations to disregard values in the form of tangible assets. No question is raised as to the necessity of accounting accurately for receivables, payables, and cash; but frequently doubt is expressed as to the value of a systematic accounting for plant assets.

Several explanations are offered for the failure to include plant assets in the institutional record-keeping system. One is the rapid growth in the size of colleges and universities, accompanied by a corresponding expansion in physical plant. Because the staff of the business office does not grow proportionately, it is forced to leave some work undone and thus neglect the inventory of plant assets. Also, after a college or university becomes relatively large, time, effort, and the expenditure of funds are required to establish a plant inventory; therefore, it may be difficult to convince governing boards of the necessity of installing accounting controls over plant assets. Furthermore, the size and value of the physical plant have no immediate or direct bearing on the financing of the institution. Cash, receivables, and payables are current and by nature demand a current accounting. Physical plant assets, representing funds already invested, are easily ignored.

Advantages of Plant Inventory Systems. The advantages of physical plant accounting and adequate inventories of plant assets are recognized by many institutions. Inventory control through the accounting system serves several practical purposes. A current record of investment in plant is justified on the grounds that one of the purposes of the accounting system is to accumulate all financial information concerning the institution. Without currently recording those transactions representing additions to or deductions from the physical plant, the financial history of the institution is incomplete. Also, the maintenance of a current account of plant investment obviates the necessity of taking a complete physical inventory of equipment each year and of having costly appraisals made of such items as land and buildings.

Another purpose of inventory control of plant assets is to fix responsibility for the custody and use of institutional property. In setting up the plant records by departments, the responsibility for the safekeeping of property is localized in department heads. With their aid and cooperation, physical checks can be made frequently to prove both the accuracy of the accounting records and the existence of the assets. When plant items, especially equipment, are purchased, they should be considered institutional property, not departmental property, even though they are charged to departmental budgets. If property is no longer needed by the department for which it was originally purchased, yet no provision has been made whereby this equipment can be transferred to other departments, the purchase of more equipment of the same kind results in the needless expenditure of institutional funds. The chief business officer should be given authority over the use and disposition of all institutional property regardless of its location. Classroom property, buildings, and other property of general usefulness should be placed under the custodianship of the director of physical plant.

An inventory system also provides information valuable for administrative purposes. As suggested, it enables the purchasing agent to utilize existing property more efficiently and avoid the purchase of duplicate equipment. Such a system assists the administration in determining over a long period of time the maintenance and upkeep costs of plant assets, as well as replacement requirements of equipment and buildings. An inventory system helps the administration in reviewing the departmental requests for new equipment, and it is essential in establishing use allowances in connection with indirect cost determinations on government grants and contracts. Also, it enables the purchasing agent to take advantage of savings resulting from quantity trade-ins of old equipment. Equipment and building inventory records are useful in determining the extent of losses in case of fire or theft and in establishing values for recovery. Finally, adequate records and inventories of plant assets are useful in the work of periodically adjusting insurance values in light of major changes in price levels.

Classification of Plant Assets. The plant assets of educational institutions may be classified according to the following outline:

1. Land
2. Buildings
   a. Educational
   b. Auxiliary enterprises
   c. Service activities
3. Improvements other than buildings
   a. Athletic field and recreational areas
   b. Gas system
   c. Gateways
   d. Lighting systems
   e. Heating and air conditioning systems
   f. Plantings and landscaping
   g. Roads, streets and sidewalks, and parking facilities
   h. Sewer and storm drainage systems
   i. Water supply systems
4. Equipment
   a. Aircraft
   b. Athletic and recreational
   c. Automotive
   d. Building and general plant
   e. Cleaning and laundry
   f. Instructional and research
   g. Household
   h. Hospital
   i. Library equipment
   j. Livestock
   k. Office furniture and equipment
5. Library
6. Art museums

Each of these subdivisions can be broken down further; for example, office furniture and equipment can be divided into desks, chairs, typewriters, adding machines, and filing equipment.

Valuation of Plant Assets. The basis for valuing plant assets for inventory purposes is generally either original cost (plus additions and minus abandonments at cost) or appraisals. Sometimes a combination of the two methods is used in which original valuations are established by appraisals, subsequent additions are recorded at cost, and deductions are recorded at either the appraised value or at cost. This last plan is resorted to when inventories must be determined long after the original acquisition of the property items. Property obtained through gift should be valued by the appraisal method. Whenever the appraisal method is used, this fact should be disclosed in all financial records and reports.

Ordinarily, original cost is the recommended basis for the valuation of educational property. Original cost is the outlay required to obtain plant fund items in condition ready for use. Thus, in ascertaining the cost of land, all the following items should be added to the invoice or contract price: assessments, taxes and fees, or commissions necessary to obtain the land; conveyances and notarial fees; and the cost of demolishing old buildings and grading or otherwise clearing the land. In case of buildings undergoing construction, cost includes all payments to contractors, taxes, and fees or commissions, as well as the cost of all permanent fixtures and appliances installed as a part of the buildings. If the institution constructs the building with borrowed funds, interest paid during the construction period should be included in determining cost. Similar elements of cost are included in the purchase or construction of improvements other than buildings. Items of equipment also would be valued at total cost of acquisition. In the case of mechanical equipment, original cost includes cost necessary to install, test, or otherwise prepare the machine for operation.

Regarding equipment, it is necessary to establish more or less rigid rules as to which items will be added to the inventory records and which will be excluded. Many items, such as desks, typewriters, and automobiles, clearly should be inventoried; but other items, such as laboratory slides and glassware and minor replacement items, may present problems. As a rule, the cost and probable serviceable life of equipment items are the two factors used in determining whether a specific piece of equipment should be taken into the equipment inventory records. Most institutions exclude items of small original cost value, *e.g.*, those ranging in cost from $25 to $100 or even $500 and those having a probable useful life of less than two years. Elements of cost and length of life must be considered together in deciding whether items of equipment are to be inventoried. In any event, it is necessary to establish working rules, and it is desirable to make these rules known to department heads and all those concerned with the inventory of equipment and plant asset accounting.

In the case of certain types of equipment such as furniture and linen for dormitory rooms and china and glassware for dining halls, the practice sometimes is followed of inventorying the original equipment but charging replacements to current expense. This is justified on the grounds that average loss through breakage should be replaced each year as a charge to current operations, so that the original equipment inventory possesses a fixed value.

Library books create no particular problem from the accounting viewpoint, since they are recorded at cost. The same rule applies to microfilms and binding of periodicals. When volumes and materials are removed, discarded, lost, or stolen, adjustments should be made in the library records. In most institutions, the details of the inventory are kept in the library, the business office maintaining only control accounts.

In the case of equipment manufactured on the campus, the approved procedure is to accumulate through the cost system (see Chapter 14) all costs of constructing the equipment and to bring it into inventory at such cost.

Depreciation of Fixed Assets. Closely related to the valuation of fixed assets is the question of depreciation. Authorities in the field of educational finance are in general agreement on the following points:[1]

1. The principles of depreciation accounting essential to proper accounting and financial reporting in commercial and business organizations do not apply to nonprofit educational institutions. Depreciation expense is reported neither in the statement of current funds revenues, expenditures and other changes nor in the current

1. *College and University Business Administration* (3rd Rev. ed.; Washington, D.C.: National Association of College and University Business Officers, 1974), 179.

funds section of changes in fund balances. This does not preclude the use of depreciation data in evaluating performance and in making management decisions on operating activities. Moreover, depreciation allowances may be reported in plant funds, if so desired, by charging investment in plant and crediting reserve for depreciation.

2. Some colleges and universities employ a procedure to which the term *depreciation accounting* is applied, but which is in reality the provision of funds for future renewal, replacement, or expansion of plant facilities. The distinction between depreciation accounting and providing for renewals, replacements, and the expansion of plant assets should be clearly recognized so that the practices employed by educational institutions and the ensuing transactions can be properly identified, classified, and reported.

3. If the financial program of an educational institution provides for the setting aside of funds for the renewal, replacement, and expansion of educational plant assets, the process should be recognized as such and should not be considered as depreciation accounting.

4. Depreciation accounting as found in commercial and business organizations is not recommended for plant used by auxiliary enterprises. The financial program of the institution may provide for setting aside funds from the revenues of auxiliary enterprises for the replacement of plant facilities and assets. If it does, such provision may be based on equivalent depreciation computed in accordance with generally accepted practices, or it may be based on the anticipated replacement costs of the assets, adjusted in accordance with the recognized price index. Such provision should be identified as funds for renewals and replacements; they should not be identified as depreciation. The annual additions to such funds should be shown in the statement of changes in fund balances—funds for renewals and replacements. Cash or other liquid assets must be transferred from current to plant funds and reported in the funds for renewals and replacements group.

5. Depreciation concepts and accounting should be followed in the case of real properties, except land, held as investments of endowment funds. Funded reserves for the accumulated depreciation charges should be established by the transfer of cash from

the revenues of endowment properties and reported in the endowment and similar funds portion of the balance sheet. The asset values of property should be reported net of the amount of such depreciation reserves.

Establishment of Inventory of Plant Assets. The initial step in establishing a perpetual inventory system for plant assets in an institution not having an inventory is to classify all properties in the manner described above and, with the assistance of department heads and the director of physical plant, to locate, count, and value all items of the physical plant. Various problems arise in inventorying each of the six classes of assets—land, buildings, improvements other than buildings, equipment, library books, and art museums. Inventorying the land begins with obtaining and filing deeds to the land. Maps should be drawn showing the location and boundaries of each parcel of land owned. Other items of information necessary to establish the inventory of land are original cost of the land, cost of subsequent additions or improvements, means of financing the original purchase, and date of acquisition. Form 13.1 is a suggested record for parcels of land owned. One card is prepared for each tract of land, each tract being indexed by number to the map.

In the case of buildings, some of the more important items of information to be gathered for each building are the building number (or name), the type of construction, the year of completion, the names of the architect and construction company, the gross and net square feet of floor space, the cubic footage, detailed floor plans showing the number and location of all utility outlets, the cost or appraisal value, and the source of funds used in acquiring the building. Photographs of the building, showing adjoining structures or improvements, are a useful addition to the buildings section of the plant ledger. Similar information should be obtained for each improvement other than buildings. Form 13.1 will also serve as a perpetual inventory record for buildings and for improvements other than buildings.

Two points should be noted in connection with the establishment of inventories for plant assets. First, most of the responsibility for constructing the inventories should be placed in the business office; however, the director of physical plant can be of

FORM 13.1

BLANK COLLEGE

R E A L P R O P E R T Y L E D G E R

(Land, Buildings, and Improvements)

Description__________	Plant Book
__________	Page No. ______
__________	Land No. ______
__________	Building No. ______
Location __________	Improvement No.______
Size __________	______
Type of Deed ______ Date______	If Gift, Exact Conditions
Recorded ______ Vol.______ No.______	Donor______ Date______
	Purpose______

Cost	Valuation Data	Insurance
Date______ Amount______	Date______ Amount______	Date______ Amount______
Date______ Amount______	Date______ Amount______	Date______ Amount______

Type of Construction ______	Completed Year______
Name of Architect ______	Square Feet ______
Construction Company ______	Cubic Feet ______

Date	Description	Ref.	Debits	Credits	Balance

valuable assistance in this work. Second, in many cases the original cost method is not practicable because of lack of documentary information concerning costs. In such cases, the appraisal method must be employed to establish beginning inventory values.

The equipment inventory can be taken best with the assistance of department heads. Form 13.2 is a type of tabulation sheet used to accumulate the inventory data. It is filled in by the department head, or by a representative of the business office working with the department head, then sent to the business office for a determination of values. The inventorying of equipment of a general nature, such as classroom furniture, can be assigned either to the departments adjoining the classrooms or to the physical plant department. The inventory of general plant equipment should be prepared by the director of physical plant. For certain classes of equipment, checklists may be mimeographed and distributed to department heads for convenience in inventorying. As an example, this method is feasible in inventorying the contents of dormitories where the same type of equipment is used in all rooms. Some of the more important information needed for each item of equipment includes the description and location of the article, its serial number, make, model, estimated life, and the source of funds from

FORM 13.2

BLANK COLLEGE

MOVABLE EQUIPMENT INVENTORY

Department__________ Date Taken__________

Location__________ (Room) (Building) Inventory Date__________

Source of Funds__________ Estimated Life__________ (Years)

College Serial Number	Description Including Name, Model, Size, Mfg. Serial No., and Number on Hand	Date Purchased	Condition (Good Fair Poor)	Cost or Appraised	Not Needed (Obsolete)

Prepared By__________ Approved as Correct__________ (Department Head)

which it was purchased. Form 13.3 is an inventory record for movable equipment. For items that can be grouped together conveniently both by nature of the item and by location—such as chairs and tables of the same kind used in a given building—Form 13.4 may be used.

Marking or tagging each item of equipment with an identifying serial number is an important part of inventorying movable equipment. Some institutions employ elaborate systems of codes, one part of the code referring to the department using the equipment and the other part being a number for the equipment. Thus, a typewriter purchased for the business administration department would be marked BA–1. Marking or tagging equipment can be accomplished through one of several methods. Sometimes more than one method should be used because of the type, make, and form of the item. Small metal tags attached to the article are probably used more than any other marking device. Another method is the decalcomania transfer process. Its advantages are that it can be used on a great number of items, it presents an attractive appearance, and it can be affixed easily; yet it is relatively permanent and can be replaced quickly and easily. Other methods of marking utilize stencils, glass acid, electric stylus, electric etchograph, laundry tags, and India ink, and printing and engraving. Some institutions mark only those articles of equipment not identified by a serial number of the manufacturer. In marking equipment, an important rule to follow is that the marking should be accessible for inventory-checking purposes, yet it should not interfere with normal use of the equipment. Also, it should not be placed in a position where constant usage of the article will cause deterioration in the tag.

Having established the inventory of plant assets and valued each item of each class by appraisals or through reference to purchase orders, invoices, and other original sources, the next step is to set up the inventory on cards. The inventory cards for land, buildings, improvements other than buildings, equipment, library books, and art museums constitute the plant ledger and are subsidiary to, and must be in agreement with, proper control accounts in the general ledger.

Operation of Perpetual Inventory System. Establishing a physi-

FORM 13.3

BLANK COLLEGE

E Q U I P M E N T   L E D G E R   C A R D

No.____________

Description____

Department____

Serial No.____________ Make____________ Model____________

Date Received____________ P.O. No.____________ Life____________

Transfer Record:

Date____________ Department____________ Place____________

Date____________ Department____________ Place____________

Date	Description	Ref.	Additions	Deductions	Balance

FORM 13.4

BLANK COLLEGE

G R O U P   P R O P E R T Y   R E C O R D

Article____________________ Department____________________

Description____________________ Building____________ Room____________

Date	Ref.	Received		Dropped		Balance	
		Quantity	Value	Quantity	Value	Quantity	Value

cal plant inventory in accordance with the procedure explained above involves considerable work. Its yearly repetition would be prohibitive. Therefore it is necessary to operate the inventory system on a perpetual basis. This may be accomplished through the following procedure under the direction of the purchasing agent. Requisitions, purchase orders, and invoices for plant assets are prepared and recorded the same as for other purchases, and they flow through the same channels. The invoices, however, are routed to an inventory clerk who, in small colleges, usually is assigned duties in addition to those of keeping inventory records. When the inventory clerk receives the invoice, he prepares an addition-to-property card (Form 13.5) in duplicate, one copy going to the department head who is to be custodian of the property, the other being retained in the business office. The business office copy is used to record the purchase of the item in the plant journal (Form 13.6) and is later filed by departments. As the asset is recorded in the journal, it is given a serial number; this number is then attached to the article by one of the methods of marking described above. Deductions from fixed assets, as in the case of trade-ins or abandonments, may be entered in red in the plant journal. The purchase is then posted to the formal inventory cards (Forms 13.1

FORM 13.5

BLANK COLLEGE

A D D I T I O N   T O   P R O P E R T Y

Type of Property__________ Req. No.__________

Date Purchased__________ P.O. No.__________

Purchased From__________

Description__________

Cost: Inv. Price	$______	Department______
Extras	______	Location______
Total	$______	Manufacturer's No.______
		College Serial No.______
Source of Funds______		Disposed of______

FORM 13.6

BLANK COLLEGE

PLANT JOURNAL

Date	From Whom Purchased and Type of Fixed Asset	College Serial Number	How Acquired		
			Current Funds	Plant Funds	Gift

FORM 13.7

BLANK COLLEGE

No. 1

TRANSFER OF EQUIPMENT

Date________________

Transferred From________________________

Transferred To________________________

Item	College Serial Number	Remarks

The above items are no longer in my custody. ________________ Department Head Date__________	Transfer Approved: ________________ Business Manager Entered__________ Inv. Clerk	I hereby accept the custody of the above items. ________________ Department Head Date__________

and 13.3). At the end of the month, the plant journal is summarized, the summary being posted to the investment in plant section of the plant funds group. (See journal entry on page 264, herein.)

The department head is held responsible for reporting to the business office any equipment that is worn out, broken, lost, transferred, or no longer needed by the department. Form 13.7, trans-

FORM 13.8

BLANK COLLEGE

D I S P O S I T I O N   O F   E Q U I P M E N T

Date____________________

The following equipment should be removed from the inventory of

the Department of______________________________

D e s c r i p t i o n	Inventory Number	Room and Building	Reason For Disposal

Posted:____________________ Inventory Clerk   ____________________ Head of Department

fer of equipment, and Form 13.8, disposition of equipment, should be used in connection with adjustments to the perpetual inventory records.

The above procedure not only results in a correct inventory record of movable equipment, but it also furnishes the business office with information regarding the location of the equipment, the number and value of each type of equipment owned by the institution, and a chronological record of equipment purchases. The additions to property cards, filed by departments, furnish information relative to the location of each item. The inventory cards, filed by types of fixed assets, afford information relative to the number and value of the articles in the inventory; and the plant journal provides a chronological and numerical listing of all additions to and deductions from investment in plant.

Institutions using electronic data processing equipment can place the entire inventory on tape or disc packs that can be updated as new items are acquired or old items removed. As a by-product of recording the data, printouts can be produced by departments, which provide all the details necessary to verify that the equipment is on hand.

At least once each year, physical inventories should be taken of all movable equipment to prove the existence of the institutional equipment and to verify the accuracy of the perpetual inventory records. Another purpose of the physical inventory is to assist in bringing up to date the records regarding the present condition of the equipment. Some institutions require each department head to submit an inventory of equipment under his custody. This list is verified by the accounting office and reconciled with the equipment cards in the plant ledger. Under an EDP system, a hard copy printout giving appropriate details about all equipment in each department can be produced routinely and sent to the department head for verification.

As an alternate proposal to the detailed inventory system previously discussed, some institutions have developed equipment inventory systems that are adequate and yet cost considerably less in terms of maintenance than the detailed system mentioned above. One technique employs the use of a wide-angle lens camera to photograph the entire contents of a room or equipment cabinet. The pictures can be used to identify each item in the room and in the entire building. Identification is achieved by including in each picture a sign showing the name of the building, the room number, and the date of the record. Pictures can be enlarged subsequently to ascertain details of the contents of the room. Costs are obtained from accounting records and these form an acceptable basis of insurance claims.

When it is necessary to compute indirect cost rates, an institution can document equipment values by reference to lists of items originally purchased and to accounting documents for subsequent purchases. When these lists are accompanied by photographs of the equipment on hand, an audit can determine whether the values used in the computation are accurate.

14

Cost Accounting

COST ACCOUNTING FOR governmental agencies can be described as "that form of accounting activity which is designed to furnish information concerning the cost of units of services or goods produced. To a large extent, governmental expenditure accounting and statements have been confined to recording and reporting how much was spent; unit cost accounting, on the other hand, is an endeavor to record, measure, and report how much was accomplished and at what price."[1]

In this discussion of college and university accounting systems, attention has been focused primarily on expenditure accounting, not on cost accounting. Two basic considerations differentiate these two types of accounting. First, expenditure accounting is designed primarily to account for cash payments or the incurring of liabilities, and cost accounting is concerned with that portion of materials or services rendered which has been consumed. Second, expenditure accounting is concerned with liabilities incurred and funds paid out without specific reference to the work performed, whereas cost accounting attempts to relate cost to units of work. Moreover, expenditure accounting provides for a distribution of costs by departments but does not indicate what has been accomplished by incurring these costs.

It does not follow that expenditure accounting and cost accounting are mutually exclusive in the college and university system, the differences between the two being a matter of emphasis and degree. Thus, expenditure accounting by departments or budgetary units is closely related to cost accounting in that all direct costs applicable to a given department are collected in the accounts.

1. R. M. Milesell and Leon E. Hay, *Governmental Accounting* (3rd ed.; Homewood, Ill.: Richard D. Irwin, Inc., 1961), 619.

However, the emphasis in expenditure accounting is not so much on costs in terms of units of work as on gross expenditures in terms of the budget. An extension of expenditure accounting in the direction of cost accounting is in the allocation of salaries among departmental budgets, primarily to secure a correct determination of departmental costs. The accounting procedure in connection with central storerooms closely approximates cost accounting in that the chief emphasis is not on the expenditure of funds to acquire supplies but on the consumption of those supplies as withdrawn for use.

Cost accounting developed slowly in governmental agencies in general, particularly in institutions of higher education. Cost accounting in educational institutions involves three definite phases: (1) cost accounting for certain service departments and auxiliary activities, (2) cost accounting for the physical plant department, and (3) cost accounting for instructional activities and programs in terms of the number of students taught, credit hours, and other measurements of service.

Cost Accounting for Service Departments and Auxiliary Enterprises. Some of the usual service departments in which cost accounting methods are useful include printing shops, photographic and blueprinting studios, mimeographing and duplicating bureaus, and telephone exchanges. Each of these types of service enterprises has its own particular problems of cost analysis and record keeping. In the college printing shop, for example, the same type of job-order cost accounting records are kept as those found in commercial printing establishments. Many auxiliary activities, such as dormitories and dining halls, have the same need of cost records as comparable enterprises owned and operated by private capital. In these instances, reference should be made to the accepted principles of record keeping in appropriate accounting fields such as hotel accounting and restaurant accounting.

Cost Accounting for the Physical Plant Department. Several reasons exist for applying the principles of cost accounting to the physical plant department of educational institutions.

First, an adequate system of cost accounting helps to prevent waste, theft, and inefficiency. Expenditures for salaries and materials to maintain the physical plant usually constitute a substantial percentage of the annual budget. The work performed in this connection is highly varied. Cost accounting makes possible close scrutiny of labor, materials, and equipment used by relating costs to the work performed.

Second, cost accounting aids the administrative offices of educational institutions in the preparation of the budget. Without adequate cost records showing costs of the various jobs and other activities performed by the physical plant department over a period of years, the preparation of that part of the budget relating to plant operation and maintenance is a difficult task. Colleges having no cost records are forced to rely on records of past gross expenditures; this practice leads, in many instances, to continued excessive and uneconomical expenditures. With the aid of cost data, an intelligent program for the operation and maintenance of the physical plant can be established.

Third, a cost system helps in the execution of the budget by serving as a guide in formulating policies regarding certain phases of the operation and maintenance of plant.

Fourth, an adequate cost system assists in answering such questions as: (1) Should a given job be performed by the college force or by an outside agency? (2) When is it economical to abandon old equipment and purchase new? (3) When should equipment be rented rather than purchased?

Fifth, since the physical plant department services the entire institutional plant and all departments, both educational and auxiliary, a cost accounting system is necessary if charges for work performed are to be assessed on a meaningful basis.

Sixth, cost figures are useful in that they afford a comparison of costs of the various activities over a period of years, as well as comparisons with similar activities in other institutions.

Principles of Cost Accounting for Physical Plant. The physical plant department services auxiliary enterprises such as dining halls, bookstores, and dormitories. All costs of operating auxiliary enterprises should be accumulated and charged against those agencies. This procedure is based on the assumption that auxiliary enterprises are quasi-business activities and should be operated as is private business—namely, by ascertaining profit or loss on operations. Although in some instances auxiliary enterprises may not be expected to earn a profit, normally they should operate without loss to the institution. This requires the assessment of all proper charges against them. This reasoning does not apply to teaching and administrative departments; hence, costs of ordinary plant operation and maintenance, such as janitorial services, repairs to buildings, and utilities, are not charged to these departments. On the other hand, if work of an extraordinary and nonrecurring nature is performed by the physical plant department for instructional departments, the cost of such work is a proper charge against the budget of the departments affected. Thus, the cost of constructing desks, tables, and bookcases, which otherwise would have to be purchased in the open market, should be charged to the capital expenditures budget of the department.

If the principles outlined above are followed, the cost system effects a complete separation between general overhead applicable to academic or instructional departments and that attributable to auxiliary or noninstructional departments. Thus, the net expenditures charged to the various activities of the physical plant department represent the costs of maintaining that portion of the physical plant devoted to instruction, research, and public service, and to the administration of such activities. The budget for the various divisions of the physical plant department represents the outlays necessary to operate and maintain the buildings, grounds, and utilities used in the academic and instructional plant and excludes the costs necessary to maintain the auxiliary enterprises and activities.

Two different practices are followed by colleges and universities in keeping cost records. The cost records can be kept in the physical plant department, and control accounts can be maintained in the central accounting office; or, all cost records can be kept in the central accounting office. In normal circumstances, the former method is preferable and is the one described here.

Classification of Expenditures by Activities. The chart of expenditure accounts given in Chapter 4 divides the physical plant department into eight subdepartments, each possessing a separate budget. For purposes of cost accounting, each of these subdepartments is classified according to the activities carried on by that department. The following outline is a suggested classification of physical plant expenditures by activities for purposes of cost accounting:

1. Administration
2. Custodial services
3. Maintenance of buildings (and equipment)
4. Maintenance of grounds
5. Utilities
6. Trucking service
7. Fire protection
8. Property insurance

Optional additions to plant accounts are:

1. Planning and construction
2. Electrical and mechanical services
3. Waste disposal
4. Police and security (if supervised by the physical plant department)
5. Major repairs and renovation

Methods of Cost Accounting. In accounting for costs of the above activities, three different procedures are employed. First, job-order cost accounting, sometimes called specific service cost accounting, is used for those activities whose costs are associated closely with specific jobs or orders. Thus the cost of repairing buildings or furniture, the cost of landscaping a particular part of the campus, or the cost of constructing equipment should be accumulated by specific jobs. Second, the cost of some activities that are recurring or continuous in nature necessitates the employment of a form of cost accounting known as continuous-process costs, sometimes called continuous service cost accounting. Under the continuous-process method, all costs applicable to a specific activity are collected for a given period of time. This method of cost accounting is employed in collecting the costs of operation and maintenance of each building on the campus. Third, certain costs of plant operation and maintenance must be allocated to specific jobs or to operating departments. Thus, in the operation of utilities it is necessary to apportion costs of heat, electricity, gas, and water to the different buildings, as well as to auxiliary enterprises. Trucking service and college automobiles, insurance, and administration of the operation and maintenance department are other examples of costs that must be apportioned.

The following chart lists each activity of the plant operation and maintenance department under the appropriate cost procedure. The discussion of cost accounting which follows is based on this outline.

1. Job-order cost accounting
   a. Special projects under care and maintenance of grounds
   b. Repairs to buildings
   c. Repairs to furniture and equipment
   d. Construction of equipment
2. Continuous-process cost accounting
   a. Campus upkeep
   b. Operation of buildings
3. Allocation of costs
   a. Supervision
   b. General overhead
   c. Heat
   d. Electricity
   e. Gas
   f. Water
   g. Sewage
   h. Trucks and automobiles
   i. Property insurance
   j. Police and security

1. ***Job-Order Cost Accounting.*** All jobs performed by the physical plant department for other departments originate with a formal requisition. This requisition, prepared by the department desiring to have work done, is sent to the purchasing agent. The regular purchase requisition (Form 3.1) may be used for work requests, or a special form may be used. The requisition follows the usual channels—going first to the purchasing agent, where a work order is issued. In some institutions, certain types of work or jobs costing in excess of a stipulated amount may have to be approved by the chief business officer or other official. The requisitioning department may be required to obtain an estimate of the cost of the job from the physical plant department. If so, the request for estimate (Form 14.1) is prepared in triplicate by the department head, all copies going to the physical plant department. The latter department estimates the total cost of the job and sends two copies of the estimate back to the department head. The department head attaches one copy of the estimate to the purchase requisition and for-

FORM 14.1

BLANK COLLEGE

R E Q U E S T   F O R   E S T I M A T E

Date____________________

To Director of Physical Plant:

Please prepare an estimate of the cost of the following job:

Quantity	Description	Estimated Price
	Work order will be issued for this project by the Purchasing Dept. following confirmation of requisition clearance by the Comptroller. Please return this form to: (check one) ( ) Purchasing Department ( ) Originating Department	

Analysis of Estimated Cost:

Labor $__________

Materials __________

Equipment __________

Other __________

Total $__________

Prepared by:____________________
Director of Physical Plant

Requested for Department of:____________________

Location:____________________

Requested by:____________________

Approved by:____________________

Charge Account:____________________

wards it to the purchasing office. Upon receiving the purchase requisition together with attached request for estimate, the purchasing office sends the document to the accounting office, where availability of funds is checked. If funds are available, the purchasing office issues a work order (Form 14.2) to the physical plant department, authorizing the job to be placed in process.

FORM 14.2

BLANK COLLEGE

W O R K   O R D E R

Date____________________

Work Order Number

NO. 5485

R____________
Requisition No.

To

This authorizes you to perform the work indicated below for:

____
Department

____
Building

____
Room

Charge Code

Estimated Cost

Partial Liquidations

Estimated Completion Date____________________

To____________________
Foreman

Signed____________________
Purchasing Agent

Begin Work____________________
Department Head

Funds Available____________________

One copy of the work order is sent to the director of physical plant, one copy to the accounting office, and one copy is retained by the purchasing agent. In some institutions, the department head roughly estimates the cost of the job, leaving it to the purchasing office to obtain refined estimates from the physical plant department.

The above procedure is generally applicable, but there are two situations which call for deviation from the usual routine. First, many jobs may be characterized as recurring maintenance—such as replacing light bulbs and broken window panes—affecting only the budget of the physical plant department. In such cases, the director of physical plant is authorized to proceed without submitting a formal request to the purchasing agent. Second, many jobs are characterized as emergencies. The director of physical plant has authority to originate such jobs. In such cases, an informal maintenance order is issued by the director or by one of his subordinate officers or foremen.

Accounting for job costs begins with the approval of the requisition and the work order by the accounting office. The work order is treated like any other order, being encumbered in the usual way.

Encumbrances
  Provision for encumbrances

Detailed accounting for job costs in the physical plant department begins when the director of physical plant receives his copy of the work order. A job-cost sheet for that particular job is set up in the job-cost ledger (Form 14.3). The function of this ledger is to accumulate the costs of each job so that the efficiency of the job can be measured and the department benefiting from the job may be charged. As shown in the illustration of the job-cost ledger (Form 14.3), costs are accumulated for labor, materials, equipment use, and other (overhead). Some institutions, however, do not allocate overhead and equipment use to jobs.

Labor costs are ascertained from daily, weekly, biweekly, or semimonthly time reports showing the number of hours of work per day devoted to each particular job and to the usual operation and maintenance activities for which specific jobs are not set up. Form 14.4 illustrates a type of daily time report. These daily time reports are accumulated in weekly, biweekly, or semimonthly reports, such as the one illustrated in Form 14.5. The time reports are used to post charges against the appropriate jobs in the job-cost ledger. At the end of the payroll period, the physical plant department prepares the regular payroll vouchers for operation and maintenance labor. The time indicated on the payroll vouchers is

FORM 14.3

BLANK COLLEGE

JOB COST LEDGER

Job No.__________

Department__________
Account__________
Description of Job__________

Requisition No.__________
Date Ordered__________
To Be Completed_____ Int. Inv. No._____

Cost Summary	Estimated	Actual
Labor	$	$
Materials		
Equipment		
Other		
Totals	$	$

Date	Reference	Labor	Materials	Other	
				Description	Amount
	Totals				

checked against the time allocated to various jobs and activities on the weekly, biweekly, or semimonthly time reports; if the two reports are in agreement, the payroll vouchers are sent to the accounting office, where checks are drawn in the usual manner. In journal form, the accounting entry to record the issuance of the labor payroll checks is:

Expenditures (for labor chargeable against usual operation and maintenance accounts)
Work in process (for labor chargeable against specific jobs)
  Cash

The salaries of foremen and superintendents cannot be charged directly against particular jobs and hence must be allocated. This allocation is made when the job is completed, as explained later in this chapter.

Materials for use on jobs are procured either through direct pur-

FORM 14.4

BLANK COLLEGE

DAILY TIME REPORT

Group #

Date:

Name of Employee

Description	M.O. #	Code																	

I certify that this time report is correct and that the work was properly performed.

Supervisor________________________________

chase or from institution storerooms. When acquired through direct purchase, the individual job accounts in the job-cost ledger are posted directly from a copy of the invoice. In the central accounting office, the following entry is made:

Work in process
  Vouchers payable

When materials are issued to jobs from storerooms, the stores order (Form 14.6) serves as the record of materials used. Each day the storekeeper transmits the stores orders to the physical plant department office where they are checked and posted to the job-cost ledger. They are accumulated until the end of the month,

FORM 14.5

BLANK COLLEGE

T I M E   S H E E T

Name________________ Date________________

Employee No.________________ Department________________

Day of Month																Total Time	Rate	Amount	Code No.	Description
1	2	3	4	5	6	7	8	9	10	11	12	13	14	15						
16	17	18	19	20	21	22	23	24	25	26	27	28	29	30	31					
Totals Forward																				
Totals																				

FORM 14.6

BLANK COLLEGE

No. SO 74111

STORES ORDER

Date________________

Item Number	Quantity	Description	Price Unit	Price Total	✓

Delivered by________ Date________	Maintenance Order Number	Charge Code________ Department________
Posted by________ Date________	Work Order Number	Requested by________ Received by________

FORM 14.7

BLANK COLLEGE

NO. SRO 1638

STORES RETURN ORDER

Date________________

Item Number	Quantity	✓	Description	Price Unit	Price Total	✓

Delivered by________ Date________	Maintenance Order Number	Credit Code________ Department________
Posted by________ Date________	Work Order Number	Returned by________

FORM 14.8

BLANK COLLEGE

SHOP MATERIAL REPORT

No.

For ______________________
Name or Description of Job

Work Order No. ____________

Maint. Order No. ____________

Charge No. ____________

Date ____________

Quantity	Description	Unit	Total

Approved By:	Received By:	Voucher No.

and then an interdepartmental invoice is prepared and sent to the accounting office, where the following entry is made:

Work in process
  Stores inventory

When materials are returned, Form 14.7 is used. Appropriate adjustments are made to the inventory records and credit is given on the job-cost ledger. Stores return orders are accumulated until the end of the month and then forwarded to the accounting office, where the following entry is made:

Stores inventory
  Work in process

Materials used on jobs processed in the various maintenance shops, such as carpentry and electrical, are accounted for by the use of the shop material report (Form 14.8). Overhead expenses, such as salaries of the foremen, charges for the use of institutionally owned equipment, costs of renting equipment (unless rented for specific jobs), and office expenses of the director's office, cannot be related directly to any job and, hence, must be prorated to jobs on some reasonable basis. As overhead costs are incurred, they are charged to expenditures accounts for administration of the physical plant department in the allocations ledger. As jobs are completed, overhead is allocated on the basis of a fixed percentage of direct labor cost. The journal entry to record the charging of overhead to jobs is:

Work in process
  Expenditures (Credit the administration budget of the physical plant department.)

As soon as a job is completed, the director of physical plant determines its cost from the job-cost ledger and prepares an interdepartmental invoice. The interdepartmental invoice (Form 14.9)

FORM 14.9

BLANK COLLEGE

INTERDEPARTMENTAL INVOICE

Date__________

Credit Department of__________
Rendering Service or Furnishing Material

Charge Department of__________
Receiving Service or Material

Description	Amount

Charge: Account	Amount		Credit: Account	Amount
		Posted Charge______ Posted Credit______		
Service or Materials Received __________ Head of Dept.		Approved______ Auditor	Service Rendered or Materials Delivered __________ Head of Dept.	

FOR ACCOUNTING OFFICE

Voucher No.

is prepared in triplicate, one copy being retained in the physical plant department and two copies going to the department for which the work was performed. The department approves the invoice and transmits one copy of it to the accounting office. This copy serves as the basis for the following entry:

Expenditures (Charge appropriate departmental account in allocations ledger.)
  Work in process

At this time, the entry encumbering the cost of the job is reversed as follows:

Provision for encumbrances
  Encumbrances

Some institutions have found it useful to institute a different policy on work orders where the cost is small, say, less than $50 or some other amount fixed by agreement. This kind of order is shown as Form 14.10. A department may initiate a request for service or a repair job simply by calling the physical plant department. This procedure eliminates having to submit a request through the purchasing department and the accounting office prior to the time the work is performed. After the service has been delivered, the low-cost work order (Form 14.10) is completed by filling in the appropriate cost information and is forwarded to the accounting office for recording as follows:

Expenditures (Charge appropriate departmental account in allocations ledger.)
  Work in process

Observe that for low-cost work, no encumbrance is made. It is assumed that the department will have funds to cover the small amounts involved.

At any time during the year, after all entries have been posted, the work in process account in the general ledger should agree with the sum of the individual job accounts in the subsidiary job-cost ledger. The work in process account appears in the unrestricted current funds section of the balance sheet. Some institutions charge out all jobs, including those in process, at the end of the fiscal year. In such cases, the work in process account will show

FORM 14.10

BLANK COLLEGE
Physical Plant Department

L O W - C O S T   W O R K   O R D E R

Charge To:__________ Date__________

Credit To: Physical Plant Dept - Work in Process   Account Code__________

A charge is made against your budget for materials and/or services rendered by this department as authorized by telephone call from your department. Authorization for this charge and services requested are shown below.

Authorized by__________

Services Requested__________

Cost:

Labor __________

Materials__________

Equipment__________

Other __________

Total Charge__________

Charge: Account	Amount		Credit: Account	Amount
		Posted Charge______		
Authorized by telephone conversation with:		Posted Credit______		
		Approved______ Auditor	Director of Physical Plant	

Accounting Office - White Physical Plant - Green Department Requesting Service - Pink Job Cost Accounts - Canary Job Foreman - Goldenrod	Voucher No. 10401

no balance after the entries are made and will not appear on the balance sheet.

The following illustration is presented for the purpose of supplementing the preceding discussion of job-cost accounting.

JOB-COST ACCOUNTING

A. Transactions

1. The department of art requests the physical plant department to construct a table at an estimated cost of $40. A work order (Job 63) is issued to the director of physical plant authorizing him to proceed with the work.

2. A work order (Job 69) is issued to the director of physical plant authorizing him to begin painting the dining hall. The job is estimated to cost $2,000.

3. Payrolls are received in the accounting office which include $20 charged to Job 63 and $1,000 to Job 69.

4. Interdepartmental invoices are received in the accounting office indicating material costs of $21 charged to Job 63, $460 charged to Job 63, and $460 charged to Job 69.

5. Paint in the amount of $500 is purchased for exclusive use on Job 69.

6. Job 63 is completed. A job-cost voucher is prepared for $42, including $20 for labor, $21 for materials, and $1 for overhead.

B. Entries in Journal Form

1. Entry to record issuance of work order for Job Order 63 (orders placed and liquidated journal):

Encumbrances	40	
Provision for encumbrances		40

In allocations ledger:

Charge equipment budget of department of art.

2. Entry to record issuance of work order for Job Order 69 (orders placed and liquidated journal):

Encumbrances	2,000	
Provision for encumbrances		2,000

In allocations ledger:

Charge supplies and expenses budget of dining hall.

3. Entry to record labor charges on Jobs 63 and 69 (payrolls):

Work in process	1,020	
Cash		1,020

In job-cost ledger:

Charge Job 63 $20 and Job 69 $1,000.

4. Entry to record materials from stores used on Jobs 63 and 69 (interdepartmental invoices):

Work in process	481	
Stores inventory		481

In job-cost ledger:

Charge Job 63 $21 and Job 69 $460.

5. Entry to record purchase of paint for Job 69 (voucher):

Work in process	500	
Vouchers payable		500

In job-cost ledger:

Charge Job 69 $500.

6a. Entry to record allocation of overhead to Job 63 (journal voucher):

Work in process	1	
Expenditures		1

In job-cost ledger:

Charge Job 63 $1.

6b. Entry to record completion and invoicing of Job 63 (journal voucher):

Expenditures	42	
Work in process		42

In job-cost ledger:

Credit Job 63 $42

In allocations ledger:

Charge equipment budget of department of art.

6c. Entry to liquidate encumbrance on Job 63:

Provision for encumbrances	40	
Encumbrances		40

In allocations ledger:

Credit equipment budget of department of art.

C. Ledger Accounts

General Ledger

Work in Process

(3)	1,020	(6b)	42
(4)	481		
(5)	500		
(6a)	1		
(Balance 1,960)			

Stores Inventory

		(4)	481

Expenditures

(6b)	42	(6a)	1
(Balance 41)			

Encumbrances

(1)	40	(6c)	40
(2)	2,000		
(Balance 2,000)			

Provision for Encumbrances

(6c)	40	(1)	40
		(2)	2,000
		(Balance 2,000)	

Cash

		(3)	1,020

Vouchers Payable

		(5)	500

Job-Cost Ledger

Job No. 63

(3)	20	(6b)	42
(4)	21		
(6a)	1		

Job No. 69

(3)	1,000		
(4)	460		
(5)	500		
(Balance 1,960)			

D. Reconciliation of General Ledger Control with Job-Cost Ledger

Control account in general ledger--work in process	$1,960
Sum of individual job accounts in job-cost ledger	$1,960

2. ***Continuous-Process Cost Accounting.*** Continuous-process cost accounting in educational institutions differs fundamentally in two respects from job-cost accounting. First, the activities for which costs are collected are continuous in nature and hence cannot be subdivided into specific jobs. Second, activities in this category are, for the most part, within the jurisdiction of the physical plant department and therefore need not be initiated by means of requisitions to the purchasing agent. There are two important activities in which costs are accounted for in this manner: (1) the ordinary operation of buildings, including janitorial services and supplies, and repairs of a minor nature, and (2) the ordinary operation of grounds, such as cleaning and campus upkeep. Accounting for the costs of continuous activities is accomplished by opening a series of standing job accounts in which the cost of each activity is col-

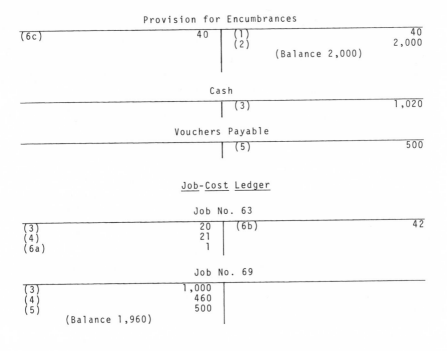

lected. In the case of buildings, a number of standing job accounts are set up to collect cost data pertaining to the various types of supplies and activities involved in the operation and maintenance of buildings. To illustrate the extent of the detail that can be furnished by the cost system, an excerpt from the chart of standing job accounts used by one university is given:

Standing Job Numbers

31. BUILDING OPERATION

31.01	Janitor labor and unclassified supplies (suffix building number)
.0101	Toilet paper
.0102	Paper towels
.0103	Cloth towels (laundry)
.0104	Soap (liquid and bar for hand use)
.0105	Soap (scrubbing) and soap powders
.0106	Powdered cleansers (detergents)
.0107	Sani-flush, lye, etc.
.0108	Sweeping compound and sawdust
.0109	Push brooms, straw brooms, and counter brushes
.0110	Mop handles, mops (cotton, linen, dust)
.0111	Chalk and erasers
.0112	Doormats, sand, and salt
.0113	Roller towels
31.02	Window washing and venetian blind cleaning, labor and materials (suffix building number)
.0201	Window washing
.0202	Venetian blind cleaning
31.03	Departmental moving
31.04	Floor treatment (suffix building number)
.0401	Prepare, seal, and wax wood floors
.0402	Clean, re-treat, and wax sealed floors
.0403	Prepare and wax linoleum floors
.0404	Prepare and seal terrazzo floors
31.05	Operation of sanitary cabinets
.0501	Repairs on sanitary cabinets
.0502	Units used
.0503	Credits
31.06	Vacations
31.07	Sickness
31.08	Holidays
31.09	Foremen
31.10	Elevator operation (suffix building number)
31.11	New equipment (inventoried)

The chart of standing job accounts for this university, in addition to the section for building operation illustrated above, includes sections for building maintenance, grounds maintenance, trucking service, steam generation, power generation, auxiliary equipment, superintendence and records, gas, water station, electrical and mechanical services, fire protection, police and security, and administration. By suffixing a building number to each standing job number, cost information of the type described is available for each building on the campus. Ordinarily, this amount of detailing is feasible only with the use of EDP systems. In less elaborate systems, costs are collected by buildings for main items of expense such as compensation of janitors, cleaning and janitorial supplies, minor repairs, and allocation of utility costs and overhead. At the end of the month, the standing job accounts are closed into the regular operation and maintenance budget accounts.

3. ***Allocation of Costs.*** Certain costs of the physical plant must be allocated on some reasonable basis to departments or to specific or standing jobs. A method of allocation of the physical plant overhead has been described above. Other costs to be allocated include utilities, trucks and automobiles, and insurance. The problem of utility allocation depends on whether the institution operates its own power plant. If so, it is necessary to design the cost system so as to accumulate the costs of the power plant, including overhead and supervision, then to allocate these costs to the various buildings and jobs. If the college does not operate a power plant, the problem is simply one of allocation. The unit to which utility costs are allocated is the building. The best way to determine the amount of the charge to each unit is to install in each building meters which will show the amount of utilities used in that building. An alternative method is to prorate the costs on a reasonable basis. Electricity may be allocated on the basis of the relative number of kilowatt hours used in each building. This is determined by three factors: (1) the number of electrical outlets in each building, (2) the voltage of each outlet, and (3) the number of hours the building is used. In the absence of meters, gas, water, and heat must be allocated on a more or less arbitrary basis, taking into account the number of outlets, the cubic feet of space in the building, and the number of hours the building is used in a day or month.

Insurance costs may be allocated to buildings based on the insurable value of the buildings covered. Auto insurance usually will be shown on a vehicle-by-vehicle basis. If not, then costs can be allocated to each vehicle on the fair market value of the vehicles or by requesting the insurance carrier to provide a cost breakdown. General liability insurance and fidelity bonds, etc., may be allocated to the departments covered based on their budgets. In similar fashion, allocations of other insurance coverages may be undertaken.

Trucks and automobiles are used by many departments on the campus; thus it is necessary, first, to accumulate the costs of operating and maintaining the vehicles and, second, to allocate the costs to jobs and departments. The usual procedure is to charge all items of expense for operating and maintaining the equipment to a truck and automobile clearing account. These items include gasoline and oil, tires, repairs and replacements, insurance, registration and license plates, and the wages of the truck and car drivers. Many institutions find it convenient to establish a service enterprise for this motor pool operation.

Depreciation may be included as an item of expense. An individual equipment record (Form 14.11) is maintained for each piece of equipment. As trucks or automobiles are used, a record is kept of the exact nature of the operations; and summary reports are made daily on a truck report (Form 14.12). The truck report serves as the basis for charging a particular job or department for the use of the truck. The usual method is to allocate the expenses of operating the equipment by means of rental charges. The following entries, in journal form, illustrate the procedure:

1. To record payment of salary of truck driver:
   Expenditures (Charge trucking services in the allocations ledger.)
       Cash

2. To record invoice for truck repairs:
   Expenditures (Charge trucking service.)
       Vouchers payable

3. To record withdrawal of gasoline from storeroom:
   Expenditures (Charge trucking service.)
       Stores inventory

FORM 14.11

BLANK COLLEGE

INDIVIDUAL EQUIPMENT RECORD

FOR THE YEAR ENDED JUNE 30, 19__

Equipment No.________________________________
Motor No.______________ Serial No.______________
Make________________________________
Type________________________________
Date Purchased________________________________
Original Cost________________________________

Estimated Salvage Value________________________________
Estimated Life________________________________
Deprec.--Current Year________________________________
Estimated Miles or Hours This Year________________________________
Rental Rates: Date__________ Rate________ Per__________
Date__________ Rate________ Per__________

Month	Gasoline		Oil		Repairs	Deprecia-tion	Total Cost	Miles Run	Hours Run	Cost per Mile or Hour	Miles per Gallon	Rental Credits Earned
	Gals.	Amt.	Qts.	Amt.								

FORM 14.12

BLANK COLLEGE

DAILY TRUCK REPORT

Physical Plant Department

Truck No.________ Rental Rate Per Hour $______ Date____________ 19____

Name of Operator__________________ Rate Per Hour $________

Description and Place of Work	Hours	Job No.

Entered By________________ ________________Foreman

4. To record use of truck on a specific job:
   Work in process
   Expenditures (Credit trucking service.)
5. To record use of truck by college department:
   Expenditures (Charge departmental budget.)
   Expenditures (Credit trucking service.)

The trucking service account is a clearing account and should be closed at the end of the year. Over- and under-absorptions of cost can be corrected by adjusting the rental rates.

Application of the accounting methods presented thus far in this chapter results in a complete separation of the cost of maintaining the educational plant and the cost of maintaining the auxiliary plant. As already explained, the physical plant budget is divided into several departments—administration, custodial services, maintenance of buildings, maintenance of grounds, utilities, trucking service, fire protection, property insurance, planning and construction, electrical and mechanical services, waste disposal, police and security, and major repairs and renovation. The budget for each of these departments provides only for the operation and maintenance of that part of the plant devoted to administration and instruction. The cost of maintaining the property used by auxiliary activities is included in the budgets of these activities.

Incomplete Cost Accounting System. The cost system described in the preceding sections of this chapter is complete and detailed and would require considerable personnel to operate it. Many colleges, particularly smaller ones, may be served better by a less elaborate cost system, such as the one outlined below.

One of the essential purposes of an institutional cost accounting system is to effect a separation of costs between the maintenance of the academic and the auxiliary plant. In the complete cost system, this is accomplished primarily through job-cost accounting methods. The following procedures are designed to accomplish the same results less elaborately for the small institution:

1. Labor costs are charged to auxiliary enterprises from time sheets similar to the one illustrated in Form 14.5. No attempt is made to relate to particular jobs the work performed by the operation and maintenance department. The only concern is to charge the auxiliary activities for all labor costs involved in work performed in their behalf. This charge is made monthly on interdepartmental transfer vouchers through the following entry:

Expenditures (In allocations ledger, charge personal services account of respective auxiliary enterprises.)
  Expenditures (In allocations ledger, credit personal services account of the physical plant department.)

2. The cost of materials used by the physical plant department in performing services for auxiliary enterprises is charged directly to the enterprise concerned. This charge is made monthly from storeroom receipts indicating the cost of materials used for auxiliary activities. The following entry is made on an interdepartmental invoice:

Expenditures (In allocations ledger, charge individual auxiliary enterprises—supplies and expense accounts.)
  Stores inventory

3. Utility costs, operation of trucks and automobiles, janitorial services, and insurance are allocated to auxiliary activities in a manner already described in the discussion beginning on page 303,

herein. The monthly entry, made on interdepartmental invoices, is as follows:

Expenditures (In allocations ledger, charge account of appropriate auxiliary activity.)
    Expenditures (In allocations ledger, credit appropriate account of the physical plant department.)

If the above procedure is followed, the costs of operation and maintenance of the physical plant used by the auxiliary enterprises will be clearly separated from the costs of the plant used for educational purposes. Although the cost system as described is incomplete, it is simple and achieves at least some of the purposes of a more complete cost accounting system.

Unit Costs of Educational Institutions. The expression of educational cost per student enrolled, cost per credit hour, and cost per course, etc., is the subject of much discussion. The determination of unit costs has both advantages and disadvantages. Unit costs, properly computed, are of value in managing educational institutions. Inasmuch as unit costs relate the expenditures of a given course, department, or curriculum to the number of students served in that division, it affords a more satisfactory index of financial performance than do gross expenditures. Various courses of study, departments, or colleges in an institution can be compared with other similar divisions through the use of per-student costs, so that the administration can determine which departments or courses of study are being developed or utilized and which ones need increased allocations. In this connection, unit costs render important assistance to the administration in preparing the annual budget.

Unit cost studies may be used as the basis of planning a reorganization of departments or colleges within an institution. Even more helpful is the use of unit costs in effecting satisfactory coordination between similar institutions within a state system of higher education. Unit costs have been used by accrediting agencies in determining whether a given college should be given an accredited standing. Finally, if used cautiously and judiciously, unit costs may be employed to make comparisons between institutions.

Certain qualifications in the use of unit costs should be noted. Unit costs in themselves do not solve financial and administrative problems, nor should they be used as the sole basis or guide for administrative action. Instead, unit costs are only a point of departure in any analysis and should be interpreted in view of all factors concerned. Furthermore, in comparing one department or curriculum with another, the inherent differences in the nature of the instruction in each division should be taken into account. Certain departments or curricula are basically more costly to operate than others; therefore, the results reflected in the unit costs should be weighted to allow for such basic difference in costs. If one department has lower unit costs than another, it does not necessarily follow that it is operated more efficiently. The fact that a department has a high unit cost certainly does not in itself justify condemning that department as uneconomical.

One danger in the use of unit costs is that they may be employed without qualification and interpretation. Legislatures and state administrations sometimes attempt to justify a division of funds on the basis of per capita costs at the various state colleges and universities. Frequently, judgments are formed without taking into account the size of the institution or the type and grade of work it performs. A small institution may sometimes show a higher unit cost than a large one because of the relatively large amount of overhead in its budget, which is fixed without regard to enrollment. All attempts to determine per capita costs by general methods or use of totals without proper analysis and interpretation are strongly discouraged.

It should be obvious that all unit cost figures are open to question because of the many assumptions upon which they are necessarily based. It is also obvious that they will change with every shift of enrollment, registration, salary scale, and price level. For that reason, comparisons of unit cost figures, even when these figures have been computed in accordance with the same formulas, should be made only with great caution. Comparisons between institutions are particularly difficult. Comparisons between similar departments of the same institution and between different years for the same department will be of some service. No institution should be without figures of unit expense of instruction, but it should use them only with due regard for their uncertainty and complexity.

Two basic factors are involved in the determination of unit costs

—the unit of measure and the expenditures by departments or colleges. The unit of measure most commonly used is the student-credit hour, which is defined as the measure of load represented by one student carrying a one-hour course. Other units that may be employed include the number of students enrolled, the student-clock hour, and the semester-credit hour. For the calculation of the unit cost of the institution as a whole, the full-time student equivalent is generally recommended as the unit of measure. A full-time student equivalent is defined as one student taking a normal academic load.

Information on expenditures should be obtained, so far as possible, from the financial records of the institution. The expenditures of a department or a college for purposes of determining unit costs are classified according to the following outline:

1. Departmental or college expenditures, divided into
   a. Personnel compensation
   b. Supplies and expenses
   c. Departmental or college administration (including salaries, clerical help, and office supplies)
2. Overhead, divided into
   a. Institutional support and student services
   b. Academic support
   c. Operation and maintenance of physical plant

Unit costs can be determined for each instructor, course, curriculum, department, or college, and, in addition, for each level of student achievement—freshman, sophomore, junior, senior, graduate—and for the institution as a whole. Usually a separate calculation is made for extension courses and for the summer session. The study may cover a semester or an academic year. In any event, it is essential that the enrollment and financial data apply to the same period of time.

Procedure for Calculating Unit Costs. Procedures for calculating unit costs are described fully in the *Cost Analysis Manual* and other publications of the National Center for Higher Education Management Systems, as well as in various publications of the National Association of College and University Business Officers; therefore, these procedures are not discussed in this book.

15

Internal Control and Audit

INTERNAL CONTROL and internal audit are important phases of the college and university accounting system. The accounting procedures outlined in the preceding chapters are predicated upon an adequate system of internal control. In the chapters on purchasing, expenditures, and income, references were made to the techniques of internal auditing, but it remains until now to discuss completely the many aspects of this phase of the fiscal system.

Internal control is defined as the system of procedures, accounting records, methods, and details through which the work of each employee or group of employees is continually checked and verified by the work of some other employee or group of employees, without duplication of effort and within the normal flow of operations. According to *College and University Business Administration*, internal control "comprises the methods and procedures adopted by an institution to safeguard its assets, to insure the accuracy and reliability of its accounting data, to promote operational efficiency, to protect its personnel, and to help insure adherence to prescribed policies and institutional regulations."[1] It implies that no one employee shall have complete or independent control over all phases of a business transaction; on the contrary, the work is so arranged and the responsibilities so assigned that the work and responsibility of one employee is complementary to that of another and provides an automatic verification of the activities of each. Internal control contrasts with external control, which assumes that an outside person or organization provides the means of verifying the work of the staff. It should be emphasized that

1. *College and University Business Administration* (3rd Rev. ed.; Washington, D.C.: National Association of College and University Business Officers, 1974), 167.

internal control is aimed not only at prevention of fraud but also at reduction of errors. If errors are made, a good system of internal control provides the means of their automatic and prompt discovery.

Internal audit is part of a complete system of internal control and consists of the deliberate and planned checking by one staff member of the work of other staff members. Internal auditing provides the same type of inquiry into the integrity and correctness of financial transactions as does postauditing by an outsider. In larger colleges and universities there is generally found an internal auditing staff whose function is to maintain a continuous audit on the operations of the business office and all outlying departments conducting affairs of a business nature. The internal auditor is responsible directly to the chief business officer and is as independent as possible of the other institutional business officers. He should have formal training in the principles and techniques of auditing and a thorough knowledge of accounting procedures and practices, including some familiarity with electronic data processing. He should be a person with considerable judgment and tact. Previous experience in auditing is desirable.

The obligation to protect the integrity of the institution and to administer its financial affairs efficiently and honestly justifies internal control and internal auditing procedures, regardless of the size of the institution. Small institutions may not be able to utilize a full-time auditing department or even a full-time internal auditor. Some staff member from time to time assumes the role of internal auditor by conducting a planned review of the work of his associates or of the operations of outlying departments. Regardless of the completeness of the internal auditing facilities, however, the presence of such a system does not remove the desirability of the annual postaudit by an outside firm of reputable accountants or by a state auditing agency.

Principles of Internal Control. The major principles or cardinal parts of a good system of internal control are as follows:

1. *Proper Organization for Business.* There should be a proper organization for the performance of the business and financial operations of a college or university, regarding both the place of

the business office in the institutional framework and the internal organization of that office. All institutional business operations should be the responsibility of a central business office headed by one or more business officers accountable to the president. The business office should be solely responsible for the control and custody of cash, the entering of obligations against the institution, and the payment of claims. This concept does not preclude the possibility of some decentralization in the collection process or in the maintenance of accounting records. For example, some auxiliary enterprises may serve as collection agencies for the business office and may keep certain detailed operating records. The important point is, however, that the ultimate responsibility and control for all business transactions should reside in the central business office. The practice of some institutions in setting up several autonomous, independent business offices on the same campus is not recommended.

Regarding the internal organization of the business office, the primary purpose is to fix responsibilities and assignments so that the work of one employee or of one division serves constantly to check and verify that of another. The following chart depicts a satisfactory organization of the college business office from the point of view of internal control:

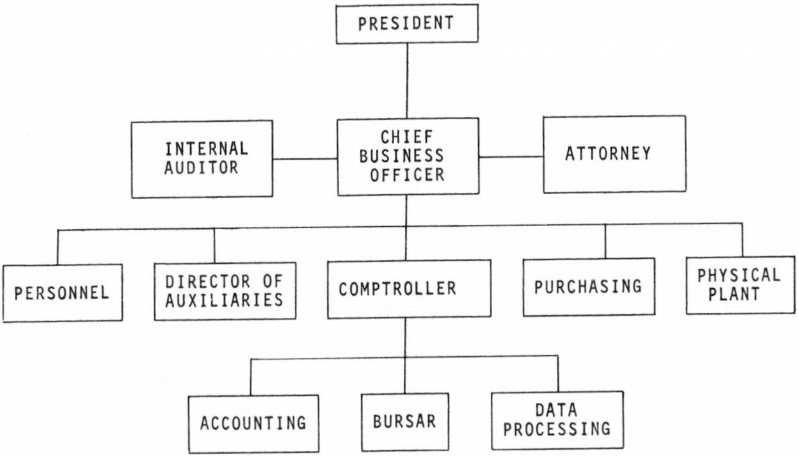

The merit of the above organization lies in the fact that the important functions of purchasing, receipt of cash, and record keeping are the responsibilities of coordinate divisions, independent of each other and each responsible directly or indirectly to the chief business officer. In addition, the internal auditor and, hence, the chief business officer have review responsibilities over all divisions. Whereas the actual organization of college business offices will vary from the one portrayed above, the basic separation of functions, consistent with the size of the institution, is one of the prime requisites of internal control.

2. *Definite Fixing of Responsibilities.* Closely related to proper organization is the principle that there should be a definite fixing of responsibilities and a clear delineation of duties. This concept applies to the internal organization of the business office as well as to the relationship between that office and operating departments. Each employee of the business office should have a clear, unmistakable assignment of responsibility. If the organization is large, a manual describing the duties of all positions will be helpful. The external responsibilities of the business office should also be clearly and completely set forth. It is especially important that the relative responsibilities of the business office and other departments conducting affairs of a business nature be definitely fixed. The institution should establish overall procedures and assign responsibilities by developing a comprehensive manual of procedures, rules, and regulations relating to the business administration of the institution.

3. *Subdivision of Work.* There should be a subdivision of the work of the business office so that no one person has complete charge or control over a transaction. For example, no one employee should bill the student, collect the cash, and deposit it in the bank. Similarly, no one person should hire the employee, prepare the payroll, audit computations, and issue the check. In a large organization it is not difficult to subdivide the work so that no employee has complete control over one transaction or function. In even the small office, however, by judicious allocations of duties, the work of one employee in a given task can be made to serve as a check on the work of another employee. The business

office should be organized to insure the validity of every transaction by having it authenticated by two or more responsible members of the staff.

4. *Use of Controlling Accounts and Subsidiary Ledgers.* When conventional mechanical accounting equipment is in use, detailed information should be segregated into subsidiary ledgers controlled by one or more accounts in the general ledger. Postings to the subsidiary ledger should be made by an employee other than the one who keeps the general ledger. In this way, the same information reaches the records through two different channels, thereby providing a means by which errors are discovered, the incidence of fraud is reduced, and the work of one employee serves as a check on that of another. The principle just expressed is best illustrated in connection with records of accounts receivable. If possible, different employees should take turns in reconciling subsidiary ledgers with the general ledger. If an electronic data processing system is in use, the detail accounts as well as the control accounts are likely to be posted by the EDP equipment. More will be said about the EDP internal controls later in this chapter.

5. *Use of Mechanical Equipment and Prenumbered Financial Documents.* The use of mechanical equipment enhances the efficiency of the system of internal control by providing additional checks and balances on the work of the staff and by reducing the possibility of error. Cash registers with locked-in counters and lists, accounting machines with automatic totaling devices, and check-writing machines are important types of mechanical equipment used in colleges and universities. The proofs and checks built into the modern office machine reduce errors to a minimum and serve not only to produce better records but also to eliminate possibilities of fraud. Prenumbered financial documents, such as receipts, checks, and purchase orders, are also valuable aids in the system of internal control. The supply of prenumbered documents should be carefully controlled by employees other than those actually using the documents as part of the regular routine.

6. *Use of Electronic Data Processing Equipment.* Fundamental to the use of EDP equipment for institutional accounting is the establishment of the data processing center as a separately orga-

nized department or unit. The center will operate as a separate service unit and as such will require special controls over its operation. The computer, with its capabilities for sorting, editing, proving, and processing data, makes the control system for computer installations somewhat different from the conventional machine accounting system. This difference shows up primarily in controls that are exercised over the data sent to the computer and controls that are built in—both in the program of instructions and in the equipment itself.

7. *Miscellaneous Factors Governing Personnel in the Business Office*. Personnel factors in the system of internal control include the bonding of employees, compulsory vacations, and rotation of employees. Every employee in the business office should be bonded for at least two reasons. First, a definite psychological effect is produced on the employee who is placed under bond, and it serves as a deterrent to fraudulent activity. Second, the institution is protected in the event of a loss due to defalcation. Employees in the business office should be required to take annual vacations. Not only does the institution benefit indirectly from the rest and relaxation thus afforded the employee, but the discovery of any fraud that a given employee may have successfully covered up during the year is facilitated. Rotation of employees in jobs, if practicable, is another successful method of turning up fraud that may have remained undiscovered for a long time. Rotation also has other advantages: it reduces the monotony of routine tasks and helps in training a well-rounded office staff.

8. *Internal Auditing*. There should be as much internal auditing as practicable, with regard to the size of the institution. The internal auditor should proceed in accordance with a planned audit program, just as the outside auditor does. He should test check the preauditing of vouchers and cash receipts and should make careful investigations into the activities of branch offices and outside departments. He should be constantly vigilant concerning the adequacy of the system of internal control and should check to see whether the policies of the chief business officer, the president, and the governing board are being constructively obeyed. As a representative of the chief business officer, the internal auditor is in a position to conduct various special investigations. Included in

the responsibilities of the internal auditor is a review of business systems and processes, with suggestions for change and improvement. This part of the internal auditor's function is called operational or performance audits. Operational auditing is increasing in significance because efficiency requires that equal or improved results be obtained at lower costs. The operational audit is usually performed with the full knowledge and consent of the department that is being audited. This differs from the internal financial audit, which often is initiated without prior notice.

At the conclusion of review, the internal auditor should prepare a formal report. This report should include a description of the activity examined, the period of time covered by the audit, exceptions noted, and recommendations for correction. The audit report should be addressed to the chief business officer, who will determine what action, if any, is to be taken.

A formal, written program for internal auditing operations should be prepared. This program will define the extent and frequency of reviews and list the departments and activities subject to regular audit. The following outline indicates the scope of a well-rounded program of internal audit for the office of the chief accountant and the office of the bursar for a medium-sized university.[2]

I. OFFICE OF THE CHIEF ACCOUNTANT

Item *Description*

1. Review payroll procedures to determine authority for payment of salaries and wages.
2. Determine propriety of deductions.
3. Determine that deductions are properly reported to the affected agencies.
4. Determine propriety of bank transfers.
5. Reconcile bank statements and check endorsements.
6. Preaudit vouchers in payment of claims presented for agreement in price, items, and quantity and for compliance with purchasing regulations.
7. Review cash receipt vouchers for source and disposition of receipts, bank deposit slips, and correctness of summary and total of receipts.
8. Review cash receipt forms and checks to verify the sequence of numbers.

2. The information is based on the internal auditing procedures of the University of Mississippi.

9. Review registration cards for correctness of assessment of registration fees based on classification, curriculum, residence, housing, and correctness of distribution of fees.
10. Vouch distribution of undistributed endowment income to restricted income accounts.
11. Determine propriety of journal entries to general ledger and subsidiary accounts.
12. Vouch authority of miscellaneous wage payments.
13. Determine (on preaudit) propriety of terminal pay.
14. Conduct general review to determine adequacy of the process of banking cash receipts.
15. Review internal control.

II. OFFICE OF THE BURSAR

Item *Description*

1. Age accounts receivable to determine rapidity in collection of charges.
2. Confirm all balances in excess of $25 and spot-confirm others in less amount that are in excess of 120 days.
3. Investigate credit balances over 30 days old.
4. Check to see that subsidiary accounts receivable records, security and room deposits, and other deposits agree with general ledger accounts.
5. Count petty cash.
6. Determine that cash receipts are being used numerically.
7. Reconcile notes receivable to general ledger control accounts.
8. Verify that notes receivable are properly supported by duly prepared and approved applications as required by university regulations.
9. Verify safekeeping receipts.
10. Investigate cash advances outstanding in excess of 30 days.
11. Verify that proper approval has been obtained for cash advances.
12. Review internal control.
13. Check credits for collections against referenced cash receipts.

In the small institution, the functions of internal auditing cannot proceed to so great a degree of specialization as that indicated above. Even so, some internal auditing is necessary, particularly in connection with departments outside the business office.

According to *College and University Business Administration*, the auditor's work should include the following general objectives:

1. Determining that the overall system of internal control and the controls in each activity under audit are adequate, effective and functioning.

2. Insuring that institutional policies and procedures, state and federal laws, contractual obligations, and good business practices are followed.
3. Verifying the existence of assets shown on the books of accounts and insuring maintenance of proper safeguards for their protection.
4. Determining the reliability and adequacy of the accounting and reporting systems and procedures.[3]

The internal auditor normally reports to the chief business officer and ideally should have direct access to the president. He should not be assigned line or operating responsibilities.

9. *Internal Auditing of Records Maintained with Electronic Data Processing*. The above internal audit program is based on the use of conventional machine accounting equipment. If electronic data processing is used, major changes in internal auditing take place. The auditor, confronted with a review of electronic data records, finds the usual accounting journals and ledgers are no longer present. In place of the conventional records are magnetic tapes, punched cards, and printouts. The computer eliminates the customary audit trails and forces the auditor to rely more on a review of other types of control procedures as well as to conduct portions of the audit with the computer itself. The internal auditor working with EDP systems will be concerned with three major areas of control: control over input, built-in controls, and program controls.

In connection with control over input, it has already been suggested that the EDP unit be organized as a separate department. As such, it would have no authority to originate data, its responsibility being limited to processing data that it receives. Such data should be processed through the utilization of approved programs. A machine log should be made so that a record of all stops and interventions is recorded, thereby providing a check against operator manipulation of data. Further, control over input is enhanced if predetermined totals are recorded for batches of data being sent to the EDP unit. The internal auditor will want to be certain that tight controls exist over data being sent to the EDP unit and that such controls are working.

Built-in control refers to those controls designed into the ma-

3. *College and University Business Administration*, 168.

chine itself to assure reliability. These controls help to insure that data are correctly received and processed and that appropriate results are produced. The internal auditor should be familiar with such built-in controls of the equipment as double circuitry, double track, double arithmetic, and parity bits. He should be able either to test these controls or to require the equipment manufacturer to test them for proper functioning.

Program control can be exercised by requiring the EDP unit to use only programs approved by proper officials. The auditor should be furnished an exact copy of each program. Changes in the programs should require the same official approval. Thus, at any time, the internal auditor can compare programs with the EDP units or even rerun data to verify the use of approved programs. It should be observed that the EDP equipment cannot ignore the program of instructions and will operate exactly as instructed by such programs. Certain checks to further assure accuracy of processing data can be built into the written programs. For example, in processing payrolls, all checks in excess of a certain amount can be determined by including a step in the program requiring a printout of such payments. These printouts may then be reviewed by proper officials.

The use of the computer as a tool of internal auditing is still being explored. As computer systems become more sophisticated, internal auditors will be forced to become more intimately acquainted with them and to make better use of them in auditing processes. Institutions using the total systems approach to business and administrative problems will have highly developed systems with a minimum of audit trails. Auditors will be required to develop written audit programs for use with the computer in order to make the tests necessary for the satisfaction of review requirements. In this connection it is noted that the larger public accounting firms have developed generalized computer audit programs which usually are made available to their clients for internal use.

10. *External Auditing or Postauditing*. The external audit or postaudit by independent certified public accountants, while not a part of internal control in the usual sense, does constitute a type of internal control from the point of view of the president and the governing board. The independent auditor should be engaged by

the governing board and should report directly to that body. In the case of public institutions the audit may be conducted by a state auditing agency; or the state, rather than the governing board, may employ an independent firm to audit the institution.

In addition to audits made by independent public accountants, the institution is frequently subject to audits conducted by the federal government. Federal programs that are audited periodically include research grants and contracts, loans, facilities, and others.

After examination by the external audit firm or state or federal agency, formal reports on findings and recommendations are addressed to the institution. The audit report frequently contains recommendations for improving operations or managerial controls. The independent audit produces important results in addition to verification of the accuracy and integrity of the records. It brings into the college business office a fresh point of view regarding possible improvements in the accounting system, and it affords expert advice and assistance to the staff on accounting and fiscal problems.

Detailed Requirements of Internal Control. The detailed requirements of a satisfactory system of internal control will be discussed under the following three headings: control over cash receipts, control over disbursements, and control over inventories.

1. *Control Over Cash Receipts*. A proper subdivision of duties is a principal requirement of internal control with regard to the safekeeping of cash. The individual or division responsible for the receiving, handling, and depositing of cash should be separated from the individual or division that keeps the records. The cashier's division is responsible for (a) receiving cash, (b) preparing receipts for all cash received, and (c) depositing cash daily and intact. The accounting division, insofar as cash is concerned, is responsible for (a) keeping all records of cash received, including bank accounts, student accounts, and detailed revenue accounts, (b) auditing daily cash receipts by comparing the receipts with bank deposits tickets, and (c) verifying accuracy of cash accounts by reconciling all bank accounts. By a proper subdivision of responsibilities in the cashier's division, the accounting division, and the preauditing division, errors are disclosed and traced automatically, and misuse of funds is discouraged.

The use of control devices such as prenumbered receipts and

mechanical equipment is another phase of the internal control of cash. In the absence of mechanical cash registers, at least three copies of a receipt should be written for every item of cash received. The original copy is given to the payer, the duplicate is routed to the accounting department, and the triplicate is retained by the cashier. Receipt forms should be numbered by the printer and controlled by an employee of the accounting or auditing division; that is, a record of the numbers received and issued to cashiers should be maintained. Spoiled receipts should be marked VOID by the cashier and should be retained by someone other than the cashiers. Far more satisfactory than manual receipting in most cases is receipting through mechanical cash registers. These machines can be obtained in all sizes and are equipped with a varying number of control registers. The more complicated cash registers provide for a distribution of cash receipts by depressing various marked keys. This device assists the accounting department in breaking down cash receipts for entry in the records, and it also assists in the daily audit of cash. Most cash registers provide a method of locking in totals, either on tapes or in registers. These totals can be read and the registers reset only by employees who do not have access to cash or to the operation of the registers.

Cash received through the mails should be listed by an employee other than the cashier before it is turned over to the latter. One copy of this list should be sent to the accounting or auditing department, where it will be checked against the cashier's daily report of cash received.

The institution should require that all checks be made payable to the institution rather than to individuals, departments, or cash. Checks should be endorsed for deposit only to the institution. Checks improperly prepared should be returned for correction.

Control over billings and assessments of student fees and charges is another important aspect of internal control over cash and revenues. Whenever practicable, assessments should be initiated in an office other than the business office. For example, all assessments of fees and charges at registration should be made by representatives of the registrar's office. The business office's duty should be to collect and deposit fees and audit documents. The assessment records of the registrar's office thus serve as a check on the collection records of the business office, and the procedure provides an excellent method of internal control on the revenues from registration and on the cashiers who handle large sums of money during the registration period. In the case of deferred payments for fees and room and board, the amount deferred is set up as accounts receivable, with a subsidiary student ledger card established for each debtor. The student ledger is kept by an employee of the accounting office and is not accessible to the cashiers.

Monthly statements are sometimes prepared by an employee other than the one who regularly maintains the student ledger in order to prevent collusion between the cashier and the student ledger bookkeeper. In machine accounting systems, the monthly statements usually are prepared as duplicates of the ledger card. In such cases, follow-up notices of delinquent accounts should be prepared and mailed by an employee other than one regularly engaged in posting the student ledger. No abatements, refunds, or write-offs of amounts set up as accounts receivable should be allowed without the proper authorization of a designated officer. After the registration period is over, supplementary fees, such as those for diplomas, transcripts, and special examinations, should be assessed in the registrar's office and collected in the business office. To see that fees have been collected for all students, test checks should periodically be made of the student ledger by comparing fees listed there with academic records kept in the registrar's office. Room, board, laboratory, and other charges can be verified by checking against records of appropriate auxiliary enterprises or academic departments. Periodic audit of the resident or nonresident classification of students should be conducted by the internal auditor. Institutions using advance billing procedures will have to adapt internal control procedures to accommodate this kind of system.

The cashing of checks for students is usually a service that most institutions provide. In such cases, the cashier should be given a separate fund for cashing checks. All checks cashed should be immediately endorsed FOR DEPOSIT ONLY and deposited separately to the credit of the institution. A reimbursement check must then be issued to the cashier to replenish his fund. The reimbursement check may be cashed out of regular receipts or out of the petty cash fund. In order that receipts may be deposited intact each day, a special change fund should also be issued to the cashier.

Cash should be deposited daily and intact. The following are advantages of this procedure: (a) the auditing of receipts and bank deposits is facilitated; (b) the possibility of recovery on checks returned by the bank because of insufficiency of funds and for other reasons is enhanced; (c) cashiers are given daily clearance; (d) the possibility of manipulation of undeposited receipts is reduced; (e) the process of balancing cash on hand at the end of the day with actual receipts results in greater accuracy in record keeping than is possible if a partial amount of receipts on hand is deposited; and (f) prompt banking of cash results in increased earnings if funds are temporarily invested. Deposit slips should be prepared by the cashier's division in quadruplicate; the original and duplicate go to the bank, the triplicate is routed to the accounting department, and the fourth copy is retained in the cashier's division. The duplicate is signed by the bank teller and returned to the accounting office, and the triplicate is used by the accounting division to verify the cashier's daily report of cash received. All legal and statutory requirements should be adhered to regarding the selection of the depository for institutional funds. State laws usually designate certain banks as eligible depositories for state funds and set forth qualifying requirements such as the amount and type of collateral needed to support deposits.

Bank statements should be reconciled by a representative of the accounting or internal auditing staff, not by an employee of the cashier's division or by one engaged in the disbursement process. Bank reconciliations should be made monthly. All endorsements on canceled checks should be carefully examined. Checks which have been outstanding for more than two or three months should be investigated through correspondence with payees. Some institutions have the notation NOT NEGOTIABLE AFTER 60 DAYS printed on checks to encourage prompt cashing or depositing of checks by payees. Reconciliation through the use of unit record or computer equipment becomes a simple routine procedure, and lists of outstanding checks are automatically produced as a by-product of the run.

The business office should maintain as complete control as possible over cash collected in outside departments. Auxiliary departments such as cafeterias, dining halls, athletic departments, and bookstores, which ordinarily must serve as collecting agencies, should be required to follow the detailed rules and regulations of the business office with regard to the receipts of cash. Necessary safeguards should be established to insure proper handling of receipts. All cash received should be deposited daily and intact with the cashiers in the business office and should be supported by sales tickets or cash receipts. All receipt forms used by outside departments should be prenumbered and controlled by the business office. When feasible, cash registers should be used and departments should be required to submit adding machine tapes in support of receipts. Normally, bank deposits should not be made directly by the outside collecting departments. The business office should institute and supervise an appropriate system of internal check and control in each outside agency or department that collects cash. One of the important functions of the internal auditor is to conduct periodic audits of outlying departments such as those just described.

2. *Control Over Disbursements*. The importance of subdividing responsibilities and duties in the business office as a prime requisite of the system of internal check has already been discussed both generally and with special reference to the control of cash. This concept is equally important in the internal control system for disbursements. The preparation of disbursement vouchers, maintenance of the voucher register, auditing of claims, signing of checks, and handling of the general ledger should be the responsibility of different individuals. In the small business office, of course, such specialization is not possible; however, the processes involved in disbursing can be allocated in such a way as to provide adequate internal control. Under an integrated EDP system, such subdivision of responsibilities is impossible, and reliance must be placed in the controls over input, built-in machine controls, and program controls.

All disbursements, except those insignificant in amount, should be made by check. Small items may be paid out of a properly controlled petty cash fund. Petty cash should be handled in accordance with the so-called imprest method.[4] Other important concepts concerning the proper handling of petty cash disbursements are:

(a) The amount of the fund should be limited to the absolute minimum necessary to carry on the work. The fund should be made the definite responsibility of one employee.

(b) A definite set of rules governing the use of the fund, and the items and amounts payable out of it, should be established. Payments from petty cash should be limited to small amounts.

(c) Vouchers for disbursing petty cash funds should bear the approval of a responsible person before cash is paid out.

(d) The petty cash cashier should not have access to the file of canceled petty cash vouchers. Such vouchers should be marked in order to prevent their being used to support fraudulent disbursements.

(e) Refunds of student fees or charges should be initiated in a department outside the business office. If fees are to be refunded, the registrar's office should issue the refund order. If charges for room and board are to be refunded, the manager of the dormitory or dining hall should issue the order calling for the refund.

(f) There should be a thorough audit of petty cash vouchers by the accounting or auditing division before reimbursement is made. Occasionally a surprise count of cash on hand and an analysis of the petty cash vouchers on hand should be made. Petty cash funds issued to departments outside the business office should receive particularly careful attention.

Centralized purchasing and departmental requisitioning are essential to a good system of internal control. All purchases should originate in departments, which make their needs known by addressing requisitions to the central purchasing authority. No purchase should be made without a requisition checked and approved by proper budgetary officers. Based on the approved requisition, a written purchase order showing actual or estimated cost is prepared and sent to the accounting office to determine availability of funds prior to release to vendor. The accounting office should also satisfy itself that all statutory requirements with respect to

4. See Chapter 6 for a complete discussion of accounting for petty cash.

bids and quotations have been adhered to fully. The purchase order should be prenumbered and controlled by number in the accounting office or auditing division.

When the invoice is received, it should be checked by the purchasing office as to price and quantity and then subjected to complete audit by the accounting office. This audit should consist of (a) certification by the department receiving the goods or service that the articles ordered have been received in good condition and that an invoice based on the order is properly payable; (b) comparison of the vendor's invoice with the purchase order and requisition; and (c) verification of computations and footings on the vendor's invoice. Under this procedure, duplicate payments of vendor's claims are rendered virtually impossible because, for a double payment to occur, it would be necessary to duplicate not only the vendor's invoice but also the requisition, purchase order, and receiving report.

As stated previously, all disbursements should be made by check and supported by properly audited vouchers. As to the number of signatures needed on the check, the facts of the individual situation will govern. In small colleges, the president and the business manager frequently sign checks. In the larger institutions, the treasurer and comptroller, auditor and comptroller, or bursar and comptroller are the usual combinations of signatures. If the countersignature on the check is not considered a formality, and if the countersigner actually scrutinizes the supporting vouchers, the two-signature method has definite advantages with respect to internal control. A check-signing machine is satisfactory from the point of view of internal control and is essential in the large institution. When the machine is not in use, care should be taken to keep it properly locked and to remove the signature plate. Institutional checks should be prenumbered, with all numbers accounted for. Signed checks should be mailed directly to the payee by the division in which the checks are signed. Checks should never be mailed by the purchasing division.

Prompt recording of expenditures is an aid to the system of internal control. A useful device in recording charges to departmental budget accounts is the provision of a duplicate copy for the department head. This procedure enables him to bring errors to the attention of the accounting office and assists in exposing incorrect or dishonest postings.

Payroll procedure is an important phase of the disbursement process. The responsibility for the various phases in the preparation of the payroll should be allocated so as to separate as much as possible the functions of employing, timekeeping, and computing and checking payrolls from the paying process. No person should be listed on a payroll whose name has not been certified officially by a dean, director or department head outside the business office. Salaried personnel are generally approved by the governing board at the time the institutional budget is adopted. Changes in salaried personnel after that date should be made in strict conformance with procedures laid down by the board. Nonsalaried or wage personnel are paid on the basis of payrolls prepared by individual departments. No name on a wage payroll should be honored unless proper authorization has been received from the personnel office of the institution. Payment to all types of personnel should be made by check.

Checks are distributed directly by the payroll department, or they may be given to department heads who, in turn, distribute them to the individual employees. At irregular and unannounced intervals the internal auditor or other representative of the business office should distribute the checks directly to the individual employees. This procedure assists in exposing padded payrolls. In the event payments are made in cash, a signed receipt should be obtained from each employee. Checks may also be distributed by mailing to banks as directed by the employees. Separate payroll bank accounts, operated on the imprest method, are frequently employed.

An earnings record on each employee has the following advantages with respect to the system of internal control: (a) it serves as a check on duplicate salary payments, since an individual record is set up for authorized employees only; (b) it calls attention to changes in earnings from prior periods, thus assisting the auditor in verifying the authenticity of salary increases; (c) it serves as a valuable aid in checking and verifying deduction accounts, since it records all deductions made from the employee's salary. Under EDP systems, the employee's earning record will be on tape or in other memory devices. Information needed for audit purposes can be acquired by the auditor through the use of a written program of instructions to the computer.

3. *Control Over Inventories*. There are several types of inventories in colleges and universities—namely, consumable supplies, merchandise for resale, food supplies, and movable property. The system of internal control is concerned with safeguarding these inventories. Control over all inventories, with the possible exception of merchandise for resale, can be obtained by establishing perpetual inventory systems and having control accounts in the business office. Withdrawal of supplies from storerooms should be made only upon properly signed and approved requisitions and should be made in reasonable quantities by departments. Periodically, the business office should make a physical count of the inventories and investigate differences between physical and book inventories. It is generally not practicable to maintain perpetual inventories over merchandise for resale, as, for example, in the bookstore. In such cases, the business office should require frequent physical inventories and should carefully test and analyze operating results. In regard to movable property or equipment, the responsibility for the safekeeping of institutional property should be allocated to the department head in whose custody the property is placed. The business office should establish and maintain accounting records of movable property and, with the cooperation of department heads, should make periodic physical checks in order to verify the accuracy of the perpetual inventory of equipment maintained in the business office.

16

Financial Reports and Statements

FINANCIAL REPORTING is a logical extension of the accounting system. If the accounting records are adequate, the preparation of financial reports and statements is primarily a matter of regrouping and classifying the information supplied by the books of account. Financial support for higher education is provided by many segments of society—by governments, private philanthropy, business and industry, and by parents of students. For this reason, the financial information pertaining to the operations of a college or university is of considerable interest to many people. Those who administer educational institutions are obligated to report on the results of their financial operations.

The publicly supported institution is financed by taxpayers who have a right to expect an accounting of the use of their contributions. The privately supported institution is financed by gifts and endowments from donors, who have a right to know how their donations are being expended.

The annual published report of a college serves not only to inform the supporters of the institution about the results of the period's operations, but also to convey important facts about the institution to legislators, alumni, parents of students, donors, and the public at large. Well-prepared financial reports do much to inspire the public with confidence in the work of educational institutions and their leaders. One of the important responsibilities of the chief business officer is to decide to what extent the publication of financial data about the institution will justify the cost of preparing, printing, and distributing the report.

In addition to the published report, other forms of financial statements serve important purposes in colleges and universities. Reports to administrative officers and governing boards furnish current information concerning the operations of the institution and make intelligent administration possible. Reports to division heads and deans concerning the status of budgets are an essential part of the system of budgetary control. Reports to heads of auxiliary enterprises and other organized activities, such as bookstores and dining halls, render important assistance to the managers of those enterprises.

Financial reports for the institution as a whole serve also to provide a permanent record of financial transactions as well as data for budgets and programs of subsequent periods. Especially valuable is that type of report which makes the financial statements of one institution reasonably comparable to reports of other similar institutions. The codification of the principles of accounting and reporting as it appears in *College and University Business Administration* has been the greatest single influence in establishing uniform financial reports and statements for educational institutions.

As indicated above, there are four types of financial reports:

1. The budget report to department heads
2. The internal report to the president and governing board
3. Interim reports for management
4. The annual financial report

Each of these types of reports is discussed in the subsequent sections of this chapter.

The Budget Report to Department Heads. The ideal form of departmental budgetary statement, as discussed in Chapter 5, is an allocations ledger devised to provide a duplicate copy for the head of the budget unit. This type of statement has three advantages. First, it provides the department head with a complete budget statement showing budget allocations, outstanding orders, expenditures, and free balances. Second, by furnishing the department head with a complete transcript of the formal accounting record, the accounting department is assisted in locating errors. Third, because this type of report is produced automatically as the by-product of posting the account, no additional effort or work is required in its preparation. A departmental statement of this kind is feasible only if records are kept on bookkeeping machines or

FORM 16.1

BLANK COLLEGE

MONTHLY BUDGET REPORT

For the Department of Art

Month of May, 19__

Budget	Budget Allocation	Less: Expenditures	Less: Encumbrances	Free Balance
Personnel compensation	$25,500	$23,400		$ 2,100
Supplies & expense	4,000	3,900	$ 50	50
Capital expenditures	1,000	500	500	
Totals	$30,500	$27,800	$ 550	$ 2,150

tabulating or computing equipment. If mechanical posting devices are not employed, the statement illustrated in Form 16.1 serves as an adequate report to department heads.

The Internal Report for the President and Governing Board. Reports for internal use should be made monthly or at other intervals that are considered necessary. The statements illustrated below are essential components of the internal report to the administrators of the institution. Other types of reports should be included as the individual situation requires:

1. Balance sheet (Form 16.2)
2. Summary budget report (Form 16.3)
3. Summary of expenditures compared to budget (Form 16.4)
4. Detailed statement of allocations, expenditures, and encumbrances (Form 16.5)
5. Statement of realization of revenues (Form 16.6)
6. Operating reports for auxiliary enterprises (Forms 16.19–16.23)

The balance sheet is illustrated in Form 16.2. It differs in few respects from the balance sheet included as part of the annual report. The primary difference is that the interim balance sheet includes among the current funds accounts certain budgetary and nominal accounts which reflect the progress of the institutional budget and which will be closed into current fund balances at the end of the fiscal year.

The summary budget report shows increases and decreases in estimated revenues and anticipated expenditures since the original

FORM 16.2

BLANK COLLEGE

Balance Sheet
(Before Closing)

ASSETS

CURRENT FUNDS:		
Unrestricted:		
Cash		$ 216,420
Investments, at cost (market June 30--$310,000)		296,000
Accounts receivable:		
Students, less allowance for doubtful accounts of $5,620)	$ 130,080	
Others, less allowance for doubtful accounts of $2,000)	311,000	441,080
State appropriations receivable		300,000
Inventories, at cost		191,800
Prepaid expenses and deferred charges		5,400
Transfers to other funds:		
Unexpended plant funds	$ 69,000	
Retirement of indebtedness	110,000	179,000
Estimate of revenues	$11,906,000	
Less realized revenues	11,917,600	(11,600)
Total unrestricted current funds		$ 1,618,100
Restricted:		
Cash		$ 387,200
Investments, at cost (market June 30--$460,000)		452,000
Accounts receivable--principally agencies of the U.S. government		887,500
Total restricted current funds		$ 1,726,700
TOTAL CURRENT FUNDS		$ 3,344,800
LOAN FUNDS:		
Cash		$ 47,640
Notes receivable, less allowance for doubtful loans of $10,000		1,171,500
Due from other funds		70,000
TOTAL LOAN FUNDS		$ 1,289,140

LIABILITIES AND FUND BALANCES

CURRENT FUNDS:			
Unrestricted:			
Accounts payable			$ 410,110
Retirement system deductions			9,600
Due to other funds			80,000
Deferred revenues			160,000
Provision for encumbrances--current year			175,000
Departmental allocations		$11,888,690	
Less:			
Expenditures	$11,552,350		
Encumbrances	175,000	11,727,350	161,340
Fund balances			622,050
Total unrestricted current funds			$ 1,618,100
Restricted:			
Accounts payable			$ 188,000
Fund balances			1,538,700
Total restricted current funds			$ 1,726,700
TOTAL CURRENT FUNDS			$ 3,344,800
LOAN FUNDS:			
Fund balances:			
U.S. government grants refundable			$ 954,140
University funds:			
Restricted			260,000
Unrestricted			75,000
TOTAL LOAN FUNDS			$ 1,289,140

ENDOWMENT AND SIMILAR FUNDS:	
Cash	$ 97,800
Investments at cost:	
Real estate (market June 30, 19__, $3,704,000)	2,650,000
Securities (market June 30, 19__, $12,500,000)	11,448,200
TOTAL ENDOWMENT AND SIMILAR FUNDS	$14,196,000
ANNUITY AND LIFE INCOME FUNDS:	
Annuity funds:	
Cash	$ 30,000
Investments, at cost (market June 30, 19__, $2,609,000)	2,573,200
Due from other funds	5,000
Total annuity funds	$ 2,608,200
Life income funds:	
Cash	$ 17,500
Investments at cost (market June 30, 19__, $2,348,000)	2,340,200
Total life income funds	$ 2,357,700
TOTAL ANNUITY AND LIFE INCOME FUNDS	$ 4,965,900
PLANT FUNDS:	
Unexpended:	
Cash	$ 88,600
Investments, at cost (market June 30, 19__, $2,150,000)	2,027,100
Due from other funds	5,000
Total unexpended plant funds	$ 2,120,700
Renewals and replacements:	
Cash	$ 24,000
Investments, at cost (market June 30, 19__, $301,000)	295,600
Deposits with trustees	100,000
Total renewals and replacements funds	$ 419,600
Retirement of indebtedness:	
Cash	$ 10,000
Deposits with trustees	52,200
Total retirement of indebtedness funds	$ 62,200
Investment in plant:	
Land	$ 785,000
Buildings	15,039,710
Improvements other than buildings	299,790
Equipment	6,481,000
Library books	428,500
Construction in progress	2,200,000
Total investment in plant	$25,234,000
TOTAL PLANT FUNDS	$27,836,500
AGENCY FUNDS:	
Cash	$ 42,700
Investments	74,350
TOTAL AGENCY FUNDS	$ 117,050

ENDOWMENT AND SIMILAR FUNDS:	
Fund balances:	
Endowment	$ 8,450,000
Term endowment	3,200,900
Quasi-endowment--unrestricted	2,545,100
TOTAL ENDOWMENT AND SIMILAR FUNDS	$14,196,000
ANNUITY AND LIFE INCOME FUNDS:	
Annuity funds:	
Annuities payable	$ 1,700,500
Fund balances	907,700
Total annuity funds	$ 2,608,200
Life income funds:	
Income payable	$ 7,200
Fund balances	2,350,500
Total life income funds	$ 2,357,700
TOTAL ANNUITY AND LIFE INCOME FUNDS	$ 4,965,900
PLANT FUNDS:	
Unexpended:	
Accounts payable	$ 26,000
Notes payable	90,000
Bonds payable	900,000
Fund balances:	
Restricted	893,700
Unrestricted	211,000
Total unexpended plant funds	$ 2,120,700
Renewals and replacements:	
Accounts payable	$ 32,400
Fund balances:	
Restricted	127,500
Unrestricted	259,700
Total renewals and replacements funds	$ 419,600
Retirement of indebtedness:	
Accounts payable	$ 2,500
Fund balances	59,700
Total retirement of indebtedness funds	$ 62,200
Investment in plant:	
Notes payable	$ 90,000
Bonds payable	1,700,000
Net investment in plant	23,444,000
Total investment in plant	$25,234,000
TOTAL PLANT FUNDS	$27,836,500
AGENCY FUNDS:	
Deposits held in custody for others	$ 117,050
TOTAL AGENCY FUNDS	$ 117,050

FORM 16.3

BLANK COLLEGE

SUMMARY BUDGET REPORT
(End of Month)

	July 1, 19__	Increases to date	Decreases to date	Adjusted budget
REVENUES:				
I. Educational and general:				
Student tuition and fees	4,655,000	12,000		4,667,000
Governmental appropriations	1,800,000			1,800,000
Federal grants and contracts	2,420,400			2,420,400
State grants and contracts	150,000			150,000
Local grants and contracts	12,500		2,000	10,500
Private gifts, grants and contracts	237,850			237,850
Endowment income	605,000	10,000		615,000
Sales and services of educational departments	19,500	2,000		21,500
Other sources	13,000			13,000
Total educational and general	9,913,250	24,000	2,000	9,935,250
II. Auxiliary enterprises	1,965,600	9,500	4,350	1,970,750
TOTAL REVENUES	11,878,850	33,500	6,350	11,906,000
EXPENDITURES:				
I. Educational and general:				
Instruction	3,912,865	2,750	1,000	3,914,615
Research	2,450,800	10,000		2,460,800
Public services	377,500			377,500
Academic support	984,900	11,000	6,500	989,400
Student services	697,475			697,475
Institutional support	736,500	4,000	1,500	739,000
Operation and maintenance of physical plant	643,000	2,000		645,000
Scholarships and fellowships	60,150			60,150
Total educational and general	9,863,190	29,750	9,000	9,883,940
Mandatory transfers for:				
Principal and interest	50,000			50,000
Loan fund matching grant	2,000			2,000
Total educational and general and mandatory transfers	9,915,190	29,750	9,000	9,935,940
II. Auxiliary enterprises:				
Expenditures	1,750,000	9,500	4,350	1,755,150
Mandatory transfers for:				
Principal and interest	187,600			187,600
Renewals and replacements	10,000			10,000
Total auxiliary enterprises	1,947,600	9,500	4,350	1,952,750
TOTAL EXPENDITURES AND MANDATORY TRANSFERS	11,862,790	39,250	13,350	11,888,690
Unallocated revenues	16,060			17,310

approval of the annual budget. Expenditures to date are compared in summary and in detail with the original budget allocations to each department (adjusted by any recorded amendments). These statements serve to inform the administration of the progress of the entire institutional budget. The statement of realization of revenues informs the administration of the progress of the revenue phases of the budget by showing the original estimate of revenue, the amount realized to date, and the balance expected to be realized.

Operating statements for auxiliary activities are essential components of the system of interim financial reporting. Not only is the information in these reports of vital significance to the managers

FORM 16.4

BLANK COLLEGE

SUMMARY STATEMENT OF EXPENDITURES
COMPARED TO BUDGET
(End of Month)

	Budget allocations	Expenditures to date	Outstanding encumbrances	Free balance
I. Educational and general:				
Instruction:				
College of Liberal Arts	1,582,950	1,092,235	5,580	485,135
College of Business and Government	327,900	226,250	6,200	95,450
College of Education	103,500	71,250	2,950	29,300
College of Engineering	887,185	576,437	11,900	298,848
School of Law	480,000	352,800	1,050	126,150
School of Pharmacy	209,000	148,800	1,100	59,100
Graduate School	74,500	53,340	120	21,040
Summer Session	247,580	198,918	300	48,362
Other instructional expenses	2,000	1,000		1,000
Total instruction	3,914,615	2,721,030	29,200	1,164,385
Research:				
Institutes and research centers	2,000,000	1,922,932	17,800	59,268
Project research	460,800	442,368	3,900	14,532
Total research	2,460,800	2,365,300	21,700	73,800
Public services:				
Community service	22,100	14,800	200	7,100
Cooperative extension	16,900	11,660		5,240
Conferences, institutes and short courses	17,000	11,220	800	4,980
Radio	91,500	66,790	1,100	23,610
Television	230,000	149,230	900	79,870
Total public services	377,500	253,700	3,000	120,800
Academic support:				
Academic administration	210,000	149,000	1,100	59,900
Computing services	390,900	277,540	9,200	104,160
Audiovisual services	21,500	15,910	1,000	4,590
Curriculum development	30,000	22,500	700	6,800
Libraries	275,000	209,000	1,000	65,000
Museums and galleries	62,000	35,312		26,688
Total academic support	989,400	709,262	13,000	267,138
Student services:				
Registrar	47,900	33,530	1,200	13,170
Admissions	33,000	23,760	600	8,640
Student counseling and guidance	17,000	12,070	400	4,530
Dean of students	33,000	23,700	1,200	8,100
Financial aids	26,500	19,000	750	6,750
Cultural activities	12,000	9,000	1,000	2,000
Health services	170,000	120,700	750	48,550
Intramural athletics	60,000	44,400	1,150	14,450
Intercollegiate athletics	264,575	180,314	3,050	81,211
Student organizations	21,500	15,050	900	5,550
Remedial instruction	12,000	9,058	600	2,342
Total student services	697,475	490,582	11,600	195,293
Institutional support:				
Governing board	25,000	16,500		8,500
President	80,000	53,600	400	26,000
Chief academic office	41,000	29,930	260	10,810
Business office	98,500	70,920	1,100	26,480
Comptroller's office	26,000	18,720	200	7,080
Budget office	16,000	11,680		4,320
Bursar	30,000	21,050	95	8,855
Legal services	10,000	11,500		(1,500)
Administrative data processing	110,000	76,680	2,050	31,270
Internal audits	12,000	8,880		3,120
Security	53,600	38,800		14,800
Safety	10,000	7,450		2,550
Alumni activities	21,000	15,200	650	5,150
Development office	17,200	12,900	1,200	3,100
Commencement	9,000	5,940		3,060
Convocations	2,000	1,200		800
Catalogs and bulletins	4,000	3,020		980
Personnel services	31,000	22,320		8,680
Memberships	1,500	1,500		
Public relations	17,500	13,300	400	3,800
Publications	19,400	10,970	975	7,455
Printing	17,500	17,000	1,000	(500)
Purchasing	31,000	22,000	300	8,700
Telephone services	39,800	27,250	720	11,830
Transportation services	16,000	8,800	400	6,800
Total institutional support	739,000	527,110	9,750	202,140

	Budget allocations	Expenditures to date	Outstanding encumbrances	Free balance
Operation and maintenance of physical plant:				
Administration	39,700	26,560	400	12,740
Custodial services	112,875	71,050	4,050	37,775
Maintenance of buildings	103,200	73,700	3,270	26,230
Maintenance of grounds	42,500	28,450	1,200	12,850
Trucking service	39,600	29,220	2,850	7,530
Fire protection	17,000	11,850	1,180	3,970
Utilities	197,700	130,480		67,220
Property insurance	81,225	50,490		30,735
Other maintenance	11,200	10,300		900
Total operation and maintenance of physical plant	645,000	432,100	12,950	199,950
Scholarships and fellowships:				
Scholarships	34,150	27,900		6,250
Fellowships	14,000	11,220		2,780
Fee waivers	12,000	9,000		3,000
Total scholarships and fellowships	60,150	48,120		12,030
Total educational and general	9,883,940	7,547,204	101,200	2,235,536
Mandatory transfers:				
Principal and interest	50,000	50,000		
Loan fund matching grant	2,000	2,000		
Total mandatory transfers	52,000	52,000		
Total educational and general and mandatory transfers	9,935,940	7,599,204	101,200	2,235,536
II. Auxiliary enterprises:				
Expenditures:				
Student union	20,000	14,520	3,200	2,280
Cafeteria	580,500	422,690	12,800	145,010
Residence halls--single	521,500	381,730	4,320	135,450
Residence halls--married	120,000	88,970	3,790	27,240
Bookstore	513,150	369,052	15,290	128,808
Total expenditures	1,755,150	1,276,962	39,400	438,788
Mandatory transfers for:				
Principal and interest	187,600	138,200		49,400
Renewals and replacements	10,000	10,000		
Total mandatory transfers	197,600	148,200	39,400	49,400
Total auxiliary enterprises	1,952,750	1,425,162	39,400	488,188
Total expenditures and mandatory transfers	11,888,690	9,024,366	140,600	2,723,724

of the auxiliary enterprises, but the statements are also an important source of information to the chief business officer, the president, and the governing board.

Interim Reports for Management. Other types of interim reports include reports concerning the operations of restricted current funds, sponsored research projects, gifts received, inventories, construction projects, and cash flow. It is useful also to prepare periodic reports, usually monthly, on the performance of the investments of endowment funds, as well as periodic reports of gifts received, which should be classified by types of donors and by the purposes for which the gifts were made.

The number, frequency, and general content of internal reports will vary according to the needs of the institution. Small institutions usually require less formal reports. The large, complex university generally requires a variety of interim reports dealing with different phases of business and fiscal administration.

FORM 16.5

BLANK COLLEGE

DETAILED STATEMENT OF ALLOCATIONS, EXPENDITURES, AND ENCUMBRANCES*
(End of Month)

	Budget allocations	Expenditures to date	Outstanding encumbrances	Free balance
I. Educational and general:				
Instruction:				
College of Liberal Arts:				
Office of the Dean:				
Personnel compensation	33,650	23,200		10,450
Supplies and expense	8,000	6,000		2,000
Capital expenditures	350		350	
Total	42,000	29,200	350	12,450
Aerospace studies:				
Personnel compensation	25,550	18,140		7,410
Supplies and expense	4,000	2,947		1,053
Capital expenditures	150		150	
Total	29,700	21,087	150	8,463
Art:				
Personnel compensation	17,000	11,800		5,200
Supplies and expense	3,700	2,595	100	1,005
Capital expenditures	300	200	100	
Total	21,000	14,595	200	6,205
Biology:				
Personnel compensation	166,500	113,280		53,220
Supplies and expense	9,000	6,600	1,155	1,245
Capital expenditures	1,500	480	980	40
Total	177,000	120,360	2,135	54,505
Chemistry:				
Personnel compensation	273,100	192,600		80,500
Supplies and expense	9,500	7,950		1,550
Capital expenditures	900		780	120
Total	283,500	200,550	780	82,170
Classics:				
Personnel compensation	25,800	17,780		8,020
Supplies and expense	1,000	690		310
Capital expenditures	700	480		220
Total	27,500	18,950		8,550
English:				
Personnel compensation	33,400	22,740		10,660
Supplies and expense	1,200	860		340
Capital expenditures	300	300		
Total	34,900	23,900		11,000
History:				
Personnel compensation	23,900	17,360		6,540
Supplies and expense	500	200	150	150
Total	24,400	17,560	150	6,690
Home economics:				
Personnel compensation	14,000	10,010		3,990
Supplies and expense	900	420	95	385
Total	14,900	10,430	95	4,375
Mathematics:				
Personnel compensation	161,680	87,950		73,730
Supplies and expense	1,370	763		607
Capital expenditures	950	400		550
Total	164,000	89,113		74,887
Military science:				
Supplies and expense	9,600	7,550		2,050
Capital expenditures	400	50	350	
Total	10,000	7,600	350	2,050
Modern languages:				
Personnel compensation	16,200	11,625		4,575
Supplies and expense	300	75	100	125
Total	16,500	11,700	100	4,700
Music:				
Personnel compensation	13,000	9,150		3,850
Supplies and expense	600	350	200	50
Capital expenditures	400	200	200	
Total	14,000	9,700	400	3,900

	Budget allocations	Expenditures to date	Outstanding encumbrances	Free balance
Naval science:				
Supplies and expense	6,000	4,920		1,080
Capital expenditures	4,000	3,280	200	520
Total	10,000	8,200	200	1,600
Philosophy:				
Personnel compensation	46,200	36,500		9,700
Supplies and expense	1,100	800		300
Capital expenditures	900	390		510
Total	48,200	37,690		10,510
Physics:				
Personnel compensation	286,000	198,690		87,310
Supplies and expense	4,600	3,050	190	1,360
Capital expenditures	4,000	3,010	280	710
Total	294,600	204,750	470	89,380
Psychology:				
Personnel compensation	176,750	129,800		46,950
Supplies and expense	4,000	2,100		1,900
Capital expenditures	1,100	900		200
Total	181,850	132,800		49,050
Sociology and anthropology:				
Personnel compensation	132,300	92,600		39,700
Supplies and expense	6,000	4,100		1,900
Capital expenditures	4,200	3,050	100	1,050
Total	142,500	99,750	100	42,650
Speech and theater:				
Personnel compensation	37,000	26,090		10,910
Supplies and expense	7,200	6,310	100	790
Capital expenditures	2,200	1,900		300
Total	46,400	34,300	100	12,000
Total College of Liberal Arts	1,582,950	1,092,235	5,580	485,135
College of Business and Government:				
Office of the dean:				
Personnel compensation	38,100	26,810		11,290
Supplies and expense	8,500	4,790	1,240	2,470
Capital expenditures	600	500	100	
Total	47,200	32,100	1,340	13,760
Accounting:				
Personnel compensation	65,050	46,825		18,225
Supplies and expense	6,000	3,000	2,300	700
Capital expenditures	700	400	300	
Total	71,750	50,225	2,600	18,925
Economics and business administration:				
Personnel compensation	64,850	45,010		19,840
Supplies and expense	4,500	3,290		1,210
Capital expenditures	1,700	900		800
Total	71,050	49,200		21,850
Journalism:				
Personnel compensation	30,200	21,530		8,670
Supplies and expense	1,900	1,470		430
Total	32,100	23,000		9,100
Business education and office administration:				
Personnel compensation	49,450	35,000		14,450
Supplies and expense	3,000	1,950	850	200
Capital expenditures	800	650	150	
Total	53,250	37,600	1,000	14,650
Political science:				
Personnel compensation	49,150	31,665		17,485
Supplies and expense	3,000	2,060	250	690
Capital expenditures	400	400		
Total	52,550	34,125	250	18,175
Total College of Business and Government	327,900	226,250	5,190	96,460
College of Education:				
Office of the dean:				
Personnel compensation	26,800	18,700		8,100
Supplies and expense	4,200	3,050	400	750
Capital expenditures	500	300		200
Total	31,500	22,050	400	9,050

	Budget allocations	Expenditures to date	Outstanding encumbrances	Free balance
Health, physical education and recreation:				
Personnel compensation	40,000	28,200		11,800
Supplies and expense	5,000	4,100	470	430
Capital expenditures	1,000	300	500	200
Total	46,000	32,600	970	12,430
Library science:				
Personnel compensation	8,700	6,620		2,080
Supplies and expense	1,900	1,200	500	200
Capital expenditures	400	100	300	
Total	11,000	7,920	800	2,280
Reading clinic:				
Personnel compensation	12,000	8,100		3,900
Supplies and expense	3,000	580	780	1,640
Total	15,000	8,680	780	5,540
Total College of Education	103,500	71,250	2,950	29,300
College of Engineering:				
Office of the dean:				
Personnel compensation	86,400	56,200		30,200
Supplies and expense	19,000	12,960	2,000	4,040
Capital expenditures	1,000		1,000	
Total	106,400	69,160	3,000	34,240
Chemical engineering:				
Personnel compensation	99,460	66,090		33,370
Supplies and expense	5,000	3,980	600	420
Capital expenditures	2,000	1,150	900	(50)
Total	106,460	71,220	1,500	33,740
Civil engineering:				
Personnel compensation	99,700	65,800		33,900
Supplies and expense	6,000	4,360	1,200	440
Capital expenditures	3,500	3,000	500	
Total	109,200	73,160	1,700	34,340
Geology and geological engineering:				
Personnel compensation	146,800	98,650		48,150
Supplies and expense	7,500	6,000	500	1,000
Capital expenditures	2,000	150	1,700	150
Total	156,300	104,800	2,200	49,300
Mechanical engineering:				
Personnel compensation	136,000	90,980		45,020
Supplies and expense	7,200	4,720	270	2,210
Capital expenditures	3,000	2,100	730	170
Total	146,200	97,800	1,000	47,400
Electrical engineering:				
Personnel compensation	123,400	84,530		38,870
Supplies and expense	5,100	2,470	400	2,230
Capital expenditures	2,500	350	1,100	1,050
Total	131,000	87,350	1,500	42,150
Seismological observatory:				
Personnel compensation	99,625	59,775		39,850
Supplies and expense	7,000	3,372	75	3,553
Capital expenditures	25,000	9,800	925	14,275
Total	131,625	72,947	1,000	56,678
Total College of Engineering	887,185	576,437	11,900	298,848
School of Law:				
Office of the dean:				
Personnel compensation	260,000	192,400		67,600
Supplies and expense	32,000	22,400	300	9,300
Capital expenditures	4,500	3,100		1,400
Total	296,500	217,900	300	78,300
Law extension:				
Personnel compensation	71,800	53,050		18,750
Supplies and expense	10,000	7,070	200	2,730
Total	81,800	60,120	200	21,480
Legal institute for agriculture and resource extension:				
Personnel compensation	84,200	62,300		21,900
Supplies and expense	14,500	10,330	100	4,070
Capital expenditures	3,000	2,150	450	400
Total	101,700	74,780	550	26,370
Total School of Law	480,000	352,800	1,050	126,150

	Budget allocations	Expenditures to date	Outstanding encumbrances	Free balance
School of Pharmacy:				
Office of the dean:				
Personnel compensation	168,500	123,000		45,500
Supplies and expense	36,000	22,600	150	13,250
Capital expenditures	4,500	3,200	950	350
Total	209,000	148,800	1,100	59,100
Total School of Pharmacy	209,000	148,800	1,100	59,100
Graduate School:				
Office of the dean:				
Personnel compensation	49,700	35,780		13,920
Supplies and expense	6,900	4,270	120	2,510
Capital expenditures	400	400		
Total	57,000	40,450	120	16,430
City planning:				
Personnel compensation	12,000	8,760		3,240
Supplies and expense	4,800	3,750		1,050
Capital expenditures	700	380		320
Total	17,500	12,890		4,610
Total Graduate School	74,500	53,340	120	21,040
Summer Session:				
Office of the director:				
Personnel compensation	38,950	31,940		7,010
Supplies and expense	9,500	6,820	150	2,530
Capital expenditures	750	600		150
Total	49,200	39,360	150	9,690
University:				
Personnel compensation	103,900	82,950		20,950
Supplies and expense	6,200	5,050	50	1,100
Capital expenditures	400	400		
Total	110,500	88,400	50	22,050
School of Law:				
Personnel compensation	83,180	68,200		14,980
Supplies and expense	4,100	2,488	100	1,512
Capital expenditures	600	470		130
Total	87,880	71,158	100	16,622
Total Summer Session	247,580	198,918	300	48,362
Other instructional expenses:				
Supplies and expense	2,000	1,000		1,000
Total	2,000	1,000		1,000
Total other instructional expense	2,000	1,000		1,000
Total instruction	3,914,615	2,721,030	29,200	1,165,395

*This is a partial statement covering instructional budgets.

The Annual Financial Report. Every institution, regardless of size, should have an annual financial report prepared by the staff of the institution. In many cases, annual financial reports are printed or reproduced in some manner and made available to governing boards, faculty members, members of the state legislature, alumni, donors, and other interested parties. The annual financial report is divided into three sections: (1) general information, including the auditor's opinion; (2) primary statements; (3) supporting schedules; and (4) statement of significant accounting policies and notes to financial statements.

The first section on general information has as its primary purpose the presentation of summary data describing the financial operations of the institution for the fiscal year covered by the re-

FORM 16.6

BLANK COLLEGE

STATEMENT OF REALIZATION OF REVENUES
(End of Month)

	Estimated revenues	Realized to date	Balance to be realized
I. Educational and general:			
Student tuition and fees	4,667,000	4,215,605	451,395
Governmental appropriations			
State--general support	450,000	326,430	123,570
Federal	1,338,000	1,300,000	38,000
Local	12,000	5,000	7,000
Federal grants and contracts			
Grants	737,500	625,000	112,500
Contracts	1,682,900	1,439,260	243,640
State grants and contracts			
Grants	27,650	22,000	5,650
Contracts	122,350	96,300	26,050
Local grants and contracts			
University funds	6,000		6,000
Other sources	4,500	5,150	650*
Private gifts, grants, and contracts			
Business grants	4,000	3,000	1,000
Business and industry contracts	222,390	197,000	25,390
Business and industry training grants	11,460	9,265	2,195
Endowment income			
Unrestricted	565,000	425,370	139,630
Restricted	50,000	41,050	8,950
Sales and services of educational departments	21,500	23,750	2,250*
Other sources	13,000	9,020	3,980
Total educational and general	9,935,250	8,743,200	1,192,050
II. Auxiliary enterprises:			
Student union	95,000	76,435	18,565
Residence halls--single	577,900	402,650	175,250
Residence halls--married	228,600	174,000	54,600
Cafeteria	444,250	349,800	94,450
Bookstore	625,000	491,740	133,260
Total auxiliary enterprises	1,970,750	1,494,625	476,125
Total revenues	11,906,000	10,237,825	1,668,175

*Indicates excess of revenues over budget estimates.

port. It is designed to give the casual reader, particularly the layman, a condensed picture of the financial operations for the period. This section may be informal in nature and, in addition to financial summaries, may include discussions, analyses, and interpretations by the chief business officer. Frequently, graphs and flow charts are provided along with the summary information. Letters of transmittal and the certificate of the auditor usually precede the discussion of the financial operations. Increasing numbers of institutions are following the practice of printing and distributing a summary financial report, and of duplicating the details of the financial transactions for the year primarily for the use of the governing board and college administration.

The second section of the annual report, the primary statements, presents the financial data for the year's operations. *College and University Business Administration* indicates that this part of the report must include three primary statements: the balance sheet, the statement of changes in fund balances, and the statement of current funds revenues, expenditures, and other changes. The purpose of the balance sheet is to report the financial condition of the institution at the end of the fiscal year. It shows what assets the institution possesses at the close of the year and what obligations exist against these assets. Following the pattern of the accounting system, the balance sheet is divided into fund groups. Usually it is presented as illustrated in this chapter; however, it may be arranged in a multicolumnar form, having a separate column for each fund group and major subgroup. If the alternate form is used, there should be no total column in which like assets and liabilities and fund balances of all fund groups are combined, unless all necessary disclosures are made, including interfund borrowings. In support of the balance sheet, the statement of changes in fund balances shows the beginning balance in each fund group, the additions and deductions during the year, and the final balance, which is reflected on the balance sheet.

The statement of current funds revenues, expenditures, and other changes is the operating statement showing in summary form the results of the current operations of the institution during the fiscal period. In addition to revealing revenues by sources and expenditures by function, it also shows transfers made from the current funds group to other funds.

The third section of the financial report is composed of supporting schedules that supply detailed information already summarized in the preceding section. The most important schedules are those showing details of revenues by source and of expenditures and transfers by function. These schedules provide information not disclosed in the summary statement of current funds revenues, expenditures, and other changes. Other schedules include an operating statement for each auxiliary enterprise and details of the operations of loan, endowment, annuity and life income and plant funds.

A study of a large number of published reports shows that many other types of financial statements are included in annual reports of colleges and universities. Many of these statements present comparisons with previous years, which are useful sources of information to the reader. Whether additional statements should be included in the annual report depends upon the circumstances in the individual institution. Adjustments resulting from a change in accounting methods to comply with recommendations of *College and University Business Administration* or the AICPA Audit Guide should be treated as adjustments of prior periods, and the financial statements of appropriate prior periods should be restated. In order to provide adequate disclosure, the basic financial statements should be accompanied by explanatory notes on significant matters not fully disclosed in the financial statements, as well as a commentary on the accounting policies followed by the institution. Financial information pertaining to separately incorporated agencies for which the institution is fiscally responsible, such as research foundations, university presses, and athletic associations, should be (1) included in separate statements, accompanied by and cross-referenced to the basic institutional statements, (2) disclosed by footnotes, or (3) included in the statements of the institution.

A suggested outline for the annual published report is given below. The tables, exhibits, and schedules listed are illustrated on pages 346–77, herein.

I. General
   A. Letter of transmittal from the chief business officer to the president (page 346, herein)
   B. Accountant's opinion (pages 346–47, herein)
   C. General condensed summary (pages 347–50, herein)

II. Primary statements
   A. Balance sheet (Form 16.7)
   B. Statement of current funds revenues, expenditures, and other changes (Form 16.8)
   C. Statement of changes in fund balances (Form 16.9)

III. Supporting schedules:
   1. Schedule of current funds revenues (Form 16.10)
   2. Schedule of current funds expenditures and transfers (Form 16.11)
   3. Schedule of changes in fund balances—loan funds (Form 16.12)

4. Schedule of changes in fund balances—endowment and similar funds (Form 16.13)
5. Schedule of changes in fund balances—annuity and life income funds (Form 16.14)
6. Schedule of changes in fund balances—unexpended plant funds (Form 16.15)
7. Schedule of changes in fund balances—funds for renewals and replacements (Form 16.16)
8. Schedule of changes in fund balances—funds for retirement of indebtedness (Form 16.17)
9. Schedule of changes in investment in plant (Form 16.18)
10. Revenues and expenditures of auxiliary enterprises
    a. Residence halls—single students (Form 16.19)
    b. Residence halls—married students (Form 16.20)
    c. Bookstore (Form 16.21)
    d. Cafeteria (Form 16.22)
    e. College union (Form 16.23)
11. Schedule of investments by fund groups (Form 16.24)
12. Schedule of long-term notes and bonds payable (Form 16.25)
13. Statement of deposit liabilities (Form 16.26)
14. Statement of bonds payable (Form 16.27)
15. Summary of significant accounting policies (Form 16.28)
16. Notes to financial statements (Form 16.29)

The foregoing outline contains the necessary minimum of financial statements and schedules. Other information frequently found in published reports of colleges and universities includes:

1. Comparative statements for a period of years showing
    a. Expenditures
    b. Revenues
    c. Operation and maintenance costs
    d. Enrollments
2. Description and map of college
3. Expenditures by programs, projects, and other similar objectives
4. Various charts and diagrams
5. Statements of endowment and other investments

The remaining portion of this chapter is devoted to presenting a model annual report. Included are letters of transmittal, comments and summaries by the chief business officer, and the statements considered to be essential in most college and university annual reports.

MODEL ANNUAL REPORT

LETTER OF TRANSMITTAL

BLANK COLLEGE
Blank, State

Office of the
Vice-President and Comptroller

September 30, 19–

President John Doe

Dear President Doe:

I am submitting herewith the annual financial report of the college for the fiscal year ended June 30, 19–. This report contains summaries of important financial data as well as more detailed tables, statements, and schedules designed to present a complete financial picture of all phases and funds of the college.

Accounts of the college have been examined by Rohn and Company, Certified Public Accountants, and their opinion is made a part of this record.

Respectfully submitted,

David Smith
Vice-President and
Comptroller

Rohn and Company
Certified Public Accountants

Manson Building

ACCOUNTANT'S OPINION

The Board of Governors
Blank College

We have examined the balance sheet of Blank College as of June 30, 19–, and the related statements of changes in fund balances and current funds revenues, expenditures, and other changes for the year then ended. Our examination was made in accordance with generally accepted auditing standards and accordingly included such tests of the accounting records and such other auditing procedures as we considered necessary in the circumstances.

In our opinion, the aforementioned financial statements present fairly the financial position of Blank College at June 30, 19–, and the changes in fund balances and the current funds revenues, expenditures, and other changes for the year then ended, in conformity with generally accepted accounting principles applied on a basis consistent with that of the preceding year.

ROHN AND COMPANY

September 25, 19–

CONDENSED GENERAL SUMMARY

CURRENT REVENUES FOR THE YEAR

Current revenues for the year, including restricted grants and contracts and auxiliary enterprises, total $11,917,600. This compares to $11,737,450 in the previous year. Revenues increased principally from restricted grants and contracts, student tuition and fees, and unrestricted gifts and grants. The following table shows in summary the revenues for the year:

	Amount	*Percent of total revenues*	*Percent of educational and general revenues*
Student tuition and fees	$ 4,677,345	39.25%	47.10%
Governmental appropriations	1,800,000	15.11%	18.12%
Federal grants and contracts	2,398,300	20.12%	24.16%
State grants and contracts	149,365	1.25%	1.50%
Local grants and contracts	11,150	.09%	.11%
Private gifts, grants and contracts	239,600	2.01%	2.41%
Endowment income	616,295	5.17%	6.21%
Sales and services of educational departments	24,940	.21%	.25%
Other sources	14,205	.12%	.14%
Total educational and general	$ 9,931,200	83.33%	100.00%
Auxiliary enterprises	1,986,400	16.67%	
	$11,917,600	100.00%	

A detailed report of current funds revenues will be found on page 356, herein.

CURRENT EXPENDITURES FOR THE YEAR

Current expenditures for the year, including restricted funds and auxiliary enterprises, total $11,656,750, which compares to $11,430,600 in the previous year. Expenditures and mandatory transfers to other funds totaled $11,906,350 and, along with revenues of $11,917,600 and a transfer of $5,000 to quasi-endowment funds, resulted in a total addition of $6,250 to the balance of unrestricted current funds. The following table shows in summary the expenditures and mandatory transfers for the year:

	Amount	*Percent of total expenditures*	*Percent of educational and general expenditures*
Instruction	$ 3,910,604	32.85%	39.56%
Research	2,461,000	20.67%	24.89%
Public services	370,900	3.12%	3.75%
Academic support	994,700	8.35%	10.06%
Student services	701,460	5.89%	7.10%
Institutional support	742,500	6.23%	7.51%
Operation and maintenance of physical plant	648,070	5.44%	6.56%
Scholarships and fellowships	56,616	.48%	0.57%
Educational and General	$ 9,885,850	83.03%	100.00%
Mandatory transfers for:			
Principal and interest	50,000	.42%	
Loan funds matching grant	2,000	.02%	
Total educational and general	$ 9,937,850	83.47%	
Auxiliary enterprises:			
Expenditures	1,770,900	14.87%	
Mandatory transfers for:			
Principal and interest	157,600	1.32%	
Renewals and replacements	40,000	.34%	
Total auxiliary enterprises	1,968,500	16.53%	
Total current expenditures and mandatory transfers	$11,906,350	100.00%	

A detailed statement of current funds expenditures and transfers will be found in Schedule 16.11, page 357–58, herein.

Loan Funds

Loan funds totaled $1,289,140 at the end of the fiscal year, an increase of $47,240 during the year. Primarily, the increase resulted from borrowings from the U.S. government and a transfer of $35,000 from matured annuity and life income funds. At June 30, 19–, a total of $1,171,500 in loans had been issued to needy students. Detailed statements of loan funds will be found on pages 355 and 359, herein.

Endowment and Similar Funds

The college's endowment fund and the income it produces are vital sources of support for current operations. During the year, endowment investments earned $616,295, of which $590,045 was designated for current operations of the college and $26,250 for specific schools and departments.

Endowment and similar funds increased during the year in the amount of $418,600, largely from capital gains of $385,800 and gifts of $27,800. The assets of the various funds are pooled for investment purposes, and each fund shares proportionately in income and capital gains generated by the pool. To date, the college has advanced a total of $400,000 from current funds to serve temporarily as endowment.

Detailed statements of endowment and similar funds are presented on pages 355 and 360, herein.

Plant Funds

The total investment in plant at June 30, 19–, valued at cost, is as follows:

Land	$ 785,000
Buildings	15,084,710
Improvements other than buildings (fencing, parking lot, roadways, and underground piping)	299,790
Equipment	6,481,000
Library books	428,500
Construction in progress	2,200,000
	$25,279,000

Additions to the physical plant increased during the year in the amount of $826,630, which represents current expenditures of $131,710 on various buildings, a net increase of $91,020 in movable equipment, expenditures of $48,900 on library books, capitalization of $45,000 of expenditures on buildings, and an increase of $510,000 on new construction in progress.

Unexpended plant funds increased during the year in the amount of $486,900, primarily from gifts and grants and borrowings. During the year, $172,030 was expended for additions to plant facilities.

During the year, funds for renewals and replacements were expended in the amount of $50,700 for equipment. At June 30, 19–, funds for renewals and replacements had a balance of $387,200.

The college liquidated $110,000 of outstanding bonds and notes during the year through funds for retirement of indebtedness; additional borrowings of $510,000 for an addition to the married students dormitory resulted in a net increase of $400,000 of the plant funds in bonds and notes payable at June 30, 19–, over the previous year.

Detailed statements of investment in plant, unexpended plant funds, funds for renewals and replacements, and funds for retirement of indebtedness and investment in plant are presented on pages 355 and 362–65, herein.

Agency Funds

Agency funds, for which the college acts only as a fiscal agent, consist primarily of deposits of students and organizations held in trust by the college.

FORM 16.7

BLANK COLLEGE

BALANCE SHEET
June 30, 19__

With Comparative Figures at June 30, 19__

ASSETS	Current year	Prior year
CURRENT FUNDS:		
Unrestricted:		
Cash	$ 127,020	$ 86,200
Investments, at cost (market June 30, 19__, $310,000; prior year $205,000)	296,000	200,000
Accounts receivable:		
Students, less allowance for doubtful accounts of $5,620; prior year $5,000)	130,080	197,600
Others, less allowance for doubtful accounts of $2,000; prior year $1,950)	311,000	325,000
State appropriations receivable	300,000	250,000
Inventories, at cost	191,800	186,700
Prepaid expenses and deferred charges	5,400	7,200
Total unrestricted current funds	$ 1,361,300	$ 1,252,700
Restricted:		
Cash	$ 387,200	$ 196,500
Investments, at cost (market June 30, 19__, $460,000; prior year $501,000)	452,000	495,100
Accounts receivable--principally agencies of the U.S. government	887,500	737,600
Total restricted current funds	$ 1,726,700	$ 1,429,200
TOTAL CURRENT FUNDS	$ 3,088,000	$ 2,681,900
LOAN FUNDS:		
Cash	$ 117,640	$ 104,040
Notes receivable, less allowance for doubtful loans of $10,000 both years	1,171,500	1,137,860
TOTAL LOAN FUNDS	$ 1,289,140	$ 1,241,900

LIABILITIES AND FUND BALANCES	Current year	Prior year
CURRENT FUNDS:		
Unrestricted:		
Accounts payable	$ 398,400	$ 253,150
Retirement system deductions	79,600	64,000
Due to other funds	70,000	105,000
Deferred revenues	160,000	277,500
Fund balances:		
Provision for encumbrances	20,000	26,000
Unrestricted	633,300	527,050
Total unrestricted current funds	$ 1,361,300	$ 1,252,700
Restricted:		
Accounts payable	$ 188,000	$ 210,000
Fund balances	1,538,700	1,219,200
Total restricted current funds	$ 1,726,700	$ 1,429,200
TOTAL CURRENT FUNDS	$ 3,088,000	$ 2,681,900
LOAN FUNDS:		
Fund balances:		
U.S. government grants refundable	$ 953,965	$ 941,900
University funds:		
Restricted	260,000	225,000
Unrestricted	75,175	75,000
TOTAL LOAN FUNDS	$ 1,289,140	$ 1,241,900

ENDOWMENT AND SIMILAR FUNDS:		
Cash	$ 97,800	$ 128,700
Investments, at cost:		
Real estate (market June 30, 19__, $3,704,000; prior year $3,900,000)	2,650,000	2,704,900
Securities (market June 30, 19__, $12,100,000; prior year $11,542,000)	11,448,200	10,943,800
TOTAL ENDOWMENT AND SIMILAR FUNDS	$14,196,000	$13,777,400
ANNUITY AND LIFE INCOME FUNDS:		
Annuity funds:		
Cash	$ 35,000	$ 47,000
Investments, at cost (market June 30, 19__, $2,609,000; prior year $2,158,000)	2,573,200	2,262,000
Total annuity funds	$ 2,608,200	$ 2,309,000
Life income funds:		
Cash	$ 39,680	$ 14,000
Investments, at cost (market June 30, 19__, $2,348,000; prior year $1,967,000)	2,340,200	2,063,500
Total life income funds	$ 2,379,880	$ 2,077,500
TOTAL ANNUITY AND LIFE INCOME FUNDS	$ 4,988,080	$ 4,386,500
PLANT FUNDS:		
Unexpended:		
Cash	$ 133,600	$ 87,400
Investments, at cost (market June 30, 19__, $2,150,000; prior year $1,580,000)	2,027,100	1,566,400
Due from other funds	50,000	89,000
Total unexpended plant funds	$ 2,210,700	$ 1,742,800
Renewals and replacements:		
Cash	$ 4,000	$ 5,500
Investments, at cost (market June 30, 19__, $301,000; prior year $274,000)	295,600	269,000
Deposits with trustees	100,000	60,000
Due from other funds	20,000	40,000
Total renewals and replacements funds	$ 419,600	$ 374,500

ENDOWMENT AND SIMILAR FUNDS:		
Fund balances:		
Endowment	$ 8,450,000	$ 8,200,850
Term endowment	3,200,900	3,106,506
Quasi-endowment--unrestricted	1,960,900	1,900,000
Quasi-endowment--restricted	584,200	570,044
TOTAL ENDOWMENT AND SIMILAR FUNDS	$14,196,000	$13,777,400
ANNUITY AND LIFE INCOME FUNDS:		
Annuity funds:		
Annuities payable	$ 1,700,500	$ 1,500,000
Fund balances	907,700	809,000
Total annuity funds	$ 2,608,200	$ 2,309,000
Life income funds:		
Income payable	$ 7,200	6,500
Fund balances	2,372,680	2,071,000
Total life income funds	$ 2,379,880	$ 2,077,500
TOTAL ANNUITY AND LIFE INCOME FUNDS	$ 4,988,080	$ 4,386,500
PLANT FUNDS:		
Unexpended:		
Accounts payable	$ 26,000	
Notes payable	90,000	$ 100,000
Bonds payable	900,000	935,000
Fund balances:		
Restricted	926,320	391,150
Unrestricted	268,380	316,650
Total unexpended plant funds	$ 2,210,700	$ 1,742,800
Renewals and replacements:		
Accounts payable	$ 32,400	29,600
Fund balances:		
Restricted	317,000	304,400
Unrestricted	70,200	40,500
Total renewals and replacements funds	$ 419,600	$ 374,500

Retirement of indebtedness:		
Cash	$ 10,000	$ 9,500
Deposits with trustees	52,200	51,150
Total retirement of indebtedness funds	$ 62,200	$ 60,650
Investment in plant:		
Land	$ 785,000	$ 785,000
Buildings	15,084,710	14,908,000
Improvements other than buildings	299,790	299,790
Equipment	6,481,000	6,389,980
Library books	428,500	379,600
Construction in progress	2,200,000	1,690,000
Total investment in plant	$25,279,000	$24,452,370
TOTAL PLANT FUNDS	$27,971,500	$26,630,320
AGENCY FUNDS:		
Cash	$ 42,700	$ 51,000
Investments	74,350	61,500
TOTAL AGENCY FUNDS	$ 117,050	$ 112,500

Retirement of indebtedness:		
Accounts payable	$ 2,500	$ 3,850
Fund balances	59,700	56,800
Total retirement of indebtedness funds	$ 62,200	$ 60,650
Investment in plant:		
Notes payable	$ 90,000	$ 100,000
Bonds payable	1,700,000	1,245,000
Net investment in plant	23,489,000	23,107,370
Total investment in plant	$25,279,000	$24,452,370
TOTAL PLANT FUNDS	$27,971,500	$26,630,320
AGENCY FUNDS:		
Deposits held in custody for others	$ 117,050	$ 112,500
TOTAL AGENCY FUNDS	$ 117,050	$ 112,500

FORM 16.8

BLANK COLLEGE

STATEMENT OF CURRENT FUND REVENUES, EXPENDITURES, AND OTHER CHANGES
FOR THE YEAR ENDED JUNE 30, 19__
With Comparative Figures for 19__

	Unrestricted	Restricted	Total	Prior year total
REVENUES:				
Educational and general:				
Student tuition and fees	$ 4,677,345		$ 4,677,345	$ 4,576,000
Governmental appropriations	1,800,000		1,800,000	1,800,000
Federal grants and contracts	10,000	$ 2,388,300	2,398,300	2,442,830
State grants and contracts		149,365	149,365	201,500
Local grants and contracts		11,150	11,150	10,000
Private gifts, grants and contracts	94,665	144,935	239,600	228,700
Endowment income	590,045	26,250	616,295	589,500
Sales and services of educational departments	24,940		24,940	23,650
Sales and services of independent operations	14,205		14,205	13,620
Total educational and general revenues	$ 7,211,200		$ 9,931,200	$ 9,885,800
Auxiliary enterprises	1,986,400		1,986,400	1,851,650
Total current revenues	$ 9,197,600	$ 2,720,000	$11,917,600	$11,737,450
EXPENDITURES AND MANDATORY TRANSFERS:				
Educational and general:				
Instruction	$ 3,757,954	$ 152,650	$ 3,910,604	$ 3,820,000
Research		2,461,000	2,461,000	2,496,500
Public services	297,500	73,400	370,900	452,710
Academic support	994,700		994,700	971,000
Student services	701,460		701,460	683,600
Institutional support	742,500		742,500	719,750
Operation and maintenance of physical plant	648,070		648,070	613,690
Scholarships and fellowships	23,666	32,950	56,616	49,650
Educational and general expenditures	$ 7,165,850	$ 2,720,000	$ 9,885,850	$ 9,806,900
Mandatory transfers for:				
Principal and interest	50,000		50,000	58,000
Loan fund matching grant	2,000		2,000	1,000
Total educational and general expenditures and mandatory transfers	$ 7,217,850	$ 2,720,000	$ 9,937,850	$ 9,865,900
Auxiliary enterprises:				
Expenditures	$ 1,770,900		$ 1,770,900	$ 1,623,700
Mandatory transfers for:				
Principal and interest	157,600		157,600	170,500
Renewals and replacements	40,000		40,000	35,000
Total auxiliary enterprises	$ 1,968,500		$ 1,968,500	$ 1,829,200
Total expenditures and mandatory transfers	$ 9,186,350	$ 2,720,000	$11,906,350	$11,695,100
OTHER TRANSFERS AND ADDITIONS/(DEDUCTIONS):				
Excess of restricted receipts over transfers to revenues		$ 342,000	$ 342,000	$ 196,000
Refunded to grantors		(22,500)	(22,500)	(16,200)
Appropriated for quasi-endowment funds	(5,000)		(5,000)	(4,500)
Net increase in fund balances	$ 6,250	$ 319,500	$ 325,750	$ 175,300

BLANK COLLEGE

STATEMENT OF CHANGES IN FUND BALANCES
FOR THE YEAR ENDED JUNE 30, 19__

	Current funds			Endowment and similar funds	Annuity and life income funds	Plant funds			
	Unrestricted	Restricted	Loan funds			Unexpended	Renewals and Replacements	Retirement of indebtedness	Investment in plant
REVENUES AND OTHER ADDITIONS:									
Educational and general revenues	$ 7,211,200								
Auxiliary enterprises revenues	1,986,400								
State appropriations--restricted		$ 450,000							
Federal grants and contracts--restricted		2,133,350							
State grants and contracts--restricted		275,800							
Local grants and contracts--restricted		113,000							
Private gifts, grants, and contracts		178,000	$ 3,000	$ 27,800	$ 415,270	$ 87,030	$ 30,000		
Expired term endowment restricted to plant						10,000			
Investment income--restricted		25,850	400		225,000	59,400	15,500	$ 2,100	
Realized gains on investments--unrestricted				69,444					
Realized gains on investments--restricted				316,356	14,930				
Interest on loans receivable			16,540						
U.S. government advances			18,000						
Expended for plant facilities, including $99,600 charged to current funds expenditures									$ 271,630
Retirement of indebtedness									110,000
Proceeds from borrowings						510,000			
Accrued interest on sale of bonds								800	
Matured annuity and life income funds restricted to endowment				10,000					
Matured annuity and life income funds restricted to loans			35,000						
Total revenues and other additions	$ 9,197,600	$ 3,176,000	$ 72,940	$ 423,600	$ 655,200	$ 666,430	$ 45,500	$ 2,900	$ 381,630
EXPENDITURES AND OTHER DEDUCTIONS:									
Educational and general expenditures	$ 7,165,850	$ 2,720,000							
Auxiliary enterprises expenditures	1,770,900								
Indirect costs recovered		127,500							
Payments to annuitants					$ 200,000				
Refunded to grantors		9,000							
Loan cancellations and write-offs			$ 24,000						
Administrative and collection costs			3,700						
Adjustment of actuarial liability for annuities payable					10,000				
Expired term endowment restricted to plant				$ 10,000					
Expended for plant facilities						$ 172,030	$ 50,700		
Retirement of indebtedness								$ 110,000	
Interest on indebtedness								97,600	
Matured annuity and life income funds restricted to endowment					10,000				
Matured annuity and life income funds restricted to loans					35,000				
Total expenditures and other deductions	$ 8,936,750	$ 2,856,500	$ 27,700	$ 10,000	$ 255,000	$ 172,030	$ 50,700	$ 207,600	
TRANSFERS AMONG FUNDS--ADDITIONS/(DEDUCTIONS):									
Mandatory:									
Principal and interest	(207,600)							207,600	
Renewals and replacements	(40,000)						40,000		
Loan fund matching grant	(2,000)		2,000						
Designation of restricted gifts to unrestricted						(7,500)	7,500		
Appropriated for quasi-endowment funds	(5,000)			5,000					
Total transfers	(254,600)		2,000	5,000		(7,500)	47,500	207,600	
Net increase for the year	6,250	319,500	47,240	418,600	400,380	486,900	42,300	2,900	381,630
Fund balance at beginning of year (June 30, 19__)	627,050	1,219,200	1,241,900	13,777,400	2,880,000	707,800	344,900	56,800	23,107,370
Fund balance at end of year (June 30, 19__)	$ 633,300	$ 1,538,700	$ 1,289,140	$14,196,000	$ 3,280,380	$ 1,194,700	$ 387,200	$ 59,700	$23,489,000

FORM 16.10

BLANK COLLEGE

SCHEDULE OF CURRENT FUNDS REVENUES
FOR THE YEAR ENDED JUNE 30, 19__

	Unrestricted	Restricted	Total
Educational and general:			
Student tuition and fees:			
Resident tuition and fees	$ 3,513,545		$ 3,513,545
Nonresident tuition and fees	705,420		705,420
Late registration fee	2,150		2,150
Course change fee	1,980		1,980
Deferred test and examination fee	2,000		2,000
Advanced standing examination fee	3,900		3,900
Music fee	7,200		7,200
Diploma fee	5,500		5,500
Thesis fee	7,650		7,650
Summer session	101,000		101,000
University extension	327,000		327,000
	4,677,345		4,677,345
Governmental appropriations:			
State appropriations--general support	450,000		450,000
Federal appropriations	1,338,000		1,338,000
Local appropriations	12,000		12,000
	1,800,000		1,800,000
Federal grants and contracts:			
Grants	10,000	736,000	746,000
Contracts		1,652,300	1,652,300
	10,000	2,388,300	2,398,300
State grants and contracts:			
Grants		28,000	28,000
Contracts		121,365	121,365
		149,365	149,365
Local grants and contracts:			
University funds		6,000	6,000
Other sources		5,150	5,150
		11,150	11,150
Private gifts, grants and contracts:			
Business grants	4,000		4,000
Business and industry contracts	87,665	135,935	223,600
Business and industry training grants	3,000	9,000	12,000
	94,665	144,935	239,600
Endowment income	590,045	26,250	616,295
Sales and services of educational departments:			
Dairy operation	22,410		22,410
Testing services	1,500		1,500
Film library rentals	1,030		1,030
	24,940		24,940
Other sources	14,205		14,205
Total educational and general	7,211,200	2,720,000	9,931,200
Auxiliary enterprises:			
Student union	36,290		36,290
Residence halls--single	590,728		590,728
Residence halls--married	147,682		147,682
Cafeteria	635,650		635,650
Bookstore	576,050		576,050
Total auxiliary enterprises	1,986,400		1,986,400
TOTAL CURRENT REVENUES	$ 9,197,600	$ 2,720,000	$11,917,600

FORM 16.11

BLANK COLLEGE

SCHEDULE OF CURRENT FUNDS EXPENDITURES AND TRANSFERS
FOR THE YEAR ENDED JUNE 30, 19__

	Unrestricted	Restricted	Total
Educational and general:			
Instruction			
College of Liberal Arts	$ 1,151,600		$ 1,151,600
College of Business and Government	165,350		165,350
College of Education	220,000		220,000
College of Engineering	425,470	$ 101,900	527,370
School of Law	371,000		371,000
School of Pharmacy	1,127,380	50,750	1,178,130
Graduate School	214,554		214,554
Summer Session	80,600		80,600
Other instructional expenses	2,000		2,000
	3,757,954	152,650	3,910,604
Research:			
Institutes and research centers		2,064,300	2,064,300
Project research		396,700	396,700
		2,461,000	2,461,000
Public services:			
Community service	31,900	10,800	42,700
Extension	29,650	10,000	39,650
Conferences, institutes and short courses	17,000		17,000
Radio	56,950		56,950
Television	162,000	52,600	214,600
	297,500	73,400	370,900
Academic support:			
Academic administration	61,950		61,950
Computing services	327,000		327,000
Audiovisual services	22,500		22,500
Curriculum development	17,290		17,290
Libraries	498,160		498,160
Museums and galleries	67,800		67,800
	994,700		994,700
Student services:			
Registrar	62,650		62,650
Admissions	43,700		43,700
Student counseling and guidance	29,000		29,000
Dean of students	47,100		47,100
Financial aids	29,740		29,740
Cultural activities	16,290		16,290
Health services	173,560		173,560
Intramural athletics	31,290		31,290
Intercollegiate athletics	250,630		250,630
Student organizations	9,000		9,000
Remedial instruction	8,500		8,500
	701,460		701,460
Institutional support:			
Governing board	32,960		32,960
President	59,750		59,750
Chief academic office	39,870		39,870
Business office	91,060		91,060
Comptroller's office	30,250		30,250
Budget office	26,790		26,790
Bursar	31,260		31,260
Legal services	10,000		10,000
Administrative data processing	96,200		96,200
Internal audits	16,000		16,000
Security	39,600		39,600
Safety	12,000		12,000
Alumni activities	39,620		39,620
Development office	41,200		41,200
Commencement	3,800		3,800
Convocations	1,950		1,950
Catalogs and bulletins	2,600		2,600
Personnel services	31,200		31,200
Memberships	1,000		1,000
Public relations	17,300		17,300
Publications	11,400		11,400
Printing	17,940		17,940
Purchasing	29,650		29,650
Telephone services	47,100		47,100
Transportation services	12,000		12,000
	742,500		742,500

	Unrestricted	Restricted	Total
Operation and maintenance of physical plant:			
Administration	39,270		39,270
Custodial services	92,730		92,730
Maintenance of buildings	87,940		87,940
Maintenance of grounds	47,260		47,260
Trucking service	17,200		17,200
Fire protection	31,640		31,640
Utilities	201,690		201,690
Property insurance	117,420		117,420
Other maintenance	12,920		12,920
	648,070		648,070
Scholarships and fellowships:			
Scholarships	15,316	24,400	39,716
Fellowships	2,150	8,550	10,700
Fee waivers	6,200		6,200
	23,666	32,950	56,616
Total educational and general	7,165,850	2,720,000	9,885,850
Mandatory transfers for:			
Principal and interest	50,000		50,000
Loan fund matching grant	2,000		2,000
Total educational and general expenditures and mandatory transfers	7,217,850	2,720,000	9,937,850
Auxiliary enterprises:			
Student union	20,270		20,270
Residence halls--single	526,130		526,130
Residence halls--married	122,250		122,250
Cafeteria	589,650		589,650
Bookstore	512,600		512,600
	1,770,900		1,770,900
Mandatory transfers for:			
Principal and interest	157,600		157,600
Renewals and replacements	40,000		40,000
Total auxiliary enterprises, expenditures, and mandatory transfers	1,968,500		1,968,500
TOTAL CURRENT EXPENDITURES AND TRANSFERS	$ 9,186,350	$ 2,720,000	$11,906,350

FORM 16.12

BLANK COLLEGE

SCHEDULE OF CHANGES IN FUND BALANCES
LOAN FUNDS
FOR THE YEAR ENDED JUNE 30, 19__

	Balances July 1, 19__	Additions: Gifts and borrowings	Additions: Endowment income	Additions: Interest and investment income	Additions: Transfers from current funds	Additions: Transfers from annuity funds	Deductions: Notes charged off and collection expenses	Deductions: Death and teachers' cancellations	Balances June 30, 19__	Cash available for loans
University loan funds:										
Unrestricted:										
General student aid loan fund	$ 10,000								$ 10,000	$ 250
Graduate School loan fund	29,600						$ 50		29,550	1,400
(List remaining funds alphabetically.)	35,400			$ 625			400		35,625	8,550
	$ 75,000			$ 625			$ 450		$ 75,175	$ 10,200
Restricted:										
John Abrams Loan Fund	$ 4,100			$ 17					$ 4,117	$ 312
Phyllis Braunson Emergency Loan Fund	7,260			22					7,282	918
(List remaining funds alphabetically.)	213,640	$ 3,000	$ 400	636		$ 35,000	$ 4,075		248,601	62,190
	$ 225,000	$ 3,000	$ 400	$ 675		$ 35,000	$ 4,075		$ 260,000	$ 63,420
U.S. government participation loan funds:	$ 232,540			$ 2,980			$ 2,150	$ 1,200	$ 232,170	$ 14,390
Health professions student loan fund	709,360	$ 18,000		12,260	$ 2,000		4,025	15,800	721,795	29,630
National Direct Student Loan fund	$ 941,900	$ 18,000		$ 15,240	$ 2,000		$ 6,175	$ 17,000	$ 953,965	$ 44,020
Total	$1,241,900	$ 21,000	$ 400	$ 16,540	$ 2,000	$ 35,000	$ 10,700	$ 17,000	$1,289,140	$ 117,640

FORM 16.13

BLANK COLLEGE

SCHEDULE OF CHANGES IN FUND BALANCES
ENDOWMENT AND SIMILAR FUNDS
FOR THE YEAR ENDED JUNE 30, 19__

		Additions				Deductions	
	Balances July 1, 19__	Gifts	Annuity funds upon death of annuitant	Net gains on investments sold or exchanged	Transfers from current funds	Transfers to unexpended plant funds	Balances June 30, 19__
Endowment funds:							
Instructional departments:							
Josiah Abramson Endowment Fund							
(List remaining funds alphabetically.)	$ 8,200,850	$ 10,000	$ 10,000	$ 229,474			$ 8,450,324
Term-endowment funds--unrestricted:							
Instructional departments:							
Sarah Conroy Educational Endowment							
(List remaining funds alphabetically.)	$ 1,679,300			$ 46,990			$ 1,726,290
Term-endowment funds--restricted:							
Professorships:							
Joseph Swanson Chair in Biology							
(List remaining funds alphabetically.)	$ 469,886	$ 11,000		$ 13,464		$ 10,000	$ 484,350
Scholarships:							
Marian Anderson Scholarship Fund							
(List remaining funds alphabetically.)	$ 957,320	$ 6,800		$ 26,775			$ 990,895
Quasi-endowment funds--unrestricted:							
Loan funds:							
General loan fund							
(List remaining funds alphabetically.)	$ 1,900,000			$ 53,125	$ 5,000		$ 1,958,125
Quasi-endowment funds--restricted:							
Building maintenance:							
Tilton Observatory Endowment							
(List remaining funds alphabetically.)	$ 570,044			$ 15,972			$ 586,016
Total	$13,777,400	$ 27,800	$ 10,000	$ 385,800	$ 5,000	$ 10,000	$14,196,000

FORM 16.14

BLANK COLLEGE

SCHEDULE OF CHANGES IN FUND BALANCES
ANNUITY AND LIFE INCOME FUNDS
FOR THE YEAR ENDED JUNE 30, 19__

		Additions			Deductions			
	Balances July 1, 19__	Gifts	Investment income	Net gains on investments sold or exchanged	Payments to annuitants	Adjustment of actuarial liability	Transfers to other funds	Balances June 30, 19__
Annuity funds:								
Joseph Adams	$ 9,900		$ 2,100		$ 2,000		$ 10,000	
Mary Parker Battle	97,620		7,000	$ 812	6,000	$ 470		$ 98,962
George L. Connolly	59,840		4,120		4,000	420		59,540
James H. Higgins	102,500		8,000	3,490	7,500	2,400		104,090
Sherman Kohlmeyer	78,000		5,420		5,000	1,500		76,920
Anderson K. Levitz	59,000		3,500		3,000	130		51,370
Manson Nomer	211,800		15,850	6,290	10,000	2,900		221,040
Emilie L. Resor		$ 92,000	3,370	(709)	3,200			91,461
Meyer Wattingly	198,340		13,742	2,516	8,281	2,000		204,317
	$ 809,000	$ 92,000	$ 63,102	$ 12,399	$ 48,981	$ 9,820	$ 10,000	$ 907,700
Life income funds:								
A. Stanley Bartwell	$ 315,000		$ 22,000		$ 20,000			$ 317,000
Marilyn Chester		$ 123,270	7,834	$ (3,012)	$ 6,000			122,092
Candice A. Donegan	247,920		16,320	4,217	17,000			251,457
Charles T. Edmonson	327,600		19,102		17,500			329,202
Bennett P. Fielding	402,680		30,900	4,090	30,000			407,670
Jackson N. Klotthar	34,820		2,600		2,420		$ 35,000	
John O. Loman	110,000		7,600	456	7,600			110,456
Mathilda B. Madison	136,700		10,702		10,702			136,700
Oscar Orlando	91,800		7,100		7,100			91,800
Mason Seals		200,000	6,950	(3,220)	3,997			199,733
Janet R. Shannon	209,720		16,000		15,000			210,720
Stella Zellinger	194,760		14,790		13,700			195,850
	$ 2,071,000	$ 323,270	$ 161,898	$ 2,531	$ 151,019		$ 35,000	$ 2,372,680
Total	$ 2,880,000	$ 415,270	$ 225,000	$ 14,930	$ 200,000	$ 9,820	$ 45,000	$ 3,280,380

FORM 16.15

BLANK COLLEGE

SCHEDULE OF CHANGES IN FUND BALANCES
UNEXPENDED PLANT FUNDS
FOR THE YEAR ENDED JUNE 30, 19__

		Additions				Deductions		
	Balances July 1, 19__	Gifts	Investment income	Transfers from other funds	Proceeds from borrowings	Expenditures for plant facilities	Transfers to other funds	Balances June 30, 19__
Restricted:								
Bell Chapel fund		$ 22,000	$ 1,000	$ 10,000				$ 33,000
Law School building fund	$ 176,450	20,000	11,400					207,850
Law School construction	114,700		6,700			$ 87,500		33,900
Richardson Hall building fund		20,000					$ 7,500	12,500
Student union building fund	100,000		31,000		$ 510,000	12,530		628,470
Wesley Recreation Center construction		10,600						10,600
	$ 391,150	$ 72,600	$ 50,100	$ 10,000	$ 510,000	$ 100,030	$ 7,500	$ 926,320
Unrestricted:								
Arts and crafts building	$ 89,500					$ 72,000		$ 17,500
Howard Hall construction	31,950							31,950
Library building fund	101,500	$ 14,430	$ 5,300					121,230
Library construction	93,700		4,000					97,700
	$ 316,650	$ 14,430	$ 9,300			$ 72,000		$ 268,380
Total	$ 707,800	$ 87,030	$ 59,400	$ 10,000	$ 510,000	$ 172,030	$ 7,500	$ 1,194,700

FORM 16.16

BLANK COLLEGE

SCHEDULE OF CHANGES IN FUND BALANCES
FUNDS FOR RENEWALS AND REPLACEMENTS
FOR THE YEAR ENDED JUNE 30, 19__

	Balances July 1, 19__	Additions: Gifts	Additions: Investment income	Additions: Transfers from auxiliary enterprises	Additions: Transfers from other funds	Deductions: Expenditures	Balances June 30, 19__
Restricted:							
Bookstore	$ 61,900		$ 2,000	$ 5,000		$ 6,000	$ 62,900
Cafeteria	39,700		1,950	7,000		11,750	36,900
Residence halls--single	109,600		5,600	17,000		14,600	117,600
Residence halls--married	52,000		2,800	9,000		7,290	56,510
Student union	41,200		1,150	2,000		1,260	43,090
	$ 304,400		$ 13,500	$ 40,000		$ 40,900	$ 317,000
Unrestricted:							
Science laboratory	$ 34,500	$ 20,000	$ 1,350			$ 8,600	$ 47,250
Wellington Recreation Center	6,000	10,000	650		$ 7,500	1,200	22,950
	$ 40,500	$ 30,000	$ 2,000		$ 7,500	$ 9,800	$ 70,200
Total	$ 344,900	$ 30,000	$ 15,500	$ 40,000	$ 7,500	$ 50,700	$ 387,200

FORM 16.17

BLANK COLLEGE

SCHEDULE OF CHANGES IN FUND BALANCES
FUNDS FOR RETIREMENT OF INDEBTEDNESS
FOR THE YEAR ENDED JUNE 30, 19__

		Additions				Deductions				
	Balances July 1, 19__	Investment income	Transfers from current funds	Transfers from auxiliary enterprises	Accrued interest on sale of bonds	Bonds retired	Interest paid	Principal repayment on notes payable	Bank charges	Balances June 30, 19__
First mortgage dormitory bonds of 1967	$ 9,400	$ 351		$ 32,180		$ 10,000	$ 22,000		$ 180	$ 9,751
Student apartment housing bonds of 1964	14,910	582		48,200		24,000	23,760		440	15,492
Student apartment housing bonds, Series B, 1975					$ 800					800
First mortgage dormitory bonds of 1971	7,150	292		15,330		6,000	7,430		100	7,442
First mortgage student union bonds of 1966	23,480	875		63,690		36,000	27,030		660	24,355
Student infirmary bonds of 1967	1,860		$ 25,000			14,000	10,780		220	1,860
Notes payable			25,000					$ 20,000		
Total	$ 56,800	$ 2,100	$ 50,000	$ 157,600	$ 800	$ 90,000	$ 96,000	$ 20,000	$ 1,600	$ 59,700

FORM 16.18

BLANK COLLEGE

SCHEDULE OF CHANGES IN INVESTMENT IN PLANT FOR THE YEAR ENDED JUNE 30, 19__

	Book value July 1, 19__	Additions: Current funds	Additions: Gifts	Deductions: Disposals	Book value June 30, 19__
Land:					
Campus grounds	$ 310,000				$ 310,000
Hospital grounds	475,000				475,000
	$ 785,000				$ 785,000
Buildings:					
Arts and crafts building	$ 1,906,000		$ 71,000		$ 1,977,000
Central building	927,000		17,000		944,000
Donnelly House	1,250,000				1,250,000
Howard Hall	1,926,000		18,000		1,944,000
Infirmary building	835,600				835,600
John T. Lattimer Memorial uilding	1,879,600		29,600		1,909,200
Married students apartment building	1,710,000				1,710,000
Lawrence T. Nelson Memorial building	1,113,100				1,113,100
Power plant	1,150,000				1,150,000
Howard Randolph Library building	1,044,600		41,110		1,085,710
Student union building	1,166,100				1,166,100
	$14,908,000		$ 176,710		$15,084,710
Improvements other than buildings:					
Fencing	$ 7,200				$ 7,200
Howard Mall	6,850				6,850
Parking lot	16,290				16,290
Roadways	21,700				21,700
Underground piping	247,750				247,750
	$ 299,790				$ 299,790
Equipment:					
Arts and crafts building	$ 294,000	$ 12,000	$ 14,600	$ 1,000	$ 319,600
Central building	427,900	6,920			434,820
Donnelly House	197,500	4,700			202,200
Howard Hall	974,000	3,690			977,690
Infirmary building	727,000	4,200	1,720		732,920
John T. Lattimer Memorial building	624,500	3,950	29,600		628,450
Married students apartment building	279,800	7,280			287,080
Lawrence T. Nelson Memorial building	849,000	6,050			855,050
Power plant	974,700	14,600			989,300
Howard Randolph Library building	737,600	3,510	4,500	500	745,110
Student union building	303,980	4,800			308,780
	$ 6,389,980	$ 71,700	$ 20,820	$ 1,500	$ 6,481,000
Library books:					
Howard Randolph Library building	$ 379,600	$ 27,900	$ 21,000		$ 428,500
Construction in progress	$ 1,690,000		$ 510,000		$ 2,200,000
Total investment in plant	$24,452,370	$ 99,600	$ 728,530	$ 1,500	$25,279,000

FORM 16.19

BLANK COLLEGE

SCHEDULE OF REVENUES, EXPENDITURES, AND TRANSFERS
RESIDENCE HALLS--SINGLE STUDENTS
FOR THE YEAR ENDED JUNE 30, 19__

Revenues:	
Room rentals--regular	$571,848
Room rentals--summer session	16,200
Guest rooms	1,700
Miscellaneous	980
Total revenues	$590,728
Expenditures:	
Personnel compensation	$192,540
Office supplies	9,000
Travel	3,450
Telephone and telegraph	4,240
Janitorial, cleaning, and laundry supplies	67,240
Heat, light, and water	161,470
Postage and freight	2,750
Insurance	69,600
Repairing and servicing to equipment	4,200
Printing, binding, and reproducing	3,250
Equipment	8,390
Total expenditures	$526,130
Transfers to plant funds for:	
Retirement of indebtedness	$ 55,000
Renewals and replacements	17,000
	$ 72,000
Total expenditures and transfers	$598,130
Excess of expenditures and transfers over revenues	$ (7,402)

FORM 16.20

BLANK COLLEGE

SCHEDULE OF REVENUES, EXPENDITURES, AND TRANSFERS
RESIDENCE HALLS--MARRIED STUDENTS
FOR THE YEAR ENDED JUNE 30, 19__

Revenues:	
Apartment rentals	$145,702
Guest rooms	1,200
Miscellaneous	780
Total revenues	$147,682
Expenditures:	
Personnel compensation	$ 44,285
Office supplies	7,000
Travel	3,100
Telephone and telegraph	4,190
Janitorial, cleaning, and laundry supplies	12,800
Heat, light, and water	18,725
Postage and freight	1,900
Insurance	21,200
Repairing and servicing to equipment	790
Printing, binding, and reproducing	980
Equipment	7,280
Total expenditures	$122,250
Transfers to plant funds for:	
Retirement of indebtedness	$ 39,000
Renewals and replacements	9,000
	$ 48,000
Total expenditures and transfers	$170,250
Excess of expenditures and transfers over revenues	$(22,568)

FORM 16.21

BLANK COLLEGE

SCHEDULE OF REVENUES, EXPENDITURES, AND TRANSFERS
BOOKSTORE
FOR THE YEAR ENDED JUNE 30, 19__

Revenues:	
Sales of books	$432,000
Sales of supplies	112,100
Other sales	31,950
Total revenues	$576,050
Expenditures:	
Cost of sales	$403,450
Gross profit on sales	$172,600
Personnel compensation	$ 89,555
Office supplies	1,290
Janitorial and cleaning supplies	780
Postage and freight	3,250
Heat, light, and water	8,900
Telephone and telegraph	1,390
Travel	1,000
Pricing supplies	675
Repairing and servicing to equipment	740
Printing, binding, and reproducing	370
Equipment	1,200
Total expenditures	$109,150
Transfers to plant funds for:	
Retirement of indebtedness	$ 30,000
Renewals and replacements	5,000
	$ 35,000
Total expenditures and transfers	$144,150
Excess of revenues over expenditures and transfers	$ 28,450

FORM 16.22

BLANK COLLEGE

SCHEDULE OF REVENUES, EXPENDITURES, AND TRANSFERS
CAFETERIA
FOR THE YEAR ENDED JUNE 30, 19__

Revenues:	
Cafeteria sales	$521,200
Faculty dining room sales	31,780
Snack bar sales	82,670
Total revenues	$635,650
Expenditures:	
Cost of sales	$311,400
Gross profit on sales	$324,250
Personnel compensation	$242,740
Office supplies	1,650
Janitorial and cleaning supplies	6,950
Laundering and uniforms	1,100
Tableware and linens	980
Heat, light, and water	12,000
Telephone and telegraph	1,640
Travel	800
Insurance	7,400
Pricing supplies	150
Repairing and servicing to equipment	740
Equipment	2,100
Total expenditures	$278,250
Transfers to plant funds for:	
Retirement of debt	$ 21,600
Renewals and replacements	7,000
	$ 28,600
Total expenditures and transfers	$306,850
Excess of revenues over expenditures and transfers	$ 17,400

FORM 16.23

BLANK COLLEGE

SCHEDULE OF REVENUES, EXPENDITURES, AND TRANSFERS
STUDENT UNION
FOR THE YEAR ENDED JUNE 30, 19__

Revenues:	
Room rentals	$ 18,780
Games rooms	13,210
Barber shop commissions	1,700
Vending machines	2,600
Total revenues	$ 36,290
Expenditures:	
Personnel compensation	$ 12,280
Office supplies	200
Recreational supplies	680
Janitorial and cleaning supplies	490
Heat, light, and water	4,860
Telephone and telegraph	90
Repairing and servicing of equipment	170
Equipment	1,500
Total expenditures	$ 20,270
Transfers to plant funds for:	
Retirement of indebtedness	$ 12,000
Renewals and replacements	2,000
	$ 14,000
Total expenditures and transfers	$ 34,270
Excess of revenues over expenditures and transfers	$ 2,020

FORM 16.24

BLANK COLLEGE

SCHEDULE OF INVESTMENTS BY FUND GROUPS
JUNE 30, 19__

	Current funds		Endowment and similar funds	Annuity and life income funds	Plant funds			Agency funds
	Unrestricted	Restricted			Unexpended	Renewals and replacements	Retirement of indebtedness	
U.S. Treasury bills	$ 296,000	$ 302,000	$ 800,000	$ 600,000	$ 1,677,100	$ 395,600	$ 52,200	$ 74,350
U.S. Treasury notes			900,000	1,940,000	200,000			
Corporate bonds			1,250,000	140,000				
Preferred stocks			312,500					
Common stocks			7,865,700	2,133,400				
Mortgage notes			120,000					
Certificates of deposit		150,000	200,000	100,000	150,000			
Real estate, less accumulated depreciation			2,650,000					
Total	$ 296,000	$ 452,000	$14,098,200	$ 4,913,400	$ 2,027,100	$ 395,600	$ 52,200	$ 74,350

FORM 16.25

BLANK COLLEGE

SCHEDULE OF LONG-TERM NOTES AND BONDS PAYABLE
FOR THE YEAR ENDED JUNE 30, 19__

	First mortgage dormitory bonds of 1967	Student apartment housing bonds of 1964	Student apartment housing bonds, Series B, 1975	First mortgage dormitory bonds of 1971	First mortgage student union bonds of 1966	Student infirmary bonds of 1967	Notes payable	Total
Balances, July 1, 19__	$ 500,000	$ 540,000		$ 140,000	$ 600,000	$ 400,000	$ 200,000	$ 2,380,000
Additions:								
Proceeds from borrowings			$ 510,000					510,000
Deductions:								
Bonds retired and note payments	10,000	24,000		6,000	36,000	14,000	20,000	110,000
Balances, June 30, 19__	$ 490,000	$ 516,000	$ 510,000	$ 134,000	$ 564,000	$ 386,000	$ 180,000	$ 2,780,000
Unexpended plant funds:								
Notes payable								$ 90,000
Bonds payable								900,000
								$ 990,000
Investment in plant:								
Notes payable								$ 90,000
Bonds payable								1,700,000
								$ 1,790,000
Total								$ 2,780,000

FORM 16.26

BLANK COLLEGE

STATEMENT OF DEPOSIT LIABILITIES
JUNE 30, 19__

Alumni Fund	$ 41,200
Alpha Phi Omega Fund	419
American Accounting Association	325
Glendy Burke Tournament	1,240
Campus Nite Program Fund	2,115
Ronald Chamberlain Art Fund	4,975
Curtain Club	500
Foreign Students Fund	3,900
Graduate School Microfilming	8,050
Guidance Agency	7,250
Gymnastics Fund	1,075
Handball Club	560
Judo Club	1,700
Karate Club	1,120
Law School Special Events	4,100
Miscellaneous Club Sports	4,950
Program on Science and Technology	17,700
Resident Government Fund	3,900
Rugby Club	1,100
1975 Senior Class	800
Soccer Club	2,500
Student Activities--School of Engineering	1,450
Student Directory	3,500
Tax Institute	2,621
Total	$117,050

FORM 16.27

BLANK COLLEGE

STATEMENT OF BONDS PAYABLE
JUNE 30, 19__

Name of bond issue	Description of bonds	Amount of original issue	Amount retired to date	Amount outstanding
Student apartment housing bonds of 1964	3-3/4% serial bonds maturing annually to 2004	$ 760,000	$ 290,000	$ 470,000
First mortgage student union bonds of 1966	4% serial bonds maturing annually to 2006	1,200,000	360,000	840,000
First mortage dormitory bonds of 1967	3-7/8% serial bonds maturing annually to 1997	300,000	90,000	210,000
Student infirmary bonds of 1967	3-1/2% serial bonds maturing annually to 2007	600,000	140,000	460,000
First mortgage dormitory bonds of 1971	4% serial bonds maturing annually to 2011	250,000	30,000	220,000
Student apartment housing bonds, Series B, of 1975	4-1/8% serial bonds maturing annually to 2005	400,000		400,000
Total		$ 3,510,000	$ 910,000	$ 2,600,000

FORM 16.28

BLANK COLLEGE

SUMMARY OF SIGNIFICANT ACCOUNTING POLICIES
JUNE 30, 19__

The significant accounting policies followed by Blank College are described below in order to enhance the usefulness of the financial statements to the reader.

ACCRUAL BASIS

The financial statements of Blank College have been prepared on the accrual basis except for depreciation accounting as explained in notes 1 and 2 to the financial statements. The statement of current funds revenues, expenditures, and other changes is a statement of financial activities of current funds related to the current reporting period. It does not purport to present the results of operations or the net income or loss for the period as would a statement of income or a statement of revenues and expenses.

To the extent that current funds are used to finance plant assets, the amounts so provided are accounted for as (1) expenditures, in the case of normal replacement of movable equipment and library books; (2) mandatory transfers, in the case of required provisions for debt amortization and interest, and equipment renewal and replacement; and (3) transfers of a nonmandatory nature for all other cases.

FUND ACCOUNTING

In order to insure observance of limitations and restrictions placed on the use of resources available to the institution, the accounts of the institution are maintained in accordance with the principles of "fund accounting." This is the procedure by which resources for various purposes are classified for accounting and reporting purposes into funds that are in accordance with specified activities or objectives. Separate accounts are maintained for each fund; however, in the accompanying financial statements, funds that have similar characteristics are combined into fund groups. Accordingly, all financial transactions have been recorded and reported by fund group.

Within each fund group, fund balances restricted by outside sources are so indicated and are distinguished from unrestricted funds allocated to specific purposes by action of the board of governors. Externally restricted funds may only be utilized in accordance with the purposes established by the source of such funds; they are in contrast with unrestricted funds, over which the board of governors retains full control for use in achieving any of its institutional purposes.

Endowment funds are subject to the restrictions of gift instruments requiring in perpetuity that the principal be invested and only the income be utilized. Term endowment funds are similar to endowment funds except that upon the passage of a stated period of time or the occurrence of a particular event, all or part of the principal may be expended. Whereas quasi-endowment funds have been established by the board of governors for the same purposes as endowment funds, any portion of quasi-endowment funds may be expended.

All gains and losses arising from the sale, collection, or other disposition of investments and additional noncash assets are accounted for in the fund that owned such assets. Ordinary income derived from investments, receivables, and similar sources is accounted for in the fund owning such assets. The exception is income derived from investments of endowment and similar funds. It is accounted for in the fund to which it is restricted; or if it is unrestricted, it is accounted for as revenues in unrestricted current funds.

All other unrestricted revenue is accounted for in the unrestricted current fund. Restricted gifts, grants, appropriations, endowment income, and other restricted resources are accounted for in the appropriate restricted funds. Restricted current funds are reported as revenues and expenditures when expended for current operating purposes.

OTHER SIGNIFICANT ACCOUNTING POLICIES

Other significant accounting policies are set forth in the financial statements and accompanying notes.

FORM 16.29

BLANK COLLEGE

NOTES TO FINANCIAL STATEMENTS
JUNE 30, 19__

1. Investments exclusive of physical plant are recorded at cost; investments received by gift are carried at market value on the date of acquisition. Quoted market values of investments (all marketable securities) of the funds indicated were as follows:

	Current year	Prior year
Unrestricted current funds	$ 310,000	$ 205,000
Restricted current funds	460,000	501,000
Unexpended plant funds	2,150,000	1,566,400
Renewal and replacement funds	301,000	274,000
Agency funds	76,200	62,600

Investment of endowment and similar funds and life income funds are composed of the following:

	Carrying value	
	Current year	Prior year
Endowment and similar funds:		
Corporate stocks and bonds (approximate market, current year, $12,100,000; prior year, $11,542,000)	$11,448,200	$10,943,800
Rental properties--less accumulated depreciation, current year, $450,000; prior year, $400,000	2,650,000	2,704,900
	$14,098,200	$13,648,700
Annuity funds:		
U.S. notes (approximate market, current year, $1,000,000; prior year, $980,000)	$ 990,000	$ 990,000
Corporate stocks and bonds (approximate market, current year, $1,609,000; prior year, $1,178,000)	1,583,200	1,272,000
	$ 2,573,200	$ 2,262,000
Life income funds:		
U.S. notes and bills (approximate market, current year, $1,540,000; prior year, $1,115,000)	$ 1,550,000	$ 1,120,500
Corporate stocks and bonds (approximate market, current year, $808,000; prior year, $852,000)	790,200	943,000
	$ 2,340,200	$ 2,063,500

Assets of endowment funds are pooled on a market value basis, with each individual fund subscribing to or disposing of units on the basis of the value per unit at market value at the beginning of the calendar quarter in which the transaction takes place. Of the total units, each having a market value of $12.10, 700,000 units were owned by endowment, 190,000 units by term endowment, and 110,000 units by quasi-endowment at June 30, 19__.

The following tabulation summarizes changes in relationships between cost and market values of the pooled assets:

	Pooled assets		Net gains	Market value
	Market	Cost	(losses)	per unit
End of year	$12,100,000	$11,448,200	$651,800	$12.10
Beginning of year	11,542,000	10,943,800	598,200	10.90
Unrealized net gains for year			53,600	
Realized net gains for year			385,800	
Total net gains for year			$439,400	$ 1.20

2. Physical plant and equipment are stated at cost on date of acquisition, or fair value on date of donation. Depreciation on physical plant and equipment is not recorded.

3. Long-term debt includes (1) bonds payable, due in annual installments varying from $6,000 to $36,000, with interest varying from 3-1/2% to 4-1/8%, and collateralized by $700,000 of endowment fund bonds and pledged net revenues from the operation of the Student union, bookstore, and the dormitories; and (2) notes payable, due in annual installments of $20,000, with interest at 7%, and collateralized by property carried in the accounts at $80,000.

4. The institution has certain contributory pension plans for academic and nonacademic personnel. Total pension expense for the year was $350,000, which includes amortization of prior service cost over a period of 20 years. The institution's policy is to fund pension costs accrued, including periodic funding of prior years' accruals not previously funded. The actuarially computed value of vested benefits as of June 30, 19__, exceeded net assets of the pension fund by approximately $200,000.

5. Contracts have been let for the construction of additional classroom buildings in the amount of $3,000,000. Construction and equipment are estimated to aggregate $4,500,000, which will be financed by available resources and an issue of bonds amounting to $3,000,000 payable over a period of 40 years.

6. All interfund borrowings have been made from unrestricted funds, and the amounts due are repayable currently without interest.

7. Pledges totaling $300,000, restricted to plant fund uses, are due to be collected over the next three fiscal years in the amounts of $150,000, $90,000, and $60,000, respectively. It is not practicable to estimate the net realizable value of such pledges.

Index